D0198631

Highway To E.S.L.

Highway To E.S.L.

A User-Friendly Guide to Teaching English As A Second Language

Rik Ruiter & Pinky Y. Dang

iUniverse, Inc.
New York Lincoln Shanghai

Highway To E.S.L.
A User-Friendly Guide to Teaching English As A Second Language

Copyright © 2005 by Pinky Y. Dang & Rik Ruiter

All rights reserved. No part of this book may be used or reproduced by any means, graphic, electronic, or mechanical, including photocopying, recording, taping or by any information storage retrieval system without the written permission of the publisher except in the case of brief quotations embodied in critical articles and reviews.

iUniverse books may be ordered through booksellers or by contacting:

iUniverse
2021 Pine Lake Road, Suite 100
Lincoln, NE 68512
www.iuniverse.com
1-800-Authors (1-800-288-4677)

Book cover design assistance: Alexander Chew
Caricatures by Sonia J. Wood
Graphics by Pinky Dang

ISBN-13: 978-0-595-34221-1 (pbk)
ISBN-13: 978-0-595-78991-7 (ebk)
ISBN-10: 0-595-34221-3 (pbk)
ISBN-10: 0-595-78991-9 (ebk)

Printed in the United States of America

CONTENTS

➢ Guided to student-centered discussions
➢ Organizing debates
➢ Correcting students
➢ Contact assignments
➢ Recipes on getting students to talk
➢ Fluency activities
➢ The world of "Improv"

➢ Who are your students?
➢ Study skills
➢ Critical reading skills
➢ Research papers
➢ Index cards
➢ Academic honesty
➢ Paraphrasing and summarizing
➢ Unity and coherence
➢ Teaching literature

➢ Validity, reliability, and practicality
➢ Question types
➢ The art of marking
➢ Oral evaluation grid

➢ The photocopy machine
➢ Teaching aids
➢ The overhead projector
➢ Video in the classroom
➢ Language masters
➢ Audio activities

➢ Songs
➢ Board games
➢ Bingo
➢ Telephone conversations
➢ Role-plays/skits

➢ E.S.L. story program themes
➢ Card games

➢ Lesson plan formats
➢ Course syllabus
➢ Sample lesson plans

➢ Student progress report
➢ Teacher observation form
➢ Interview forms for English Placement Tests
➢ Reading assessment form
➢ Writing evaluation grids
➢ Diagnostic pronunciation profile

Highway To E.S.L.

Let the Adventure Begin

INTRODUCTION

If you drive a car, you would probably remember your first time behind the wheel. Whether that first time was with a professional driving instructor or a stressed-out parent, you may have tried to drive with confidence thinking, "Hey, driving is easy. If Mom and Dad could do it, it'll be a piece of cake." Then when your instructor repeatedly reminds you that a red light has meaning or you're being told that your driving on the sidewalk is illegal, you soon discover your need for further practice. Learning to teach English can be equated with learning to drive. Driving looks easy because the experienced driver sits comfortably in his seat, maneuvers the car with ease, and knows what to look out for. The skilled driver has the potential to travel to wonders that you and I see in glossy travel magazines and feels the freedom and independence this mode of transportation brings. Teaching English may seem easy too as it's the language you've constantly used with ease all your life. Having a marketable and mobile skill such as teaching English As A Second Language (E.S.L.) can bring you travel wonders as a teacher as well, along with the feeling of employable independence and a sense of purpose in affecting the lives of people who benefit from your teachings. Both skills require a gradual learning progression in attaining a high level of expertise. When that level is attained, you experience a profound feeling of accomplishment and develop a confidence in yourself to continually improve not only your teaching or driving skills but also the other areas of your life that define who you are as a person.

Your first day of driving may have taken you on the roads of your subdivision. You felt nervous as you were forced to stick well below the speed limits and watch out for little Billy darting out on the road for an errant ball. An inexperienced and unprepared English teacher, on her first day of her teaching career, would probably feel nervous too and compelled to not step "outside of the box" in her lesson plan (if she had one). She would teach in a conservative manner by exclusively relying on the course textbook for all teaching material and command her entire lesson in a way that leaves students wonder if there is any stimulation at all in learning E.S.L. On your second day, the driving instructor may have warmed up your skills by getting you to drive around the subdivision again and when he saw you master it, he directs you to drive on a street outside the subdivision; however, you're disappointed because it seems like a repeat of the first day. From an inexperienced English teacher perspective, students have learned how boring the class was on the first day and wonder if there would be a repeat. They soon discover the second class is a yawner too. After a few days of driving on a busy local street, the instructor says it's time to advance to an even busier area like downtown. Driving on the streets of downtown went smoothly, except for your parallel parking attempt that backed up traffic for ten minutes and made irate drivers yell and honk at you to hurry your task. You then seek others for tips on how to improve your parking skills. For an inexperienced teacher, after a few days of conservative teaching, she realizes that her students are transferring to Mr. Brown's class because she heard his lessons are more exciting and challenging. The inexperienced teacher investigates what Mr. Brown's lessons have that hers don't.

Finally the ultimate driving challenge comes when the instructor tells you the highway experience is ahead. You've been waiting for the highway because it's what leads you to faraway exciting destinations you've imagined yourself in. As soon as you've mastered the highway, you can go anywhere you wish. For the English teacher, she discovers that Mr. Brown goes "outside of the box" when it comes to lesson planning. He includes creative warm-ups, stimulating lesson introductions, and engaging activities that are beyond what the conservative textbook presents. His teaching style opens a new door to a world of teaching that the inexperienced teacher never thought was possible. The inexperienced teacher learns from Mr. Brown and incorporates his techniques in her teachings. She then becomes more popular with the students and gains more confidence in effectively guiding her students closer to the exciting world of fluently navigating the "Highway to E.S.L."

In this comprehensive guide, you'll discover a plethora of valuable information that will prepare you towards the rewarding career of being an E.S.L. teacher. This guide includes valuable information that prospective teachers should consider before stepping into an E.S.L. classroom and guidelines on teaching the different disciplines of English.

Where do I start? First, you need to ask yourself some basic *wh*-questions: *What, where, when, who, why,* (and of course, *how*) Here are some questions you may ponder:

❑   What do I need to know?

- ❑ Where do I want to teach?
- ❑ When do I want to teach?
- ❑ Who do I teach?
- ❑ Why do I want to teach?
- ❑ How do I find more information about teaching?
- ❑ Oh, so many questions…

Before we begin the E.S.L. adventure, let's take a behind-the-scenes look into the backgrounds of the authors. Ms. Pinky Dang is an experienced E.S.L. teacher and teacher trainer from Richmond, British Columbia, Canada and is professionally certified by TESL Canada and is a member of the British Columbia association of Teachers of English As An Additional Language (TEAL). Ms. Dang graduated from the University of British Columbia with a Bachelor of Arts Degree in History in 1989 and from Vancouver Community College with a TESOL Certificate (Teaching English To Speakers of Other Languages) in 1999. She has been an E.S.L. teacher for immigrants, international students, local high school students, post-secondary students, and seniors. She has taught for community organizations, private language schools, a teacher training school, and a community outreach program. During her teaching career, Ms. Dang has taught all levels and disciplines of the English language and has developed and coordinated comprehensive E.S.L. programs and exam preparatory courses at various language schools around the Greater Vancouver area. In addition, Ms. Dang has developed and taught in-class and on-line teacher-training courses for prospective E.S.L. teachers studying in a TESOL program. She currently resides with her family in Richmond, Canada.

> *During preparations for an upcoming Halloween party at a private E.S.L. school in downtown Vancouver, I was determined to claim first prize in the annual costume contest. I had spent several sleepless nights designing an original costume that was sure to beat out all my competitors'. I had spent about $100 out of my own pocket and about 8 hours of my time at home, sewing, clamping, stringing and wiring a costume that I ultimately hoped would make my presence "hall-clearing". Since I had to teach a couple of classes before festivities began, my anxiety grew leading up to the unveiling. After lunch, the moment of truth arrived. I made a quick exit from my classroom and prepared to secretly adorn myself with my proud piece of work. When I finally emerged*

in all my revelry, I indeed cleared the hallways. Students from all corners of the world dropped their jaws and stood in silence. The walking tree had arrived, complete with singing birds, butterflies, and nests cleverly disguised over a human head. It was a sight to behold as cameras started flashing to record this memorable vision. I had bought brown fabric to sew a make-shift tree trunk to adorn my torso, cut and molded chicken wire into a cage-like structure to act as the tree canopy to wear on my head, strung artificial leaves, birds, nests and butterflies all over the head piece, and tape recorded sounds of singing birds onto a cassette tape to secretly play hidden under my trunk. I truly was nature at its best as I walked out in my costume and played my singing bird tape at full volume. My competitors stood in stunned silence as students whispered wondering who was the ingenious person hidden behind all those leaves. Yes, my presence was indeed "hall-clearing" as my canopy stretched to nearly the same width of the hallway. I really loved the looks on my students from the Middle East, Asia, and Africa who weren't used to seeing walking trees. In the end, I lost out to Frankenstein and claimed second prize; however, I had my moment of glory for a day and savored my tasty prize of a bag of candy.—P.D.

Dr. Rik Ruiter is an eclectic and effective therapist, motivator, theologian, educator, and visionary. He has touched many lives. Adhering to a movement in advancing human potential his life has reflected what he preaches. Dr. Ruiter has not only preached the endless possibilities and opportunities that life can hold, he has endeavored to explore and live those adventures and life experiences that reflect his teachings. With a resourceful education and much life experience, he has embarked on many interesting adventures. After accomplishing several life goals, he continues on the "Roadless Traveled." Having made several career changes, which seem to be natural progressions, from theology and family therapy to education, he brings a wealth of knowledge and experience to his latest adventure of training prospective E.S.L. (English As A Second Language) and E.S.P. (English for Specific Purposes) instructors. His theology/philosophy embraces compassion, understanding, respect, and humanness. His keen insight, sense of humour, and enthusiasm for adventure has brought him to this stage in life. Having left The Netherlands as a teenager to embark on a life in the New World, he has climbed the ladder of success, which he sees as never final. Dr. Ruiter graduated from McMaster University with a Bachelor of Arts Degree in Sociology in 1971 and completed a Master's Degree in Divinity from Knox College in Toronto in 1974. Dr. Ruiter obtained his CELTA Certificate (Certificate in English Language Teaching To Adults) from Seoul, South Korea in 1999 and completed his Doctorate in Psychology from California Coast University in 2003. He is professionally certified by TESL Canada and is a member of the British Columbia association of Teachers of English As An Additional Language (TEAL). Dr. Ruiter has taught E.S.L. and teacher-training courses overseas in South Korea, China and Thailand. He has also provided therapy, workshops and seminars for the ex-patriot community for over 8 years. He is the founder of Global Excellence International, Ltd., a teacher-training company in Vancouver, Canada. Dr. Ruiter is anticipating the expansion of teacher-training programs throughout Asia, with a focus on China.

The authors would like to thank Sonia J. Wood for her wonderful caricatures; Alexander Chew for his assistance in designing the book cover; Wayne D. Burns for his legal assistance; and the many wonderful students from all over the world that have crossed paths with the authors over the years.

I wish to thank my sons, Daniel and Jonathan for their support and encouragement

—R.R.

Thanks to Eric Dumas for being a source of inspiration; Kane and Kinman Dang for their encouragement; my mother Lee Yuit Kim for her unconditional love; and my late father Edward Dang who started life in Canada as an E.S.L. speaker and who inspired me to become an E.S.L. teacher.

—P.D.

CHAPTER 1:

Teaching Mosaics—Start Your Engine

> **In This Chapter**
>
> > Your reason to teach
>
> > Teaching at home or abroad
>
> > Who and where to teach
>
> > The hidden job market
>
> > Your qualifications
>
> > Teaching principles
>
> > The ideal teacher

Nowadays, teaching E.S.L. is big business. There are many international E.S.L. schools located in all parts of the world. Teaching E.S.L. can be a profitable enterprise that can spawn into specialized instruction in TOEFL (Test of English As A Foreign Language), TOEIC (Test of English In International Communication), LPI (The Language Proficiency Index), IELTS (International English Language Testing System), the Eiken Step Test, Business English, E.S.L. for Nursing, and other specialized E.S.L. courses. The need for a common international language with the expansion of a global communication network has made English the language of choice. A career in teaching E.S.L. can be pursued after high school, college, university, or retirement. It can act as an interim career or as a long-term profession. Many E.S.L. teachers earn good money in this business. It's a good way of making money to pay off all those student loans, especially if you're teaching in a foreign country with favorable tax advantages. Teaching E.S.L. is a respectable career at home and abroad. There are many opportunities and possibilities that present themselves in this career field every day.

Why Do I Want To Teach E.S.L.?

I.S.E.: I Speak English = It is easy = Inaccurate Formula

Not too long ago, the mere ability to speak native English was an adequate enough reason and provision to teach E.S.L. Without any qualifications, you could find a job teaching English almost anywhere. Many employers only cared about the fact that you were a native speaker. The plane landed somewhere and "Voila" you had a job…or the job found you.

Ah, the good old days.
Ah, they are gone.
Forever.

Teachers are well liked and treated with respect in many foreign countries, unlike North America where students seldom give apples to teachers anymore. Teaching E.S.L. gives you the opportunity to travel and make new discoveries. You'll have many experiences and many wonderful stories to tell your grand-children about your treks around the world. These stories would be welcome additions to the ones describing your daily 20-mile treks through blizzard conditions to get to school when you were a youngster. The world is a global village with access to every corner of the planet in a short period of time. People are continually on the move in this global village as they want to see the wonders of the world and experience different cultures. Companies send their employees to different countries to work, to set up affiliate companies, to educate the employees there, to expand product lines, etc. In this global village, English is THE international language of choice and a hot one. With the exception of Chinese, more people speak English than any other language. Airline pilots and air traffic controllers all over the world communicate in English. International business is conducted primarily in English and more than 70 percent of the world's mail is written in it; the list goes on and on.

Learning English is in high demand. With access to T.V., movies, multimedia and the internet, so many people want to learn English. From the Falkland

Islands to Vladivostok, and from the Sahara Desert to Lapland, the opportunity to teach has never been more appealing and greater than it is today. So, teaching E.S.L. is a way to see the world and to learn how to say, "Where's the bathroom?" in different languages. It allows you to experience different cultures up close. To live in a foreign country is an experience that will broaden your perspective and open your mind, if you go with an open mind. In our little global village, where we have become close neighbors, we are exposed to different cultures and traditions as more people are migrating and traveling to different parts of the earth. Thus, teaching E.S.L. has many exciting rewards that include worldwide travel, experiencing rich cultural traditions first hand, enjoying international cuisine, and learning different languages and customs. Ah, the wanderlust, the excitement, the exotic places, the draw of another country, the fantasies…Wow, what an opportunity to work, travel, experience and pay off those student loans. All that can be yours.

> English: Where is the bathroom?
> German: Wo ist der WC?
> French: Où sont les toilettes?
> Spanish: Donde esta el bano?
> Russian: Gde zeds tualet?
> Italian: Dove e il bagno?
> Mandarin: Xiv shouv jian zai-na-li?
> Japanese: Toire wa koko desu ka?
> Greek: Pu' I' ne I tauale' ta?
> Portuguese: Onde e o quarto de banho?

To Stay or Not to Stay, That is the Question

What to do as an E.S.L. teacher? Stay home or go abroad? Most teachers will do both. First, let's look at staying close to home. With many immigrants flocking to the West, there is a great demand at home to teach E.S.L. Many people come to western countries with little or no English. Not every one is as fortunate as most of us to have English as their first language. To us, speaking English comes naturally; we communicate without thinking, which isn't always wise! Immigrants coming to our shores are highly motivated to learn English in order to get jobs and establish themselves in their new community. Survival English is their primary learning objective. Their children learn E.S.L. in elementary and high schools. English is the language of university, business, technology, and travel. Many opportunities exist at home to teach E.S.L. and these opportunities will only increase. There are many opportunities in private language schools that cater to international students who come to our shores for a "learning holiday" or who wish to enter North American universities. Thus, you need to identify and customize the English needs of these types of students. Of course, acquiring a good teaching job will depend on your qualifications, your education and experience. Whether you teach in public or private institutions, they all require applicants to demonstrate appropriate credentials and teaching experience. Beginner teachers may gain experience through volunteer tutoring or teaching in community programs. The more experience you gain while learning the "ins" and "outs" of teaching, the better off you will be in preparing for your first paid teaching career.

> Just by speaking the lingo, a person can apply for more jobs, pursue that long sought-after promotion, open up new business opportunities, meet new friends from different cultural backgrounds, listen and understand the lyrics to the latest music from the West, or simply impress a sophisticated social network of friends.

Where Do You Go? Who Do You Teach?

First, sit down and decide who you want to teach and where. Do you like children? Is the environment of teaching kids comfortable to you? Keep in mind that in some countries, physical discipline is still practiced on misbehaving students. A colleague who was teaching E.S.L. in the 1980s in Korea displayed pictures of the teachers'

The internet has several E.S.L. job sources to check out:
www.eslcafe.com
www.esljobworld.com
www.teacherhunt.com
www.esljobbank.com

room that stored long sturdy sticks that were the tools of classroom discipline. Classroom discipline was defined as physically beating kids with poor behavior or poor academic performances. Fortunately Korea has since passed a law, forbidding teachers from physically harming students. More about classroom discipline can be read in Chapter 3 on Classroom Management. On the other hand, are you more interested in teaching at a university, a strategic government department, or a corporate business? There are many international schools providing education for ex-pats and often they require professional teaching certificates from your home country. What are your interests? Where would you like to go? What do you want to teach? What area of the world would you like to discover? In many foreign schools, the native teachers teach English with a focus on grammar, but not in conversation. Students graduating from high school are proficient at grammar, but cannot tune into listening and speaking English. They are usually not exposed to conversation due to the lack of opportunities to do so. Now, a shift is occurring that allows native teachers to teach conversational English in elementary and high schools in many parts of the world. Many teachers find positions in schools teaching English conversation.

Grammar Alert!!!

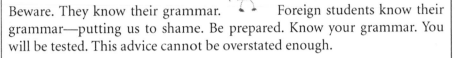

Beware. They know their grammar.   Foreign students know their grammar—putting us to shame. Be prepared. Know your grammar. You will be tested. This advice cannot be overstated enough.

So, do you want to teach children? Work in an international school? Try your hand in institutions, high schools, universities, or multinational corporations? The opportunities await you. Discovering what kind of educational institution you wish to teach at is the first step. Then, ask yourself which continent you feel drawn to living in. Do you wish to live in an urban setting or a rural one? Keep in mind that rural settings may not afford the conveniences and resources that living in an urban setting provides. Research as much as you can about the places that interest you through travel journals, the internet, the library, and through word of mouth. The more research you do, the less surprises, disappointments and frustrations you'll meet. There are many agencies out there that recruit native English speakers for various schools overseas. Refer to your community business association to check on any complaints against these agencies and investigate on the reputations of them before you deal with agents.

A good way to begin your teaching career is to do volunteer tutoring for community organizations that service the needs of new immigrants. My first tutoring student back in 1996 was Kimberly Ruan from China. Although our tutoring sessions lasted only 3 months, we've remained friends since and have even traveled to China together to visit her hometown of Zhong Shan. You may discover newfound friendships being made with your students from being involved in community-offered tutoring services.—P.D.

The Hidden Job Market

E.S.L. teaching jobs are not all focused on working in schools. There is a hidden job market out there that demands the services of E.S.L. teachers. Where is this hidden market you ask? Think about contract work that utilizes teachers for short or long-term periods. Non-traditional E.S.L. jobs that are not session-focused are great sources for employment. If there is a particular demand in learning a specialized course such as an exam prep course in passing the TOEFL and you happen to have experience in teaching it or are very familiar with the test, you can market yourself as a TOEFL teacher to different organizations that could use your services or as an entrepreneurial freelance teacher. Specialized contract work involving multinational companies, transportation companies, manufacturing sectors, tourism, hotel chains, telecommunications, government services and so on are potential marketing grounds for employment. Private tutoring is another area where you can build a solid base of clientele for your tutoring business.

English for Specific Purposes (E.S.P.) is a field you could consider too if you happen to notice a demand in a particular field. E.S.P. courses (such as E.S.L. for Nursing, Business English, E.S.L. for Accounting, etc.) can be designed and marketed by E.S.L. teachers for self-employment opportunities. You can also ask yourself if there is an area of specialization that you're knowledgeable in that can be designed into an E.S.P. course. If you are marketing a course for other schools, it's best to propose it about 2 months before their course calendars are released. You can market E.S.P. courses to private businesses as well by offering language upgrading to E.S.L. employees. Non-profit societies, community organizations, continuing education programs are other potential employment sources. However if you wish to teach at a local E.S.L. language school, you can check your local administrative body that registers post-secondary schools in your area for a list of registered or accredited schools.

If you have an E.S.L. course idea, you need to create a successful proposal that outlines your proposed course called a syllabus. A syllabus is a summary description of the main points of a speech, a book, or a course. In our case, it'll be a personally designed E.S.L. course that we're trying to market.

What should a course syllabus contain? It should contain the following:

course title; length; time required; equipment and course materials; course description; evaluation methods; identification of course units; pre-requisite restrictions; the name of the instructor; the target market for the course; and a breakdown of how the course would be taught

When you are submitting a syllabus to a potential employer, you should also submit a resume to outline your qualifications for teaching the course. Your proposed course can be based on a textbook, supplemental exercises, and on personally designed materials. If you were teaching a course called E.S.L. for Wilderness Survival, you would need more than a text-book. You'd probably need materials such as first aid equipment, camping equipment, navigation tools, toiletries, etc. You can check out a sample course syllabus with weekly and monthly lesson planning schedules in the Course Planning section of this book.

Qualifications

In the good old days, westerners stepped off the plane in almost any foreign land and were able to immediately find a teaching job. That may still happen, but the E.S.L. business has become much more organized and sophisticated. A prospective E.S.L. teacher needs to shop around and find his/her way. An analogy can be made in shopping for shoes. If you were hunting for the most comfortable pair of shoes to wear everyday, you would not settle for the first pair that you see. You'll likely shop around and compare shoes before you decide on a pair that you can live with day in and day out. Moreover, you need to set some objectives on what you want to do. Gone are the days when you hopped on a plane without any qualifications and easily found a job upon arrival.

Hello Planning!

To get the best jobs you need certain qualifications. The minimum qualifications are certificates and diplomas that say you can teach E.S.L. or E.F.L. (English As A Foreign Language). These pieces of paper will get you a job, maybe not the best one, but they will do for a start. You will be able to work at a language institute, but not a university. Most universities require you to possess a Master's Degree in addition to your teaching qualifications. Language institutes commonly require you to have a Bachelor's Degree (in any field) and an E.S.L. certificate such as CELTA (Cambridge Certificate In English

Language Teaching To Adults), DELTA (Diploma English Language Teaching to Adults), TEFL (Teaching English As A Foreign Language), TESL (Teaching English As A Second Language) or TESOL (Teaching English To Speakers Of Other Languages). There are many E.S.L. teacher-training institutions that offer these certificates and diplomas; however, not all offer the same caliber of training. Some E.S.L. teacher-training institutions will give you a certificate after 40 hours of training while others may require 320 hours of training. A good teacher-training program will usually require a minimum of 100 hours of study in addition to a practicum component. There are professional E.S.L. teacher organizations, such as TESL Canada that sets institutional standards of training and gives recognition to a list of qualified E.S.L. training institutions. See their website, www.teslcanada.org for their latest list of qualified teacher training institutions in Canada.

Be aware that if you are able to spend 40 hours of study for a TESL certificate in Joe's E.S.L. Teacher Training School, you may not be as prepared with the professional training that is demanded from a more reputable school that requires 320 hours of training. Shop around and find out what each training institution has to offer. Is the institution licensed or registered and accredited with a government agency? Are the certificates or diplomas recognized around the globe? Does the institution offer a practicum in their program? Is there any job assistance after graduation? How many hours are required for a certificate? Is it going to be cost-effective? Other considerations to ask yourself are: Do you want to attend classes in person, on-line, or through correspondence? You better do your homework or Joe's Teacher Training School may become a memory of regret.

To teach E.S.L. at a university requires a university degree in a related field. Consider an M.A. (Master's Degree) in linguistics or English. For non-university positions, a Bachelor's Degree in any field and a certificate or diploma in CELTA, DELTA, TEFL, TESL, TESOL or some related E.S.L. certificate can be sufficient to land you an E.S.L. teaching position. In non-university positions, you may still get away with merely an E.S.L. teaching certificate, but don't forget, the competition is getting stiff. Like most other academic fields, more is better: the more education and the more experience together can land you a nice plum position.

Guiding Principles

In the world of E.S.L. teaching, there are some basic principles that help guide teachers in their careers. The following list contains eight principles.

1) *A teacher's attitude is the number one influencer in effective teaching.* Teachers must be patient, understanding and encouraging to students. Teachers with a poor attitude will negatively impact students who are keen in detecting how enthusiastic their teachers are. Teachers should also add a sense of fun in the classroom as well.

2) *Teach English at a level that is appropriate to the students.* If you have a low-beginner class, use common words and short sentences to speak to them. If you have an advanced-level class, use more complex sentences to speak to them. When speaking to students, teachers should speak at a normal speed with normal intonation. Over-emphasis in a teacher's speech will negatively impact a student's receptive skills in the long run.

3) *Teaching oral English first, before reading and writing, eases language learning for students.* Low-level E.S.L. students should focus on listening and speaking skills first and read and write only what they are able to communicate orally.

4) *Student-centerd language activities optimize language learning.* Students must be able to practice the target language with minimum guidance from the teacher.

5) *Students are more receptive to language learning when used and practiced in its systemic patterns.* Enabling students to visually see and recognize language patterns will allow students to manipulate and create more diverse sentences.

6) *Non-academic students will have different language needs.* Teachers should customize the language programs of non-academic students to suit their students' specific needs as much as possible.

7) *Teachers should learn cultural differences and similarities with their students.* Nonverbal signals and body language among different cultures are important features that teachers and students should be aware of between different cultures.

8) *The ultimate goal in language learning is to have students put their skills to practical use outside the classroom.*

When considering what encompasses the ideal teacher, one should examine what would an E.S.L. student need to have in a teacher. Below is a list of characteristics of an ideal teacher.

The ideal teacher...........

➢ respects the students' culture by doing prior background research and has an interest to know more about it.

➢ is enthusiastic and inspires students to learn

➢ encourages students by providing clear positive feedback.

➢ creates a relaxing atmosphere conducive to language learning.

➢ is animated in the classroom by using facial expressions, body language, and gestures to communicate meaning.

➢ uses teaching aids that utilizes the 5 senses.

➢ observes students for non-verbal clues that may indicate lack of understanding.

➢ conducts student-centered activities so he/she isn't always the focus of every activity and gives students a chance to freely practice target language.

➢ is well-organized.

➢ knows when and how to correct. Too much correction inhibits the learning process while too little impedes progress.

➢ teaches lessons at an appropriate pace.

➢ asks comprehensive questions to ensure student understanding. Never relies on the question, "Do you understand?"

➢ is patient and attentive to the students' needs.

➢ has a good sense of humor.

➢ knows his subject.

➢ assigns relevant homework and assignments.

➢ administers periodic tests.

Which of these characteristics do you see yourself as already possessing in your plans to be a future E.S.L. teacher? Which of these characteristics do you find absent or uncertain within you and why?

CHAPTER 2:

Overseas Preparations— Your Driving Route

Psst....I've got a job for you!

After receiving your hard-earned E.S.L. teaching certificate, you may have the urge to flee your homeland and go to more exotic locales to try your hand at teaching in a foreign land. Before fleeing, it's always a good idea to do some background research not only in the destination of your choice, but to the prospective employer as well. There are many international language schools and

TESL Organizations
www.tesol.org
www.teslcanada.org

public/private schools that have agents or companies who recruit native English teachers with appropriate qualifications to teach in their countries. You may look for recruiting companies and international schools who are hiring foreign E.S.L. teachers by entering "E.S.L. teaching jobs" in various search engines on the internet. There is a great website for E.S.L. teachers called *Dave's E.S.L. Café*, http://www.eslcafe.com/, that is rich in teaching ideas, information, job postings, and forums that describe the overseas experiences of other E.S.L. teachers. It's always a good idea to read the forum on overseas teachers' experiences to get a handle on what you can expect in certain schools around the globe. You will find positive and negative stories from TEFL teachers but as with all things in life, there are always 2 sides to a story.

Keep in mind that not only are language schools sources of employment for E.S.L. teachers, a hidden job market exists for prospective teachers. Multinational companies and high technology firms often recruit language teachers for their overseas staff. In addition, hotel chains, phone companies, airlines, manufacturing companies and government offices are also potential sources of employment. The Royal Saudi Air Force often recruits English teachers for their staff. Moreover, there is a need for a level of E.S.L. called E.S.P. (English For Special Purposes) to serve the in-house English upgrading needs of business executives who need to conduct foreign business. E.S.P. can focus on English for service trades, tourism, industry, socio-cultural programs, airlines, import/export companies, etc. Your own personal work experience in clerical, hospitality or trade industries may benefit greatly when focusing on an E.S.P. program. Furthermore, personal hobbies and interests can also help you expand a custom-designed E.S.P. program.

The Teacher Draft

If you decide that teaching in a language school is the road you'd like to travel, you'll likely be faced with signing a teaching contract with either a recruiter representing a school or a representative from it. Recruiters typically arrange work permits, visas, air travel, accommodations and housing allowances, medical insurance and salary details for their new employees. Extra  benefits such as moving allowances, furniture allowances and daily transportation to and from work can also be provided or negotiated with some recruiters. Salary expectations can range from as low as $19,200 to $84,000 USD or more per year depending on your qualifications. If you keep in mind the different costs of living, a salary as low as $19,200 will provide a comfortable standard of living. The potential to live like "royalty" on an E.S.L. teacher's salary is possible. One school in China even provides regular maid and cooking services to teachers' homes!

This book will not attempt to be politically correct in its desire to give readers as much information as possible when they go job hunting locally or overseas. It had been reported by a former female colleague that from her experience, she often was turned down for E.S.L. teaching positions in Asia simply because she was of Asian descent. There are some Asian schools that prefer a non-Asian looking (a.k.a. "western") face for their E.S.L. teaching staff, regardless of the skills and experience of the job applicants.

In Canada, one E.S.L. college that I worked for was owned by a couple from China who hired a good looking, young, blonde, Caucasian receptionist. She was placed front and center at the large reception desk, among a predominantly Chinese staff and a predominantly Chinese student population. It was the owners' way to show students and visitors how "Canadian" their college was even though there was no English-Only immersion policy to prevent the Chinese language from being widely spoken all over the school; it essentially became another Chinese school that happened to be overseas. Several months later, one of the owners decided to go on a student-recruiting trip to China. Instead of bringing along a qualified teacher, an academic coordinator, a Director of Studies, or an administrator who had a thorough knowledge of the school's academic programs, the owner brought the Caucasian receptionist as his lone recruiting assistant. Although this young good-looking receptionist was friendly and personable, she had no teaching credentials, didn't contribute to the design of any of the academic programs, and lacked the experience necessary in learning how to assess and meet the needs of E.S.L. students. In essence, she was no more than a physically attractive "lure" for potential student recruitments.—P.D.

You will discover early in your teaching career that a school's management goals may not always strive for teaching excellence. Many schools with E.S.L. programs will often gear themselves towards what makes them the most money rather than what gives students the best value for their education dollar.

Not All Places Are Equal

Salary remuneration for E.S.L. teachers vary from country to country. Some countries have been in the E.S.L. business for a long time, while others have just opened its doors to it. Meanwhile there are still other countries that are just in the process of opening its doors.

When exploring different countries and places, be aware that not all places provide the same salaries and benefits. Some regions such as Taiwan have programs that aim towards sending foreign language teachers toe teach English in the countryside. The mere mention of "countryside" brings about images of meadows, streams and fresh air. Contrary to that ideal image, you may find that a country's "countryside" is often as polluted and dirty as some of the cities. When you are posted overseas in a small town, you may find that few people there may speak English and that there may be few amenities (familiar Western food, laundry service, bookstores, movie theatres, etc.). Some teachers who agree to living and working in certain rural areas often find themselves feeling lonely, frustrated and miserable. These teachers end up spending their money by heading out to the big cities on the weekends to escape. What should you look for? Research essential information such as:

❑ What is the salary? Is it paid on time? In what currency is the salary paid in? What are the pay schedules?

❑ What are the tax rules at home and abroad? Becoming a non-resident from your home country will exempt you from taxes. Check your local tax department for updated tax rules.

❑ What benefits are provided? Is there medical insurance? Medical insurance is usually the minimum provision. What is exactly covered in the medical insurance?

❑ Are there any dental benefits?

❑ Is there severance pay? A pension? Disability benefits?

❑ Who pays for the airfare and when?

❑ Is airfare paid up front or reimbursed after a certain period of time upon the commencement of employment?

❑ Are you entitled to be paid holiday time? For how long?

❑ Do I have airfare provided for my vacation time back to my home country?

- [ ] If I decide to return to my home country before the end of my contract, do I provide my own airfare?

- [ ] What consequences, if any, are there if I do not complete my contract?

- [ ] Is housing provided? Is it included in your package? Shared or not? Furnished or not? Are there any appliances? Is there a furniture allowance? Is there a moving allowance?

- [ ] How far will my residence be from the school? How will I commute to school on a daily basis?

- [ ] How can I be sure that I won't have sub-standard housing?

- [ ] Will I be forced to relocate at any time during my stay in the country? How can I be sure it won't happen? You should ask for a provision included in your contract regarding relocation matters.

- [ ] Who takes care of the working visa or work permits? Who looks after the paper work?

- [ ] Am I required to surrender my passport to the possession of the school or to the recruiter during my employment? NEVER surrender your passport out of your possession to anyone. If a school insists, you can offer them a photocopy.

- [ ] Get a list from your country's embassy of recommended medical doctors and dentists in the area you'll be based in.

- [ ] Register yourself with your country's embassy when you arrive.

- [ ] Brainstorm any other details that need to be answered before you leave

An informed teacher is a happy teacher. The more informed you are, the more pleasant and enriching the experience will be. Get as much information as possible to minimize any unexpected situations that may arise. Ensure any contract you sign is written in English and check and double check if you have to sign a translated contract that is the same as the one you signed in English. In China, the government requires Chinese-written contracts. When initially signing a contract in English, teachers have been told after a month in China to sign a contract written in Chinese. It's not a good idea to put your signature on something that you can't read. Ensure a third party translator can assist you in reading a contract written in a language you can't read. There have been occasions where some teachers weren't told about the Chinese-language contract requirement and reluctantly put their signatures on a document they couldn't read. Ensure contracts written in English are translated into the language of the native country by an independent third party who is a professional translator.

Additionally, recruiters have reported that teachers at times may initially work in China without a work permit because it sometimes takes a long time for a foreigner to acquire one from outside the country. Teachers are often told that they are to apply for a work permit once they enter the country and after they start work. It's best to check for regulations on proper procedures with the nearest embassy or consulate of your new country before you leave home. How do you know which recruiters are recommended and which should be avoided? You can check for referrals from other experienced E.S.L. teachers or check for any reported complaints to the Department of Foreign Affairs and International Trade or your local Better Business Bureau.

You may sometimes find ads from overseas schools or government departments seeking English teachers to come overseas to work. In an ad from *The National Post* newspaper in 2004, the Military Language Institute from the United Arab Emirates sought English teachers for their military college. The contract was with the UAE Armed Forces. The salary was commensurate with your university degree qualifications ($34,600–37,600 USD for BA qualified teachers; $37,900–40,800 USD for MA qualified teachers; $51,000–54,000 for program coordinators) and included the following benefit package:

- housing allowance plus utilities
- furniture allowance
- hospital medical coverage
- relocation allowance
- 45 days annual leave (excluding UAE national holidays)
- return tickets to your home for annual leaves
- professional development provisions
- family status of your spouse and up to 3 children
- children's education allowance
- annual salary increases
- end-of-contract bonus

Specific degree qualifications and 3 years of English language instruction were required for teachers while 5 years of program management experience and 5 years of teaching and administrative experience were needed for program coordinators. Interviews took place in Toronto, Canada for a 12 day period and in London, England for 11 days. Before making serious inquiries for ads such as this one, check out E.S.L. teacher website forums like Dave's E.S.L. café (www.eslcafe.com) for feedback from teachers who've worked in the countries or for the employers that interest you. It's best to obtain as much information as possible and a goldmine of information is from those who have worked in those places before.

Cross-Cultural Anecdotes

An often over-looked field of study when traveling abroad is the different cultural communication that exists around the globe. If you've decided on a particular destination to begin your TEFL career, researching the culture that you're going to commit to living in is essential. If you view the world from the vantage points of others, you will be able to function more effectively and comfortably in different cultures. Requirements that are needed to help bridge the gap between cultures are:

➤ The ability to accept ambiguity

➤ The ability to be open-minded

➤ The ability to be indiscriminate and tolerate differences

➤ The ability to show empathy

➤ The ability to communicate and motivate

➤ The ability to embrace the warmth of human relationships

➤ The ability to perceive and adapt to changes

➤ The ability to be self-reliant and flexible

➤ The ability to fail

The last requirement may surprise you but it's important to recognize that in success there are often failures along the way. Success is often built on failures. When you're faced with difficult situations, you must be strong emotionally and spiritually. You become what you believe. Your place in life is defined not by your wishes, dreams or hopes, but ultimately by what you believe. If you feel uncertain about being able to live and adapt to another culture, keep in mind that personal growth involves dealing with uncertainty. People would rather choose the certainty of a "terrible" life than the uncertainty of a possible good life.

Cultural Variables

There are many common elements in society that people often perceive as being universal. Time, for instance, is interpreted in different manners. Depending on the culture, what is considered punctual, early, or late varies. To avoid unpleasant surprises, it's best to communicate your expectations about time and inquire about those of other regions. Moreover, dropping by to visit people unexpectedly is common in some countries, such as Eastern Europe. If you prefer to be notified in advance of a visit, it's best to inform friends from a new country of your preferences. Formality also varies around the globe. In some cultures, such as in Asia, the Middle East and parts of Africa, people refrain from using the first name with elders due to their belief that it shows disrespect. You'll find values differ all over the world. Find a friend to serve as a cultural educator. Some common questions to consider as you explore your new culture are:

➤ Is individualism more important (as it is in North America) than collectivism (as it is in Asia)?

➤ Is cooperation valued more than competitiveness?

➤ How is equality viewed in your new culture? Are women and men seen as equals in society?

➤ Is there more focus on the extended family or the nuclear family?

➤ Are there special lineal relationships where past generations and ancestors are worshipped?

➤ How does religion play a part in society?

➤ What are the parents' roles in the guidance and choices they provide for their children?

➤ Is there an authoritarian design in the family structure where the father is seen as the top decision maker?

➤ What is a society's definition of success? Is it more material than spiritual?

➤ What are a society's feelings on honor and respect?

➤ What are the attitudes toward education in society? What performance expectations and reactions is made of a teacher?

➤ What are the communication styles of a classroom?

➤ What are the customs surrounding gift giving? What gifts are considered offensive? (Giving clocks as gifts in China is not a good idea)

➢ What are the dating customs of your new country? (Group-dating is common in Japan in early stages of a relationship.)

➢ What significance do friendships have? People from Asia, Latin America, and the Middle East may have higher expectations than North Americans do on friendships

➢ Are there any culinary dining rules? How are the offerings of food made? (Asian cultures typically repeatedly offer food out of courtesy to guests)

➢ How are important business discussions conducted? (In some parts of the world, important business matters can be discussed over a meal rather than in an office setting)

➢ What is considered appropriate attire for teaching or general wear?

➢ How does the society view physical contact or signs of affection?

Before settling in a foreign country, remind yourself that people's behaviors may not always reflect their values. A person who asks you your age may not mean to offend, but rather intends to initiate a friendly conversation and to figure out the appropriate way to address you. All cultures have values and ideals that are true to their members.

Culture in the Classroom

A western teacher's friendliness and informality can often confuse students who are used to conservative, placid, and closely supervised classroom environments. Such environments are characteristic in authoritarian educational systems outside of North America. Humorous banter and open expressions from teachers are not always welcomed by students as well. Teachers are often seen as authority figures to be respected, revered, and even feared, thus some students may find it difficult to assert themselves in class with questions or challenges to ideas. Teachers should also be aware of using red ink in marking students' papers. In many parts of Asia and in Mexico, seeing one's name written in red ink is a sign of death. It's best to avoid red ink and use an alternative color for marking. Discipline is also an area of concern when it comes to managing unruly students. Physical discipline of problem students may be allowed in some countries. Check disciplinary rules of your new country and school. Personally, physical discipline should not be used as a motivator for learning in any environment. It's important to identify potential generalizations. Although culture doesn't necessarily reflect behavior, it does greatly influence it. Students who are unassertive may just be giving respect to teachers. All in all, it's best not to overemphasize cultural differences or similarities, but embrace the enriching experience of learning about cultures.

Cross-Cultural Communication

The meanings of many non-verbal gestures have wide interpretations from culture to culture. According to Norine Dresser's *Multicultural Manners*, the "thumbs up" gesture has sexual connotations to some Afghani, Middle East and Australian cultures. The "okay" sign is offensive in some Latin American countries. In addition the gesture of clasping one's hands has an ominous signal, especially with babies as it supposedly predicts death because according to Dresser's research, people from some Latin American and West Indian cultures see clasped hands as a reminder of the clasped hands of a corpse lying in its coffin. Thus it's not uncommon to see child caregivers from these cultures make efforts to prevent babies from clasping their hands.

Even the simple act of smiling doesn't have a universal meaning. Many people from some Asian cultures don't smile in photos. They equate smiling as being insensitive to the "seriousness" of the photo. Even in certain situations smiling is reserved when formal relations are involved, whether it be commercial or personal transactions; thus many westerners may mistakenly equate unsmiling Asian shopkeepers as being people who lack respect or who have anti-social behavior.

Another great resource for cross-cultural learning is Orlando L. Taylor's article "Cross-Cultural Communication: An Essential Dimension of Effective Education", which can be found on the internet from the *Northwest Regional Educational Laboratory* website: www.nwrel.org/cnorse/booklets/ccc/index.html. He provides invaluable questions that you can ask when you are researching a new culture.

> *While traveling in Asia, I ran into many mistranslated signs in places like ZhengZhou Airport where I spotted a sign saying "dometic" instead of "domestic" and "Incapacited People Board First" instead of "incapacitated"; or on the highway leaving the airport I noticed a sign saying "drying lane" instead of "driving lane"; there was also a car accident reference to "rear end collusion" instead of "rear end collision"—R.R.*

Culture Shock

Imagine you've just received a free ticket to exotic Jupiter Island in the South Pacific. All expenses will be paid for you for a whole year on the island. Jupitonians don't speak English; however they speak Esperanto. Their culture is completely unlike the West. Visitors to Jupiter Island often see the native islanders conduct behavior opposite to what is expected from the West. You see this free trip as an exciting adventure, yet a challenging one too.

Many people who immerse themselves in a new culture with a new language may undergo an emotional reaction within themselves called "Culture Shock". Culture shock is a form of anxiety and can be minimized by educating oneself on the history, culture, politics, and people of the new country. Learning as much background information on your host country will be invaluable in your adaptation to a new life.

Culture shock is divided into four stages:

1) The Excitement Stage
   - A short period of excitement at being in a new culture begins.

2) The Frustration Stage (Culture Shock Begins)
   - Familiar cultural patterns begin to be missed. A period of depression, homesickness, loneliness, disorientation, irritability, insomnia, boredom, withdrawal, frustration, and so forth may pop up.
   - Pre-conceived notions of host country nationals are challenged; thus there may be stereotyping and resentment of host country nationals.

3) The Adjustment Stage (Culture Shock Managed)
   - The visitor begins seeking and learning to understand unfamiliar cultural responses.
   - There may be less judgmental moral opinions on host country nationals.
   - There may be less over-emphasis on the value of the mother-culture.
   - The visitor begins learning rather than reacting to the culture of the host country.
   - The visitor begins making friends with host country nationals.
   - The visitor begins noting some positive things about the new culture

4) The Recovery Stage (Culture Shock Gone)
   - This stage may take a long time to reach.

- This stage describes the visitor's full integration in society.
- The newcomer begins to feel at home and enjoys living in the new culture.

Let's return to the Jupiter Island adventure. If you landed on the island and began to settle in your new home for the coming year, what would your reaction be in the first month, the sixth month, the ninth month, and a year from now and why?

Western and Non-Western Students

International students in western countries add a beneficial dynamic to the student populations of western schools. Western students are enriched socially and culturally in a multinational student population; however, along with the benefits, there can be potential learning problems between these international students from diverse cultural groups and western educators. A great book that examines the issue of meeting the needs of an international student population is *Understanding the International Student* by KaiKai and KaiKai. This book is a compilation of a series of essays on international students and the multicultural classroom written by various educators. In the essay "Understanding Students From Diverse Cultural Backgrounds", written by Septimus M. KaiKai in *Understanding the International Student* there are several notable differences in attitude, expectations, and perceptions between western and non-western students.

In comparing attitudes towards education, a non-western student tends to experience heavy pressure to perform well academically due to his society's strong link between social status and academic achievement. On the other hand, social status in western society is not necessarily defined solely by academic achievement. A more open definition of excellence prevails in western society.

Another difference in attitudes between the two types of students can be observed with performance expectations. Non-western students embrace the belief that exam failure is the fault of the student and is seen as a tremendous dishonor to the family. Western students tend to blame academic failure on the instructor but at the same time see it as an individual problem rather than as a family problem. Exam results in non-western societies tend to be publicly exposed and general information on impending exams are withheld by instructors whereas in western society the opposite occurs—exam results are not publicly exposed to identify the student and instructors tend to give general information on impending exams.

The other main area where different attitudes occur involves views towards the teacher. Non-western society views the teacher as a highly honored individual with a great deal of authority and power. Teachers in non-western societies tend to control a standard of conformity in the classroom and play the role of disciplinarian if necessary. In western societies, teachers have to earn the respect of their students and they tend to encourage individual thought and assertiveness in the classroom. Western teachers see themselves as educational guides and are not responsible for discipline.

References

Dresser, Norine. (1996) *Multicultural Manners*. Toronto: John Wiley & Sons

KaiKai, Septimus M. "Understanding Students From Diverse Cultural Backgrounds". In Septimus M. KaiKai & Regina E. KaiKai, (Eds.) (1992) *Understanding the International Student* (pp.6-8). New York: McGraw-Hill.

Recommended Reading

Dresser, Norine. (1996) *Multicultural Manners*. Toronto: John Wiley & Sons

KaiKai, Septimus M. & KaiKai, Regina E. (Eds.) (1992) *Understanding the International Student*. New York: McGraw-Hill.

Taylor, Orlando L. Cross-Cultural Communication: An Essential Dimension of Effective Education. *Northwest Regional Educational Laboratory* website. Retrieved November 10, 2003 from the World Wide November 10, 2003 from the World Wide Web:www.nwrel.org/cnorse/booklets/ccc/index.html.

CHAPTER 3:

Classroom Management—Getting to Know the Vehicle

How do you make a good first impression when starting a new class? Are first impressions really important? Ask the parents of a teenage daughter who comes home to introduce her new punk rocker boyfriend who has long slick purple hair, green lipstick, black eye shadow, shredded leather pants, a stained yellow tank top, and a big spiky dog collar on his neck. He also goes by the nickname, "Killer" and has a metal tracking device on his ankle placed there by police authorities. If you take this same fellow and  introduce him to a class of students as their new teacher, you can probably be sure to experience a drop in attendance as students run for their lives. How do you begin to create a good first impression for yourself?

You can begin by making pre-class preparations before you see the faces of your smiling students. The more preparations you make, the more efficient your lesson will be and the more you become the master of time-management. If you're using audio or visual equipment for your lessons, ensure that all equipment is functioning normally and all videos, DVDs, tapes, or CDs, are positioned at the right place. If you're using a television, program it for closed captioning if a function exists for it. Locate any remote controls for easy control access on VCRs. Overhead projectors should be checked for proper illumination and magnification. Overhead transparencies, transparency pens, and a moist rag (for cleaning the transparencies) should be organized and prepared as well. Moreover, ensure that the electrical cords on all equipment are sufficient in length to reach a classroom electric outlet; otherwise an extension cord may be needed. Since you may not know the names of your students on the first day of class, it's always a good idea to prepare name-pates for students to write their names on, so you can identify who they are. Name-plates can be made by folding letter size paper to make a standing triangle (see Figure 3.1). Students can clearly write their names with a big black felt pen that you can supply.

Figure 3.1

1. Fold paper along dotted lines.   2. Make a triangle shape along the folds   3. Write name on one side.

> *While teaching in Thailand, two brothers were in my class: Ping and Pong. In*
> *China, I had a class of students whose last names were primarily Deng, Ding*
> *and Dong.—R.R.*

If a school allows teachers to arrange a classroom to suit their needs, embrace the opportunity to demonstrate your furniture arranging skills. Unneeded furniture should be pushed against walls or in an area that may be used for extra activities. If there is a "teacher's desk" in the room, push it aside so that it isn't located in front of the main board. You'll want to keep the area in front of the main board clear of obstruction to facilitate your classroom movements. When students enter a class, keep in mind that if you are working in a school populated by students from different countries, it's best to ensure that students don't sit next to a person who understands his/her first language. Students who share a common native language will tend to speak to each other with it rather than practice their English. It's imperative that this arrangement be done from the first day, otherwise students will tend to look at an altered seating arrangement in a negative light when it's done in the middle of the term. In oral discussions, students may be put in a semi-circle with you being part of the circle. Never assemble students in a semi-circle around a teacher's desk with you sitting behind it. A desk between you and the students tends to impair communication connection with students. The most ideal seating arrangement for effective language learning is the U-shape. Arrange tables and chairs so that they take on the shape of a "U" but are not physically touching each other (see Figure 3.2).

Figure 3.2

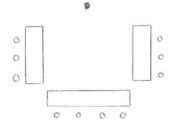

o student
● teacher

A teacher may check students' work with the U-shaped set up by standing beside a student and then switching positions to monitor the next student and continuing until all of the students have been helped (see Figure 3.3).

Figure 3.3

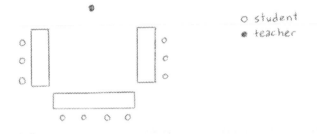

An inner U-shape seating plan where students can face each other and engage in conversations at appropriate distances (see Figure 3.4) can also facilitate interactive discussions. When there is pair work, students can be positioned in a specific pair-work seating plan as well (see Figure 3.5).

Figure 3.4

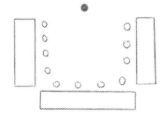

Figure 3.5

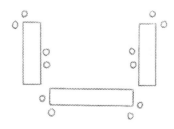

Standing Locations

Unless blood circulation in the foot is lost, teachers should not limit their standing positions to 1 or 2 locations. Variety in a teacher's position is vital for learners. Wherever you are in the classroom, there should be a reason for being in that position, whether or not you happen to have digestive gas or are monitoring students. Teach from every possible position in the room and avoid being a classroom statue that students have to lock their eyes on for an hour. It's important to note that it doesn't mean that you should pace up and down the class like a field marshal motivating his troops for battle. The main goal is to establish a relaxed and open atmosphere where students can feel comfortable in non-dominating discussions. You may sit down in a chair, but just don't sit for long periods of time. When you have a problem with a soft-spoken student, don't position yourself directly in front of the student so you can hear him/her. Such a move wouldn't be a good idea due to the fact that the other students wouldn't be able to hear what the quiet student is saying and students wouldn't be able to see your face. With this focused attention on the quiet student, you would begin to lose the attention of other students as their minds would begin to wander. Instead, position yourself between the soft-spoken student and the rest of the class (see Figure 3.6). Consequently, the other students can press their soft-spoken classmate to increase his/her volume.

Figure 3.6

Avoid this bad-teacher-position   Good teacher position with distant locations

Furthermore, if a student needs special attention, you can stand diagonally behind him as a means of providing encouragement. Finally, when standing in the classroom, teachers should not have their hands in their pockets, have their arms folded, or constantly carry a book around. Expressing body language is essential when teaching in a classroom. In essence, strategic seating plans, varied body language and teacher positioning are critical factors in producing an effective teaching environment.

Interactive Seating Plans

There are a variety of seating positions for interactive activities. Teachers should experiment with these positions to help simulate possible interactive situations in the real world and to improve listening skills (see Figure 3.7). Interactive activities can be conducted with students in face-to-face or back-to-back seating arrangements.

Figure 3.7

   (1) Pairs   (2) Small Groups

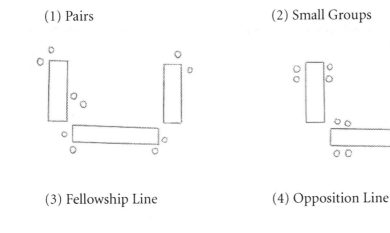

   (3) Fellowship Line   (4) Opposition Line

   (5) Expert Panel   (6) Moving Wheel

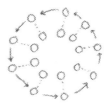

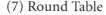
(7) Round Table

(8) Debate Formation

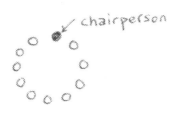

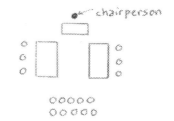

Board Work

Does your writing look like you drank a little too much? If yes, you should practice writing legibly on a board. You should avoid cursive writing in case some students are not familiar with it. Teachers should plan their board work and do it effectively so the information that they're conveying doesn't look like a confusing road map. Teachers should also write on the board by standing to the side of their writing and facing the students. Try to avoid writing on the board with your back to the students; otherwise students end up staring at the back of your head wondering what shampoo you use. Use different colored markers (if you should have a dry erase board or are using an overhead projector) to highlight potential problems in grammar form and other areas that may need to be emphasized. It's also useful to reserve a small space off to the side (such as a column) on the board for incidental vocabulary or grammar items. Avoid writing in capital letters; otherwise you're defeating the upcoming lesson on capitalization. Lastly, when doing board work during a lesson in which you want the students to listen to you first and write down information later, inform them that you will give them time to copy the information in their books after you have made your presentation.

Troubleshooting Large Classes

Problem 1
Teacher: *I can't hear my students. Should I start distributing megaphones?*

Many students are shy in speaking in a foreign language in front of a large crowd. Quiet speakers tend to lull their audiences into coma-like states that can be difficult battle.

Possible Repair:

a.   Encourage students to speak loudly with shouting dictations and interactive pair work.

b.   Do more activities that allow students to get to know one another more on a personal basis.

c.   Group quiet students together in a group or allocate the role of group secretary or chairperson to a dominant student in a group.

Problem 2
Teacher: *Students give minimal responses in front of the class.*
e.g. Teacher: *Johnny, what did you do on the weekend?*
Johnny: *I slept.* (laughter)

Students are shy and afraid of making mistakes and feeling humiliated in front of their peers. As a result, to avoid making mistakes, students will give minimal answers that are just enough to answer the question quickly with little or no added input.

Possible Repair:

a.   Give students time to think about their responses. (e.g. Have them write the answers first, then turn over their papers and give their answers.)

b.   Get students to practice answers in a less threatening environment—first, in closed pairs before giving answers in front of the class.

c.   Move from reception (listening, video, reading) to production (speaking, writing, role play).

E.g. Get students to ask you the question first, and then give them a model of the length of answer you expect, then ask them.

Problem 3
Teacher: *Taking attendance takes too long and the students get restless...(yawn).* Often attendance is the key deciding factor for passing or failing a course so keeping thorough attendance records is vital. In smaller classes, attendance taking should be done discreetly by the teacher so students shouldn't have to bear going through this daily task; however, in larger classes, discreet attendance taking may not always be efficient, especially if you haven't grasped the names of all your students.

Possible Repair (for large classes):

a. Use attendance taking as a warm-up. For example, instead of having students say "yes" or "here", get them to answer with the name of their favorite movie or actor, or play a word association game, etc.

b. Get them started on a reading or writing task and call their names out while they work so no time is wasted.

Problem 4
Teacher: *I can't remember their names. Do I need more Coenzyme Q10?*

So many students, so many names!

Possible Repair:

a. Make a class seating plan by name as you take attendance.

b. Use a badge system—students wear their names until you remember them!

c. Have students display personal paper name plates each time they are seated in class.

Problem 5
Teacher: *Students don't pay attention—they talk when I'm talking and they don't stop talking when I want them to. Is it time for me to show them who's BOSS in this classroom?*

Students feel anonymous in a big class. They may be used to attending boring university lectures with 500—600 people in a massive auditorium where paying attention is considered an option.

Possible Repair:

a. Use non-verbal cues to get their attention: for example, raise your arm or move to center stage—but inform the students what these cues mean and what they should do.

b. Don't start giving instructions until they are all quiet and listening.

c. Look at them until they become quiet.

d. Seat problem students closer to you so you can see and hear them and vice versa.

Problem 6
Teacher: *Students resist pair and group work and using English with each other. Help!*

From the student's standpoint, it's not proper to do interactive activities with a peer. It also doesn't feel natural for them to speak to their friend in English. In large foreign language classes, all communication tends to go primarily through the teacher while students listen and take notes (or sleep).

Possible Repair:

a. On the first day, explain the style of lecture and activities students will be doing throughout the course.

b. Learner training—use open pairs to get them used to working together in English.

c. Teach them functional language for doing classroom tasks: *Can you repeat that please? How do you spell...? What does...mean?*

d. Establish clear learning objectives for each activity.

e. Establish a clear English-Only Policy on the first day and consequences if students don't abide by it (Eg. You can charge an offending student 10 cents each time he/she breaks the rules and use the collected money at the end of the course to buy treats for the class.)

Problem 7
Teacher: *Students revert to their native tongue when I'm not monitoring. How can I control their tongues?!?*

Students often feel awkward with each other in a foreign language setting. Students may feel you don't know what you're doing with so many students in the class. Sometimes they don't see the point of an activity nor why they are speaking to each other in English.

Possible Repair:

a. Explain how the course evaluation is conducted and distribute reference sheets.

b. Explain and reinforce what students need to do to get top grades in the course and to improve their English.

c. Get students used to speaking to each other in English by involving them in interactive pair work.

d. Give feedback on how the task was performed and specify positive performance traits: "This group did well by using a lot of vocabulary and the correct verb forms, but this group..."

e. Give interesting/motivating tasks with clear aims: info gaps, surveys, etc

f.   Designate a leader or a monitor for group work. For example, one person in each group plays the role of a secretary who'll report the group findings to the rest of the class.

Problem 8
Teacher: *They stop pair/group work too quickly.*

Students tend to feel awkward speaking English. They may treat activities as a race or they don't see any relevance in doing the work.

Possible Repair:

a.   Give quick finishers extra tasks such as a written report of the discussion they have just finished, to stop them disturbing other students.

b.   Give feedback on the performance task: "Group A finished very quickly, group B took their time. Who do you think did the activity more carefully?"

c.   Provide plenty of variety in the types of pair or group work you give them so they don't get too bored.

d.   Communicate the learning objective clearly so students understand why they're doing the task.

e.   Assemble shy students with dominant students together in groups.

f.   Check if some women feel inhibited from participating in group-activities with men present.

Problem 9
Teacher: *Knowing students individually is impossible. How can I build a connection with them when I am vastly outnumbered?*

Building a solid teacher-student learning relationship is difficult in a large class. There are actions that teachers may do that may seem small but can have big responses.

Possible Repair:

a.   Take attendance daily so every student's name is said at least once.

b.   Learn and use students' names.

c.   Nominate a weaker student.

d.   Talk to the students when they are working in groups.

e.   Use personalized activities that build on relationships between peers and you.

<u>Problem 10</u>
Teacher: *Student circulation around the class is difficult for interactive tasks. Should I start knocking out the walls to create space?*

In large classes you may find that they are antiquated with "primitive" desks that are often fixed and too heavy to move. With so many students, having them circulate around the class for discussion tasks is like asking a herd of rhinos to use an outhouse. Students may not come from an education background that would see them regularly circulate around the class to do activities. You may have to teach them that this form of learning facilitates language learning.

Possible Repair:

a.   Divide instructions for complex activities into manageable portions.

b.   Arrange students in pairs or groups before class begins.

c.   Before class, show students how to arrange the class as you want it and then choose certain students to arrange the class in this way.

Classroom Civilities

Now that you've established a great seating plan and have checked all necessary audio and video equipment, it's time to set out some expected policies governing classroom etiquette. There are five key essentials that teachers should prepare to help establish the positive classroom environment they wish to set up to pave the way for the rest of the course. First, determine what happens when students are late. If a school already has a late policy, then teachers should abide by it; however, if a late policy is left up to the teachers' discretion, a ten-minute leeway can be established for latecomers to enter class. Beyond ten minutes, latecomers can be refused admittance until break time or when the next class begins. A teacher may also proclaim that 4 late occasions will equal 1 official absence on record. This proclamation can serve as a deterrent for late attendance.

The key to upholding a late policy or any classroom policy is to inform the students on the first day of class and to have it in writing for students to see on a handout and on a poster hung on a wall. If a school declares that latecomers should be admitted to class, there is a tip that you can consider that encourages students to be more punctual. First, don't wait for latecomers to class. Beginning class right on time tells students that you wish to get down to business and you're eager to do it. It may also irritate students who made the effort to come to class on time and are made to wait for students who are not as conscientious. Too much energy is focused on students who are late.

Fellow colleague and experienced E.S.L. teacher, Ms. Sharry Burns states that punctual students should be rewarded by being given a pop quiz at the beginning of class. Ms. Burns suggests that teachers can distribute a specially designed test at the beginning of class. Teachers can design this test so that it would be exorbitantly too long to complete in a short time frame. When teachers distribute the test at the beginning of class, they can verbally instruct their punctual students to only do the odd number questions; thus the exorbitantly long quiz then becomes a quiz of reasonable length. The key to the instructions is to verbally express them at no other time except at the beginning of class. Latecomers who arrive to class and begin the test should not be told the verbal instructions since they were not present for them. As a result, latecomers would feel the stress of frantically trying to complete every question from this exorbitantly long quiz. This teaching tip on minimizing late arrivals to class is one example of an effective way to condition latecomers to be punctual.

In addition to a teacher's handling of student lateness, another factor affecting the classroom environment is a teacher's enthusiasm. Experience has shown that when a teacher is enthusiastic about a subject, students become infected by it, regardless of the course content. Enthusiasm rubs off on students, even in courses that may seem disdainful to them. If you were required to take *Introductory Nail Filing*, it surely helps to persuade the mind to attend classes when you have an instructor who eagerly wants to pass on this life skill and see you with perfectly shaped nails. A master nail filer with 5 doctorate degrees will not be an effective instructor if he doesn't have the enthusiasm to transfer his knowledge to his students.

Thirdly, in small-size classes, avoid taking attendance at the beginning of class. The dreariness of such a task can best be left after class is finished so as not to subject the students to a mundane procedure that goes back to when there were one-room schoolhouses. Attendance can be taken discreetly near the end of class so as not to interrupt the flow of the lesson. A school should have a policy on a minimum attendance requirement for all courses. Many schools in North America outline that a minimum 90% attendance is needed for students to receive credit for a course.

Fourthly, another key preparation teachers can make is making a course outline that describes the course content, hours of instruction, learning objectives, materials required, the distribution of marks, course evaluation guidelines, student progress reporting, and dates of important tests such as mid-terms and the final exam. It's important that students know from the first day what they are going to learn, what they are going to be tested on, and how their progress is going to be evaluated in the course.

Finally, inform students of any classroom rules that have been established by the school. Are drinks allowed in the class? If yes, what are they limited to? Is there an expected student dress code? Does the school have a specific rule that forbids students from speaking languages other than English in the class? If not, can teachers outline their own English-Only rule in the classroom? A reward system, such as distributing sweet treats can be implemented for students who make concerted efforts to speak English. You can also work with the students on the first day and ask them for suggestions on how to create an English-only policy in the class. When all students contribute in making an English-Only policy in the classroom (and eventually written up and hung on the wall by the teacher) it gives students an added sense of personal responsibility and control. Likewise, you can also get students to make a list of positive behavior traits that contribute to a respectful environment in the class and then hang it on the wall. If a student needs to use the washroom, do you have to be notified? If two students need to go to the washroom, can they both go or should they go one at a time? Inform students what is forbidden in class, such as eating, using foul language, listening to personal audio players, allowing their cell phones to ring, etc. In addition, ensure that students know that interrupting fellow students during class discussions is not acceptable. If all measures are taken to inform students on the first day of expected classroom behavior, you'll minimize any potential problems that may arise and avoid any needed stress leave.

Gesturing

If you've ever driven in a car and someone in another car cuts you off, what non-verbal gesture would you instinctively make? Like many people, you may find yourself using a finger gesture that is commonly classified as being rude. Non-verbal gesturing can communicate messages well in many environments. In second language learning, non-verbal gestures serve well in helping students communicate more in the classroom. The most effective way for students to communicate amongst themselves is to minimize teacher talk time and maximize student talk time as much as possible. How? Teachers can train students to understand the meaning of certain non-verbal gestures to replace the use of common classroom instructions. For example, if a student wasn't speaking loud enough for his other classmates to clearly hear him, a teacher can motion with his hand in such a way that means. "Mr. Student, you must speak louder." If a student makes a mistake in verb tense by saying a sentence in the future when it should have been said in the past, a teacher can use a certain motion with his hand in such a way that means, "Mr. Student, you must make the sentence past tense". Many common classroom instructions can be replaced by gesturing to minimize a teacher's talk time. For example, consider developing some gestures that mean:

➤ repeat
➤ listen (to me)
➤ please stop talking
➤ finish the sentence
➤ make a sentence
➤ work with a partner
➤ change (a certain part of the sentence)
➤ five minutes left
➤ stand up
➤ don't show your worksheet to your partner
➤ past/present/future tense
➤ continuous-progressive tense

The gesture for "listen" can be a cupping of your hand to your ear; the gesture for "make a sentence" can be the lateral motion of extended arms from being together to moving laterally outwards; the gesture for "repeat" can be the motion of having the arm stretched out with the palm of the hand up and the four fingers bending towards you like a *come here* message. Gesturing should be taught early when the course begins. Teachers can train students to interpret common gestures by doing them repeatedly and consistently while simultaneously saying its verbal meaning for a couple of weeks. Students would soon be able to associate the meaning of the gestures without the teacher having to verbalize them in the class, giving way to more student-centered communication. Before you develop an inventory of personal gesturing, be cautious of some of the ones that may be mistakenly interpreted for rude meanings by people from other cultures. For example, the "okay" symbol of circling the index finger to the thumb is rude according to people from some South American and African countries as it has sexual connotations; even the gesture for the "thumbs up" is considered rude by people from parts of the Middle East, Africa and Australia.

The Art of Giving Instructions

Before implementing a language activity, teachers should pre-plan the wording of instructions to students. Often teachers get students to do complex activities by providing complex instructions interspersed with irrelevant comments on how to do them. When instructions contain unnecessary language, students tend to have a gazed look wondering what planet their teacher is from.

Here is an example of poorly worded instructions to a high intermediate class:

Now, everyone, there's twenty minutes left, let's do an activity, maybe there's no time; should be okay. John, would you pass these papers around, when you get it, don't show each other, your partner I mean, which you'll be paired with, some are the pro-side and some are the con-side. Pro-side is good and con-side is bad. The papers list some ideas for both sides, you can use these ideas to start, some are developed by experts, your discussions. Sit face to face and move your chairs so you're comfortable and you can exchange ideas with the group beside you or whatever. Pros talk with the cons, more like arguing actually. You can read your papers but then don't look at them and then you can talk or more like debate with each other. The topic, which is capital punishment, is controversial with a lot of people. These days, I mean when you talk about it together, respect the other person's opinions. Okay, not let's try this conversational activity. Each pair can write down but it doesn't have to be too long, their points of view on a paper.

After a presentation like that, students will think their teacher is from Pluto. Here are the same instructions re-worded:

(pre-teach what *capital punishment* means and any associated vocabulary that would help students form opinions; note the word "list" should be pre-taught in its verb and noun forms)

- *John, pass these papers.*
- *You will work in pairs. One student is "A" and one student is "B"*
- *"A" thinks capital punishment is good for everybody "B" thinks capital punishment is bad for everybody. (if students know what "society" means, you can replace "everybody" with "society".)*

- *Your exercise sheets list/has some ideas on why capital punishment is good and bad*
- *With your partner, decide who will be "A" and "B"*
- *All "A" students should read the ideas for the pros and remember the ideas*
- *All "B" students should read the ideas for the cons and remember the ideas*
- *After, turn your papers over (gesture) and tell your partner your ideas. You can add your own ideas too. (ensure students know what "add" means.)*
- *(Give 10 minutes for the discussion and then hand out blank poster paper.)*
- *Now, on this poster paper, list all the ideas that you gave to each other in your conversation. List all the pro-ideas on one side and list all the con-ideas on the other side. Don't look at your exercise sheets please.*

Note that the revised version of the instructions was broken down into manageable chunks with short and concise sentences. All sentences eliminated garble and focused on the task in simplified language that would be more easily understood. Moreover, to make instructions a step easier, teachers can coincide them with demonstrations to help reinforce what students are required to do in the activity.

General Drilling

Unlike a dentist's office, drilling plays a big role in controlled practice for pronunciation lessons. What is drilling? Drilling is the act of repeating an utterance with or without variation several times in succession. Its purpose is to give pronunciation practice in stress, intonation, linking, reduction, etc. It also serves to draw attention to contrastive analysis of words and structure. While drilling reinforces targeted or manipulated forms, they should be kept short otherwise students will prefer the dentist's office.

There are several kinds of drills: the choral drill; the small group drill; the pairs drill; and the individual drill. Before drilling, you should model what students have to do in terms of manipulating the form, adding and reducing stress to appropriate places, providing intonation, etc. In addition, maintain a natural speed and rhythm when conducting drills; you don't want to condition your students to learn exaggerated pronunciation when people don't speak in the same exaggerated way in the English world.

A. Repetition Drill Stages:

Stage 1: Whole Class Drill

➤ Use non-verbal gestures to indicate stress points, linking areas, contractions, and other problem areas.

➤ Problem areas can be dealt with by exaggerating pronunciation, but make it brief and return to natural speech flow.

Stage 2: Less Guided Whole Class Drill

➤ Teacher guides the drill with the whole class or small groups of student by initially making repetitions with them but then passively lip-syncing the words.

Stage 3: Individual Drill

➤ Teacher prompts the stronger students in individual drills, then prompts the other students randomly.

➤ Teacher can guide the student to self-correct any pronunciation discrepancies or prompt for peer correction.

B. Substitution Drill

This kind of drill involves substituting a word or a phrase in a sentence to manipulate its form. The substitution always occurs in the same location of the sentence. It's helpful for reinforcing rhythm and intonation of a sentence, vocabulary pronunciation, and sentence structure. The downfall of this drill is that it can be quickly boring for students to do. An example substitution drill would be using the sentence:

Jane is studying French.
(*French* would be replaced with the words below to make new sentences)

1. English	2. History	3. Biology	4. Geography	5. Chemistry
5. Law	6. Physics	7. Medicine	8. Nursing	9. Engineering

C. Modified Substitution Drill

After providing sufficient practice with the substitution drill, teachers can progress and move to a more complex drill where a modification to the sentence is needed. This kind of drill is similar to the substitution drill except it involves changing the structure of the sentence in order to accommodate the substitution. This kind of drill is valuable for manipulating the form of verbs in grammar lessons. An example modified substitution drill would be using the sentence: <u>I</u> have a big dog. (*I* would be replaced with the words below to make new sentences)

1. You   2. He   3. She   4. It   5. They
6. We   7. The bird 8. John and Jack 9. Joan and you 10. Jim

D. Complex Modified Substitution Drill

After your confident students have mastered the modified substitution drill, teachers can lead them to a more complicated drill that requires multiple modification of the sentence. Teachers may have to model an example sentence several times to train students on the complexity of this drill. Ensure that the substituted sentences make sense. An example complex modified substitution drill would be using the sentence: *John <u>wrote</u> a letter last night.* (*wrote* would be replaced with one of the words below along with other associated words or phrases to make new sentences)

1. studied   2. watched   3. sewed   4. cooked   5. fixed
6. ran   7. bought   8. ran   9. drank   10. opened

Non-violent Teaching

What do you do when you have a student whose goal is to make your life as difficult as possible during your time on earth? What do you do when a student only wants to make you feel miserable and reconsider your teaching career? First, you must refrain from using violence. Using violence is not a form of psychological therapy no matter how much you try to convince yourself. Schools usually have grievance procedures for handling problems with students. If you happen to be in an isolated teaching environment where there is minimum administration and policies are left for teachers to establish, you can utilize certain steps to resolve disputes.

The Cheater

If a student is found cheating on any quiz, test, or exam, the student should automatically receive a score of zero. Thereafter a meeting between the student, the teacher, and the school administration can be arranged. If the student commits a second cheating offence, further disciplinary measures may have to be taken up such as advising the school to issue a suspension or recommending expulsion from the school. Incidents of plagiarism by students should be dealt with in the same serious manner. Plagiarism should be discussed in detail with students as they may not be aware of what it is and how to avoid it. Any incident involving academic misconduct should be noted in a student's file and a letter should be drafted and sent to the student's parents.

Testing Your Boundaries

Students who persist in having their cell phones ring during a lesson should have their phones confiscated and taken to the school administration to be reclaimed by the student at the end of the day. Teachers must resist the urge to disassemble a student's cell phone when the sound of a ring is heard. Headsets that are attached to audio players and used in the classroom (unless they are part of a lesson plan and authorized by the teacher) should be confiscated in the same manner as the cell phones. If a student appears to suffer from a case of having heavy eyelids and falls asleep during a lesson, he/she should be woken up and quietly informed that such a regimen distracts the learning process of other students. If that student continues to count sheep, he/she should be promptly dismissed from the class. Allowing a student to sleep in class and ignoring him/her will only send a message to other students that you are a passive instructor who doesn't care about the learning environment of the class and can be taken advantage of. Therefore, please follow the equation:

Sleeping Student = Dismissed Student

Student Progress Reports

If a school doesn't require interim progress reports for students, you can create one midway into a course. It's good for students to know how they're progressing in the course. If a student's marks are lower than the Marianas Trench and you think he will not pass a course unless more effort is exerted, it's your responsibility to communicate clearly to the student that the road to failure is up ahead. A student with poor marks should be given the opportunity to conference with you and try to plan a strategy that will allow him to improve his standing in the time remaining in the course. Mid-term progress reports can be made for students by filling out a custom designed report card. A report card can reveal a student's up-to-date marks, study habits in class, participation habits, assignment and homework completions, and attendance statistics. An area on the report card can be left for any other written comments that you may like to make. Depending on the school's policies, copies of student progress reports can be given to the students and sent to their parents.

Accepting bribes from students in exchange for exemplary student reports should be refrained, even if you do need a new BMW. An example student progress report can be seen in the Appendix section of this book.

Here is part of an actual letter I wrote to the Dean of Education requesting disciplinary action for a student during my tenure at a private international college in Richmond. The college was newly established and did not have a firm disciplinary policy in place at the time. I have purposely changed the student's name to Jane:

The behavior of Jane has been consistently poor during this semester. I've asked Jane to leave my class twice in this term. On many occasions, Jane has failed to listen to my instructions and doesn't attempt classroom exercises due to her continuous conversations with other students. While students are working, I would sometimes find Jane not working. I have repeatedly asked Jane to not speak Chinese in class and she does not listen. She would purposely speak to my face in Chinese even after I've asked her not to. She clearly defies almost every request I make and has little regard for discipline in the class. During conversation exercises, she usually doesn't participate and spends more time socializing in Chinese instead. She continuously resists learning English. Her poor test marks and lack of doing homework reflect her poor efforts in the class.

The last time I ordered Jane to leave the class, she had refused to keep quiet when other students were asked to speak. When I asked her to be quiet, she replied with the work, "Shit." I asked her to repeat what she said and she replied in Chinese. I then told her to leave the class. She doesn't care if she uses profanity with the teacher and gives no respect to the study environment of the classroom.

Jane has already been warned of her poor behavior by myself on several occasions during the semester. In addition she has been warned by the Assistant to the President (Ms.———-) in the last week of November. I recommend that Jane's parents be notified of her continuous poor behavior and efforts in the class. If her behavior continues, I will continue to dismiss her from the class so that other students may concentrate on their studies. If nothing is done, she will clearly have great difficulty in being successful in any postsecondary institution in North America.

The Dean responded by writing a letter, which was subsequently translated into Chinese, to send to her parents. A copy was given to Jane. After Jane's parents were notified by phone and informed that the Dean's letter would be forwarded to them, Jane's behavior quickly changed. There were no further conflicts with Jane in the class. You will often find at least one student who will disrupt a class with negative behavior just like any other typical class with young exuberant students in western society. If Jane had repeated her actions in a university in the West, the professor would have kicked her out early in the course. Students have different motivations for studying E.S.L. Teachers will often find fewer behavioral problems with students who are self-motivated to learn English than those who are enrolled because their parents forced them to be there.—P.D

How Was I?

Schools, particularly post-secondary institutions, commonly ask students to rate and comment on their courses and teachers. This much anticipated day for teachers see instructors and courses be assessed by the all-important clientele: the students. At the end of a course, students are given surveys that ask them to rate certain aspects of a course and their instructor. Course assessments may ask students to rate, according to a provided scale, course content such as the appropriateness of activities, assignments and evaluation methods, course material and resources, teacher qualifications, instruction effectiveness, etc. The language of the survey should be carefully observed to avoid any bias against the instructor. If a "yes/no" question on a survey stated, "If I had a better teacher, I would come to class", then it's a good indication that the survey lacks a neutral stance. Additionally, if the surveys are written in English, ensure the language level is suitable for your students. Before distributing course assessments, teachers should inform students several key details:

1. Students should not write their names on the surveys.
2. Teachers should designate a student to be the collector of all the completed surveys and submit them to the school administration
3. Teachers should not be present in the class when students are filling out the surveys.

After the school administration has reviewed the completed surveys, teachers should have the right to look at the results. It's a good idea to use the results of the survey to either confirm the effectiveness of your lessons (and to pat your-self on the back for doing a job well done) or to learn how to better improve your teaching methods. Course feedback is the only way, other than teacher observations, that teachers can know how effective their instruction is. You must be willing to accept criticism along with all the praise. There will always be a student who may have different opinions on what makes a teacher a good teacher. Whether or not you possess ten degrees from Ivy League universities you may never satisfy all your students' expectations. You have to accept and be open to suggestions, criticism, praise, and indifference to your teaching per-formance.

Teacher Observations

Every teacher will experience observations at different times during his/her career. Teacher observations are assurances of "quality control" in classroom instruction. The guidelines of how teacher observations can vary from school to school. Some schools announce observations without warning while others give some advance notice. Ideally, teachers should be given advance warning of observations due to the fact that lessons for them should be ones where new language material is being introduced and not ones where simple review of previous material is being done. Observers are usually the program directors, head teachers, or department heads. An example teacher observation form is included in the Appendix.

Now that you have some tools to fill your classroom management toolkit, you should build upon them as you gain more and more teaching experience. Anticipating and taking preventative measures to avoid problems that would negatively impact the learning environment of your classroom will go a long way in assisting your students' language acquisition skills.

CHAPTER 4:

Language Needs and Placement Tests—Understanding Speed Limits

---

In This Chapter

> Assessments for adult learners

> Assessments for schools

> Conducting the oral interview

> Reading assessments

> Writing assessments

> Other sources for English Placement Tests

If you're teaching in North America, you may be assigned to teach immigrant students who may have language needs different from those of academic students. How are these language needs different? To discover what these adult learners need, you have to consider their lives. What places do they go to? Who do they have to communicate with in certain settings? How are their daily lives structured? Lesson planning will usually focus around the immediate daily needs of these students. The planning advantage of the adult learner is that these students have often already thought about where they need to focus their English and have prioritized their language goals to help them settle in the community as quickly as possible. As a result, the teacher sometimes only needs to ask the students what they wish to study. This may sound too easy for you; however on the other hand, you may have immigrant students who don't have a clue where to begin their language studies, which is where this chapter begins.

Common themes that are covered with adult learners deal with housing; the medical system; schooling and daycare; transportation; shopping; the banking and postal systems; finding a job; accessing social, community and recreational services; developing social skills; and applying for citizenship. If your student doesn't know where to begin her lan-
guage studies, you can introduce a mapping or webbing exercise to assist. Let's look at an example with an E.S.L. student named Bertha.

If Bertha is a low beginner learner and knows very little English, demonstrate the following special mapping technique by drawing pictures rather than using words. Before you have Bertha do this mapping technique, you should probably first demonstrate it with a map of your own life and draw pictures of places or people you tend to interact with. Verbally explain or mime the different English skills you would require in each area in terms of reading, writing, listening and speaking. After the demonstration, Bertha can then proceed to do a mapping of her own life. On a piece of paper, have Bertha draw a circle in the middle of the page to represent her. Then have her draw lines or arrows pointing outwards from the circle towards different areas in her life, such as the places she goes to, the people she speaks with in person or by phone, personal interests such as hobbies, or sports, etc. Under those different areas, Bertha can list in further detail names of people, places, or situations (see Figure 4.1).

Figure 4.1

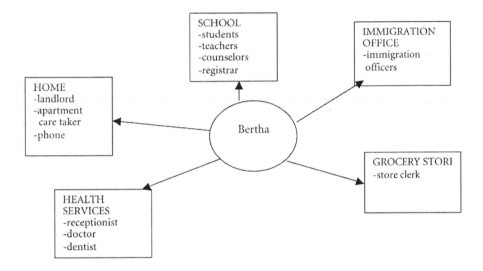

By completing this mapping exercise, you can then determine what her language needs are and plan a customized and prioritized program of study for her. Each theme can be examined in further detail by presenting different functional real world situations. Discover what language and gambits are needed for each situation and ask the student what she already knows. You can prepare material for each theme by referring to your own experience, or if you're not familiar with the theme, consult people who are, find informative books and brochures and look up information on the internet. When thinking about the different situations that arise out of themes, put yourself in Bertha's shoes and ask yourself what you would need to know if you were in her place. In addition, it's important to ask yourself if there are other situations in life that may utilize the same language patterns. For instance, learning how to make requests can be taught in a variety of functional situations such as in banks, restaurants, retail stores, phone conversations, etc.

A good example of program planning for the adult learner can be seen with an example situation of a couple who are looking for rental accommodation. A young tutor, who may not have personal experience in finding rental accommodation, can devise a program divided into four areas of study. The first area covers where to find available rental accommodation through newspapers and community notices. Vocabulary and abbreviations can be covered here. The second area will introduce the language required for checking the conditions of potential locations with question and answer forums. The third area deals with how to make requests from the landlord for any situation that should arise from the rental (example: broken heater, leaky pipes, holes in the wall, etc.). Finally the fourth area would deal with how to respond to potential questions from the landlord in an interview. In each area, a tutor can plan on the specific vocabulary needed; check for the reading and writing requirements needed for a rental agreement; pass on any useful cultural information concerning the rental process; and utilize teaching aids such as Tenant's Rights brochures and general information books on applying for phone and hydro service, etc. In addition to planning and teaching these four areas, a tutor can expand on each area to include other situations that require the same language such as preparing for a job interview, purchasing real estate, talking to a repair person, etc.

Characteristics of Adult Learners

1. Adult learners are motivated students who are eager to learn.

2. Adult learners may be affected by challenges in sight and hearing. Teachers must ensure that classroom space isn't crowded, reading material has a readable font size, lighting is sufficient, noise levels are minimal and ventilation is optimal.

3. Adult learners are mature people with different learning styles. Some may absorb material faster than others.

4. Adult learners have a preconceived notion of what they need to learn.

5. Adult learners don't always come from an educational system that has the same teaching style and attitudes in education found in western countries. They may come from a rigid system that may not accept the dynamics of western-style education.

6. Adult learners know what is the best way for them to learn a language. For example they may believe that they learn new material best by a presentation of its form first, and its meaning second, or vice-versa.

7. Adult learners want to apply new material as soon as possible

8. Adult learners are more receptive to material that's relevant in their lives

9. Adult learners have limited study time so they only want to learn what is necessary for their particular needs.

School Assessments

Imagine if it was intake week (*intake* refers to the time period when new students are registering at the beginning of a new session) and a new semester was about to start in a few days. You have a stampede of new student entering the school wanting to register but before they sign up for classes, you have to know what level of English they are at. Hiring language psychics is not necessary. To determine which classes would best suit students, assessment tests, also known as English Placement Tests, must be written. These tests have a variety of formats: oral interviews, grammar exercises, reading tasks, and writing tasks. The interview portion should be about 20 minutes in length while the exercise portion should take about 40 minutes for a total assessment time of about 1 hour. You will find that more time is often needed for the writing portion so it's best to allow a margin of another 30 minutes for the completion of the assessment. Of course, as soon as new students hear the word "test" as they're writing down their names on the registration papers, you may witness expressions of fear come across their faces followed by slow movements towards the exits. Please assure prospecting students, particularly adults who have had a long absence from a school environment, or those who may have had past negative experiences, that it's not a real test, but rather a tool to figure out which classes would be useful for them. Inform them as to what they should expect and how long it would take to assess their language level. Assessments must be respectful and serve to meet each student's needs and goals in a relaxed and friendly manner.

The Interview

Interviews should be conducted in a private and quiet setting. Forgo the large audience talk-show format, regardless of any desires on your part to imitate Oprah Winfrey or Jay Leno. Basic interviews can be done before the reading and writing assessments. Interview formats should provide the students a feeling of being involved in the planning of their education goals. Open the interview with open-ended questions as you fill-out your interview forms. Example interview forms can be viewed in the Appendix section of this book. Informal open-ended questions provide a relaxed atmosphere for students to freely communicate their needs and goals while at the same time provide you with a rough idea of their communication level. As students start to speak, explain to them that you need to report their answers on your interview form. As you acquire more information, you will discover if the program they're applying for is the one that they need. Ask general questions about facts and opinions on certain topics but be sensitive to the subject matter. Can the student understand questions at normal speed? Ask the student questions using different verb tenses in the past, present and future. Be aware that some students may be sensitive to talking about past education experiences. Ask questions that contain common idioms and commonly used vocabulary. Can the students make some kind of response to unfamiliar topics? Ask students directions to do a task or go somewhere. How often does the student make appropriate responses? Are the meanings present in the answers? Are the meanings laced with severe or moderate grammar errors? The above considerations should be made when you make up an inventory of example questions and create a corresponding interview form. Based on a school's criteria for what students should know at each level, you can observe and make a general conclusion of a student's conversational level with the oral interview. An example interview form can be found in the Appendix.

> *I was doing an oral test at a university in Korea when a student entered the room and sat down. I asked, "What is your name?" She hesitated, scratched her head and after a few moments she responded, "Repeat?" Very slowly I asked her the same question, "What...is...your...name?" She replied, "The bus." The lesson here is don't be surprised by any unexpected answers from oral testing.—R.R.*

The Reading Machine

After a pleasant 15 minute introductory interview with Bertha, your prospective student, you are now ready to engage in another level of the English Placement Test: reading comprehension. The reading part of an English Placement Test can be done orally. The reading test (we'll use the word "test" just for the sake of reference) involves instructing Bertha to read a passage in silence to herself and then having her read it aloud to you. The purpose of this oral reading is to discover Bertha's "instructional reading level" which refers to a student's ability to identify 90% of the words in a passage and have 75% comprehension of it. Some schools may require different percentages to obtain the instructional reading level. Word identification can range from 80–95% while comprehension can range from 75–80%. In this book we will use the 90% word identification and 75% comprehension figures. The instructional reading level will determine the reading level of a student and the assigned writing task to follow. As Bertha reads the passage aloud, you should record any errors on a reading assessment form that can be found in the Appendix. Errors during reading can be word substitution errors; ("those" is replaced with "these"); long pause errors (allow a maximum of 3 seconds for the student to say a word); words pronounced correctly but lacking meaning with the student; mispronounced words; etc. If Bertha identifies less than 90% of the words in a passage, you do not need to ask comprehensive questions because you have then found her instructional reading level. However, you should verify results by giving another passage at the same level and repeating the procedure because sometimes students are simply nervous the first time around and their first-time results may not be reflective of their true performance. If Bertha identifies 90% or more of the words in a passage, you can then proceed to ask questions about the passage to check her comprehension. Comprehensive questions and answers should be administered orally. While Bertha is answering comprehensive questions, encourage her to answer in her own words and allow her to look back at the passage. Remember, you're not testing her to see how much she recalls; rather you're investigating her comprehensive abilities. If Bertha answers 75% or more of the questions correctly, you may then repeat the procedure at the next reading level. If Bertha answers less than 75% of the questions correctly, you have then found her instructional reading level. If you have discovered Bertha cannot identify at least 90% of the words in a passage nor at least 75% of the comprehensive questions correctly, you have then targeted the instructional reading level. At the conclusion of this oral reading exercise, inform Bertha of her reading strengths and areas that you feel need improvement.

How do you devise the reading passages for testing? Reading passages can be made for each level based on a school's guidelines that define each academic level. As students progress through the levels, the passages become more difficult as well. Beginner passages can be short simple sentences of 30–180 words in length. Intermediate passages can be 200–250 words in length from short stories, easy-to-understand newspaper articles, letters, etc. Advanced reading material can be derived from non-fictional sources and consist of 250-400 words in length. Remember to put together at least 2 passages at each level and have a copy for the student and one for the teacher. When creating your own passages, make you sure use an easy-to-read font, double-spaced beginner and intermediate passages, and single-spaced advanced ones. Fonts such as Times New Roman, Book Antiqua or Arial have simple typefaces. Beginner passages should have a large font size such as 16; intermediate passages should have a font size of 14; advanced passages should have a font size of 10–12.

The instructional reading level will serve to place students in the appropriate reading class in their E.S.L. program. Each school will have their own guidelines for what students should know at each level. If guidelines are not defined in writing, you can get a general idea by taking a look at the school's textbooks for each level. There isn't a definite boundary that defines levels but many grammar books will feature common structural areas of teaching. Moreover, you should be aware of 2 kinds of guidelines that help determine what a student should know at each level: the functional criteria (specific situations that require specific language structures) and the grammatical criteria. Nancy Yildiz's book, *English As A Second Language: An Experimental Curriculum*, defines in detail what an E.S.L. student should generally know at each level. For example, an intermediate level student should functionally learn how to make consumer telephone inquiries, offer assistance to people, give directions in an emergency, fill out employment applications, etc. In terms of grammar, intermediate students should know adjective phrases, direct and indirect speech, indirect questions, conditionals, etc. Ultimately when you're teaching at a school, you should always consult the school's criteria of what defines each level. If the school doesn't have precise definitions, you can have a general overview by consulting the school's text books or refer to Yildiz's useful book that will not only help you define each level, but will also give you ideas on developing a progressive E.S.L. curriculum.

The Writing Machine

Before commencing this portion of the assessment, reassure worried students that they should not be concerned with making errors and that you are only trying to discover which writing class would suit them best in their language program. Based on the instructional reading level of students, specific writing assignments can be administered. Students who scored at the beginner instructional reading level need not perform a writing assignment. According to Laurie Gould in her book, *Intake Assessment Materials*, she suggests that students who scored at the high beginner reading level can be given a simple dictation as a writing task. For example, she describes that a list of grocery items can be slowly read aloud by the teacher while a student writes down the list. Inform intermediate and advanced students to double-space their writing. Intermediate students can be presented with a simple situation (they are late for class and their teacher requires a written excuse for the lateness) that requires a simple written response of a short note or a ½ page. Advanced students can be presented with a simple letter-writing task. The letter can be written to a mentor, a friend, a celebrity, an influential person, etc. The task should be 1 page long and formatted to resemble a letter. At the conclusion of the writing task, thank the student for taking the time to write the placement test and provide information on where and when the results will be. After you've collected all of the writing papers, you can use evaluation sheets to help you grade them. Example writing evaluation sheets can be found at the end of this chapter. It's important to note that the placement scores from a student's oral interview may place him in a conversation class that's not necessarily the same level as his reading, writing, and grammar classes.

The English Placement Test Market

You now have a framework to create an English Placement Test for students and adult learners, but what if you don't have the time or energy to create one? There are some ready-made tests on the market that schools can purchase, such as The Michigan Test of English Language Proficiency (MTELP) which was developed by The University of Michigan's English Language Institute; The Secondary Level English Proficiency Test (SLEP) which is sponsored by the Educational Testing Service; and the Basic English Skills Test (BEST) from the Center for Applied Linguistics. MTELP has a 95% accuracy in its assessment abilities and is used by many post-secondary institutions while the BEST is used by educational institutions and occupational businesses. You may also research other sources for placement tests such as the journals, *The Modern Language Journal, Language Testing*; the Buros Institute's *Mental Measurements Yearbook*; and *Reviews of English Language Proficiency Tests*.

Note that some schools may elect to use TOEFL scores as guidelines for placements. TOEFL scores should not be relied on for placement purposes. Data on the skills that students would be required to deliver in a program—reading, writing, listening, speaking, and grammar—should be collected with appropriate placement tests to ensure accurate evaluations. A well-designed assessment system will prevent many potential problems down the road.

E.S.L. Levels

The criteria of student assessments will be based on a school's established guidelines. Most textbooks will follow similar guidelines with each other on what knowledge beginner, intermediate and advanced level students should have. E.S.L. levels can be divided into 6 distinct groupings:

Level 1 (low beginner)
Level 2 (high beginner) (Grade 2–3 reading level)
Level 3 (low intermediate) (Grade 4 reading level)
Level 4 (high intermediate) (Grade 5–6 reading level)
Level 5 (low advanced) (Grade 7 reading level)
Level 6 (high advanced) (Grade 8 reading level)

With each level come different skills in grammar, reading, writing, and conversation.
You can refer to the following chart on what you can expect students should generally know at each level.

	Listening/Speaking	Grammar	Reading	Writing
Level 1	limited vocabulary; primarily uses content words; can express basic personal information	simple present, simple past and future, articles, nouns, verbs, objects	repeatedly reads a passage to find its meaning	very minimal writing skills if any; numerous errors in word order, subject-verb agreement, tenses, etc.
Level 2	expanded vocabulary with the use of adjectives and adverbs, repeats key words to express meaning, states basic opinions	irregular simple past, present progressive, past progressive, basic modals, comparatives, superlatives, count/non-count nouns, direct/indirect object pronouns	can extract meaning from simple passages with more ease	writes in simple sentences, lack of organization in short passages, opinions and ideas roughly expressed, uses some coordinate conjunctions
Level 3	expanded vocabulary but may choose incorrect words to express complex sentences, meaning may not always be clear	present perfect, present perfect progressive, phrasal verbs, gerunds, infinitives, modals, introduction of conditionals	able to read with a minimal level of abstract thought	uses subordinate conjunctions and coordinate conjunctions to make compound and complex sentences
Level 4	can discuss abstract or complex issues on a more proficient level but with gaps in vocabulary	past perfect, past perfect progressive, future progressive, future perfect, future perfect progressive, negative and tag questions, passives, real/unreal conditionals, adjective clauses, direct/indirect speech, more phrasal verbs, more gerunds and infinitives	able to read complex issues and express opinions at a more proficient level	paraphrasing difficult with a lack of synonyms, basic writing errors such as verb tense and agreements are of less frequency, errors in word choice, gerunds, reported speech, writing is more organized.
Level 5	clear oral meaning but minor problems in cohesion, some problems with idioms and English usage errors	practice of all verb tenses, all modals, adjective clauses, noun clauses, adverb clauses, practice of real and conditionals, practice gerunds, infinitives, and phrasal verbs	introduction and practice with different levels of genre: poetry, fiction, non-fiction, bibliographical, can guess the meaning of words by identifying the meaning of suffixes, prefixes or base roots, etc.	able to write more formally, limited errors, minor problems with cohesion and unity, paraphrases with more fluency, can write academic essays, makes compound-complex sentences
Level 6	proficiency approaches native fluency, minor problems in English usage errors, more knowledge of idioms and idiomatic expressions	proficiency approaches native fluency	able to do extensive research on complex topics, feels comfortable with reading all levels of genre	can write assignments to suit any genre and any audience, provides good unity and cohesion in writing, fluently writes simple, compound, complex, and compound-complex sentences

References

Gould, Laurie. (1999). *Intake Assessment Materials: Fundamental Level English and Math*. Vancouver: Vancouver Community College

Yildiz, Nancy. (1983). *English As A Second Language: An Experimental Curriculum*. Vancouver: Vancouver Community College.

CHAPTER 5:

Planning Curriculum and Lessons— The Subdivision Tour

> **In This Chapter**
>
> \> Student language exposure
>
> \> Lesson planning terms
>
> \> Lesson planning philosophy
>
> \> Course book analysis
>
> \> Course book lesson planning
>
> \> Peer teaching practice

Now that you've assessed your students' language needs and have reviewed their personal backgrounds, you've reached the "how" stage of teaching E.S.L.. What do students need to know about the English language? Many academic E.S.L. students are bombarded with grammar as they move through their native countries' school systems. They know their English grammar but their oral skills lag behind. Since many E.S.L. students don't have the advantage of being immersed in an English-speaking environment in their native countries, their main weakness is with listening and speaking; consequently many E.S.L. conversation teachers are highly sought after overseas.

New Language Items

What knowledge and wisdom can you convey to students to help them become more fluent communicators in English? As native speakers, people often take their innate language skills for granted by pronouncing words with reduced stress in sentences, linking strings of words together to increase speed; eliminating the use of function words; adopting accents; and slurring or mumbling—all while still being coherent to listeners. An E.S.L. student who was taught by a teacher from New Zealand will have been taught different pronunciation rules than a student who was taught by a teacher from Canada. Check to see where your academic student's previous teachers were from and what their credentials were. Orland L. Taylor has written an excellent article called "*Cross-Cultural Communication: An Essential Dimension of Effective Education*" which can be seen on the internet from the *Northwest Regional Educational Laboratory* website at: http://www.nwrel.org/cnorse/booklets/ccc/. His article expresses how education is affected by cross-cultural communication and how language doesn't exist in isolation.

Powerful Planning Terms

A syllabus:	A summary that extensively describes the objectives, main themes and topics, philosophy, resources, weekly plan, costs, and market potential of a course of study.
A timetable:	A weekly or monthly schedule of lesson topics. Timetables help teachers and department coordinators organize and track the progression of a course.
A lesson plan:	A specific plan that defines and outlines how lesson objectives are to be met. Daily lesson plans help teachers introduce and organize language objectives and activities in a logical order and time frame.
A disorganized and inefficient teacher:	A lazy teacher who doesn't plan ahead and tends to do lessons as ideas "pop" in his head. His students lack direction and are often confused and bored with his lessons. Unfortunately this breed of teacher is all too common in the educational world.

Me, Plan?

Model syllabus, timetable, and lesson plan formats are provided in the Course Planning section of this book. Why is it important to plan?

✓ To *pace material* so that teachers can ensure there is sufficient time to cover everything that needs to be taught in a particular time frame.

✓ To introduce teaching material in a *logical progression* so that student-centered activities follow teacher-guided target language.

✓ To ensure that weekly lessons are presented in a *logical sequence* to give students a feeling of accomplishment (i.e., so that you don't end up presenting new language structure at 4:15 on a Friday afternoon)

✓ To provide *a balance and variety of activities and skills*
   • Grammar, Reading, Writing, Listening and Speaking
   • Accuracy and Fluency practice
   • Revision versus new input

✓ To give a *sense of direction* so that students will feel like they're moving forward in their language acquisition.

Planning = Efficiency

Before making lesson plans, teachers should consider non-teaching factors that may influence their students' ability to benefit from lessons:

- Length of the course
- Time of day of the lesson
- Language level of the students
- The students' needs
- The students' interests
- Amount of homework
- Adequate classroom temperature and air circulation
- Adequate classroom space

From a student's point of view, imagine yourself on a late Friday afternoon in a hot tiny 30 degree centigrade, stuffy classroom with no windows, a closed door, sleepy classmates, and a sweaty teacher named "Killer" who starts to introduce a new unit with 20 minutes left in the class and expects you to begin practicing a new verb tense. His introduction is brief and he forces you to examine this new language structure on your own because he is anxious to start his weekend plans on a nearby island. Chances are that no matter what your academic goals are, your intellectual output won't be at its maximum capacity. Taking the non-teaching factors into consideration, it is important for you to respond appropriately to them as you plan and timetable your curriculum with any assigned course.

Textbook Analysis

In a new curriculum, decisions have to be made on which textbooks would be ideal to base a program on. There are certain factors, other than checking for cartoons, that you should consider when choosing a textbook. Before looking for the right book you have to determine what your course objectives are so that you have a set of criteria to help you judge which book would best suit your needs. If you're looking for a grammar text-book, you'll be less focused on looking for a book with a lot of phonetics or if you're looking for a reading text-book, you'll want a book that has topics that would best suit the interests of your class profile.

Look at course books and find the following information:

1. Who is the author? What's his background?
2. Is the book appropriate to its indicated level of teaching?
3. Does each unit meet the objectives of the course in terms of grammar, function and vocabulary?
4. Is the book based on a grammar (structural) syllabus, a vocabulary (lexical) syllabus, a functional syllabus, or an integrated syllabus?
5. How many hours of teaching/learning does the course book cover?

6. How many units are there?

7. How far do you think your students can reasonably cover the book each week?

8. Will the units hold the interest of the students?

9. What are the components of the book? (Are there accompanying tapes, CDs, videos, workbooks, a teacher's guide and an answer key?).

10. How do you know what grammar is covered in any given unit?

11. Does the book teach grammar rules?

12. Is there a pronunciation (phonetic) chart?

13. Does the book contain listening exercises?

14. Where are the transcripts?

15. Is there a balance between the 4 skills: Speaking, Listening, Reading and Writing?

16. Is there a book for the next level?

17. Is the book current or has it already been revised?

Ask yourself, what makes a book difficult to read?

➤ small print that is jumbled together

➤ chapters that are too long

➤ boring subjects

➤ complex vocabulary

➤ confusing organization

➤ lack of illustrations or diagrams

➤ content that is too technical

➤ too many references

The content of an ideal textbook should be written in a style with appropriate vocabulary and sentence structure. The content should also be judged for its chronicle, rhetorical and spatial elements. If a textbook is not assigned for a course, teachers would have to improvise, search, or make up material that would be appropriate for their students. Chapter Nine of this text describes how teachers can create original reading materials or manipulate existing materials following guidelines for layout and design.

Let's analyze the features of two exercises.

EXERCISE A

Bob collapsed on the couch of his two-bedroom apartment. His roommate Jim greeted Bob in the living room. Jim asked, "Bob, you look really tired. Did you have a good day?" Bob looked at Jim with tired eyes and replied, "Jim, I've never had such a stressful day in all my life. Cathy asked me to do several things before we leave on our trip on Saturday. She gave me a list of tasks to do and I finally did them all today." Jim was curious in what Bob had to do and asked him what his tasks were. Bob exhaustedly began to describe his day. Bob woke up early and phoned the car rental agency to confirm a reservation. There was a problem with the reservation so he had to skip breakfast and go down to the agency himself to speak with the manager. He then went to the travel agency downtown to pick-up their airline tickets. Next, Bob remembered he had to go to the bank to purchase some travelers' cheques but the closest one was 10 blocks away so he had to quickly hike there. It suddenly began to rain heavily during Bob's journey to the bank, thus soaking Bob who didn't bring a jacket. Later, Bob had to go to the pharmacy to buy some over-the-counter medication and toiletries to pack for the trip. Next, he had to pick-up their passports from the government office. On his way there he became hungry so he bought a small apple from a street vendor for lunch. Along the way he stopped off at the dry cleaners to retrieve Cathy's laundered dress. Finally, after picking up the passports, he drove to the local dog kennel to make arrangements for Cathy's dog Spot to stay at while they were away. As soon as Bob got home, he was drained of energy and told Jim, "I need a break from my vacation!"

Later in the evening, Cathy phoned Bob to verify if he completed all his tasks.

PRACTICE: WHAT DID BOB DO?

Cathy: Hi Sweetie. Did you reserve a car?
Bob: Yes, I reserved it <u>in the morning</u>.
Cathy: Great. Did you get the tickets?
Bob: Yes, I picked them up <u>afterwards</u>.

Continue the conversation until all of Bob's tasks have been covered. The person role-playing Bob should provide a time period for all replies.

Traveler's cheques
Pharmaceutical items
dress
passport
dog kennel

EXERCISE B

<u>JOB AD:</u>
ABC Software is expanding to Vancouver, Canada with a new distribution center. We are looking for an enthusiastic and experienced person to fill the position of human resources manager. The ideal applicant must have a minimum of 5 years experience as a human resources manager and must be familiar with the XYZ software program. Knowledge of a second language is an asset. We offer an attractive compensation package of $50,000 per year plus attractive benefits. Please reply with a resume and cover letter to:

Ms. Janet Walker
Personnel Manager
ABC SOFTWARE
45 Brown Road
Gabriola Island, BC
V0R 3W4 CANADA

Mr. Frank Smith submitted a cover letter and his resume to ABC Software and was successful in gaining a job interview with Ms. Walker. In the interview, Ms. Walker is asking Mr. Smith about his qualifications. Ms. Walker is asking *yes/no* questions and *wh*-questions in the present perfect and simple past tenses. Mr. Smith is answering the questions <u>fully</u> (there are no short answers) <u>and with detailed information.</u>

With a partner, simulate a conversation between Mr. Smith and Ms. Walker in a job interview.

Example:
Walker: How long have you been a human resources manager?
Smith: I've been a human resources manager for 8 years with the Ben & Howard Law Firm in Ottawa.
Walker: Did you enjoy your experience?
Smith: Yes, I enjoyed it. I learned a lot about the operations of a law firm and the functions f different personnel.
Walker: What were you responsible for?
Smith: I was responsible for...

Ask yourself the following questions to determine if the material from both exercises would be suitable in a particular course:

<u>GUIDELINES FOR MATERIAL EVALUATION</u>

1. Is the vocabulary in both exercises appropriate to the level of your students?

2. What would a teacher have to pre-teach before giving the students the exercises?

3. Are the activities conducive to the learning objectives?

4. How is the target language used?

5. How can I teacher determine if the students have been successful in acquiring the target language?

6. Would a job interview be familiar to your students?

7. Are there any cultural aspects in the exercises that should be pre-taught?

8. How would you compare the two exercises?

9. Are there any interesting graphics in the exercises?

Course Book Lesson Planning

The Director of Studies has just given you the textbook that your students will be using for a course. You look at it and ask, "Is there a teacher's guide?" The Director replies, "No." Your jaw drops because your brain had depended on the existence of a thick teacher's guide that would be jam-packed with ready-to-use lesson plans that would free up your lesson preparation time. Your next step could be to contact the publisher to try to get a copy of a teacher's guide, or you could tell yourself that a lack of a teacher's guide is a molehill of a problem in life that can be hurdled. How do you hurdle this molehill?

Hurdling the Molehill

The following 2-part plan will make lesson planning from any course book a simple process:

Part 1: Pre-teaching Preparation

Look at the course book carefully and be prepared to do the following steps:

1. Analyze—What is the aim of the material?

2. Evaluate—What language/skills are being developed?

3. Adapt, reject, supplement, organize, develop tasks/activities, and gather materials.

<u>Part 2: Teaching Preparation</u>

Negotiate your aims, materials and activities for the teaching stage.

4. Stage the lesson—How will the material logically break into "teaching slots" and provide a cohesive lesson for your eager learners?

5. State the procedure—How will the individual teaching slots be staged? What procedures will be implemented?

6. Allocate—What kind of interaction will you allocate for each stage of the lesson?

Lesson Planning

Lesson plans follow a logical progression. Usually a short time is spent at the beginning of a lesson practicing material that is familiar to the students. This material may be from a previous lesson or from general knowledge that the student is familiar with. This initial stage is called the "Warm-Up" or "Review" stage. The purpose of this initial stage is to get students to start thinking in English.

Following this initial stage is a "Lead-In" stage in which situational contexts, story telling, multimedia, classroom surveys, and so forth are used to help introduce new material. New material is accompanied by concept questions that are comprehensive in nature to ensure that student understand the new material.

After the students have demonstrated a working knowledge of the new material, the lesson progresses to a stage called the "Controlled Practice" stage in which students do guided activities of the new material with direction and correction from the teacher. Following the guided activity, students proceed to less guided activities in the "Less Controlled Practice" stage where students put their new language to use more freely with less teacher guidance and minimum correction.

There are two main parts to a lesson plan: the identification area (what and who a lesson is for) and the procedural area (how you are going to teach the lesson). A lesson plan should have the following details labeled:

PART I: WHAT/WHO

Time—Length of your lesson.

Level—Language level of students (low beginner, high beginner, low intermediate, etc.).

Class Profile—Are you teaching academic students, immigrants, children, or others?

Aims—What you intend to achieve in a lesson (try to see this from the students' point of view); your aim should be expressed as "To present_____" or "To revise _____", "To develop
      (x/structure/function/vocabulary)   (x language point)
_____" or 'To enable students to _____"
(listening/reading for gist/specific information)   (target function)

Personal Aims (of the teacher)—Personal objectives in a lesson.

Assumptions—What language (structure or vocabulary) you assume the students already know; without this information, it would be difficult to achieve your aims.

Anticipated Problems—What problems you think the students (not you!) will have with the target language; for example, there may be problems with form, meaning, pronunciation, verb tense, etc.

Solutions—How you intend to overcome the problems you have anticipated; for example, you would pre-teach unknown vocabulary before a reading exercise, model pronunciation, review specific phoneme articulation, demonstrate interactive activities, etc.

PART II: HOW

In this part of the plan you need to fill in columns stating what you are going to do in stages.

Time—How long each stage of the learning activities are going to take; timing your activities will increase your efficiency.

Stage—Which sequential part of the learning process an activity is in; for example a stage can be a lead-in, a pre-teaching of vocabulary, a presentation, controlled oral practice, less controlled practice, listening for gist or specific information, prediction, etc.

Aim—What your objectives are with each stage of your lesson.

Procedure—What you are going to do at each stage of the learning process; you may write: "Show picture to elicit vocabulary", "Model the target sentence", "Set gist questions", "Assemble students into pairs to....", etc. You should also include how many times you play audio recordings, what your concept questions are (questions testing comprehension), what diagrams you will be showing, and your blackboard organization. You may use the common abbreviations: T = teacher, Ss = students

Interaction—Your plan to change the interactive focus of your lesson. For example your focus could be student-to-teacher, students-to-teacher, teacher-to-student, student-to-student, or students-to-students. The change in interactive focus is to ensure that there is a good balance between teacher-centered and student centered activities.
Abbreviations:
S → S = Student interaction with another student
S → T = Student to teacher interaction
S = Individual student work

Material/Aids—Indicate all materials you are going to use such as tapes, pictures, cue-cards, overhead projector, handouts, etc.

The following headings may be used to describe the various stages of a lesson:

Review/Warm-Up—A review of previously learned language material.

Introduction—Initial teaching of the new skill; introduction of new skill to be taught.

Feedback—Collecting student input from an activity

Task—The initiation of a language learning activity.

Check—Check and monitor student progress of the target language.

Reinforcement—The initiation of less guided student-centered activities.

Lesson Evaluation—Student response to the lesson; areas in your lesson that may need improvement, tips or ideas for future lessons.

Lesson Plan Formats

Just as there can be more than one way for a person to arrive at a destination, there are several ways to organize a lesson plan. Depending on your personal preferences, you can organize a lesson plan however way you feel comfortable with as long as the "what", "who", and "how" parts are covered. Check the Course Planning section of this book for a look at some lesson plan formats accompanied with some example lessons.

> *Some fellow teachers reported that they sometimes find it easier to do Part II of the lesson plan in reverse sequence. They would determine what the reinforcement would be first then determine the check, the task, the feedback, the introduction, and lastly the warm-up. I sometimes work in this fashion myself and you may want to experiment which method works for you in sequentially creating your lesson plans.—P.D.*

Preparation for Peer Teaching

A great pre-class teaching preparation that prospective teachers can do is to find a willing soul, ideally a colleague, to conduct practice teaching sessions with. For example, a language point can be assigned to each participant to teach to the rest of the group. Each trainee teaches the group as if they were E.S.L. students.

When conducting peer-teaching sessions, check for some of the following guidelines in your lesson plans:

➢ Establish the context clearly.

➢ Elicit target sentence.

➢ Ask concept questions to check for understanding.

➢ Model the target sentence with focus on:
  • natural speed/rhythm
  • beat stress
  • difficult words/contractions (using finger gestures if appropriate)

➢ Drill the pronunciation.
  • chorally
  • individually

➢ Check for concept.

➢ Make substitutions with the target language by the E-M-D method (elicit, model, and drill).

➤ Highlight the structure form on the board and identify its function. For instance, the form for the sentence, *I'm going to write some letters this afternoon,* would be: <u>SUBJECT</u> + *To Be* + <u>"going to"</u> + <u>BASE VERB</u> +....

I	am	going to	write	some letters this afternoon.

After presenting the form, ask concept questions to check for comprehension:

Am I going to read or watch TV?
Did I write this morning? Did I write this afternoon?
Am I finished writing?
Am I going to write tomorrow?

➤ Show sentence stress and intonation. For instance, note that the stress and intonation of the following sentences are function (situation) oriented.

1. I'm going to write some letters this afternoon.
2. We've been robbed. The TV's been stolen. My earrings have been taken too.
3. If I were you I'd look for another dentist.
4. Have you thought about trying this new recipe?

Here is a valuable lesson I learned during my tenure at a private international college. I was assigned to teach intermediate grammar to a small class of Chinese students. During some of my lessons I would present fictitious examples of situations to reinforce grammar points. For example, one day I pointed to Cathy (many Chinese students adopt western names when they study overseas) and told the class that I was going to make some example sentences that were not true. I thought by integrating students in example sentences I could involve the class more in my lessons. The lesson at the time was introducing the comparative, "better." I repeated that the sentences were not true and were only example sentences. The class already knew the concept of "example sentence", "true", and "false." I said to the class, "Last week Cathy wrote a test. Her test result was not good. She got a poor mark. She is sad because she got a poor mark. Last week Jenny (a student adjacent to Cathy) wrote a test. Her test result was good. She got a good mark." I then proceeded to introduce the new word of "better" by saying slowly and with special emphasis the target sentence. I slowly said, "Jenny got a <u>better</u> mark than Cathy." The class instantly *understood the concept of "better" without any direct translation. I again repeated that the sentence was untrue and only an example. The fact that there was no test administered the previous week led me to believe it was safe to use that example sentence without any ill-will being created. I proceeded with asking concept-check questions on my lead-in to ensure students understood the meaning of better and proceeded to write the form on the board and present further examples using inanimate objects. The class responded well to the lesson and there were no further obstacles to this new grammar point.*

A few days later, Cathy entered the teacher's room, handed me a handwritten letter and walked away. It stated that she was hurt by my use of her name in the class and that she didn't know why I hated her. Her letter further stated she cried a lot from that day and that she didn't want me to hate her so much. It concluded by saying she would try not to bother me in the short time left in the semester. It was the hardest document I've ever read. After my state of shock dissipated, I immediately sought out Cathy in the college and managed to track her down. I privately met with her and stated her thoughts of how I felt about her were completely wrong. I had thought my repeated emphasis was clearly understood by the class that the example sentences were completely untrue. She stated how important her name was to her and her family, and that my emphasis didn't matter. She looked at the lesson as me announcing to the class that she was not smart. I said her assumptions were not true and in fact, Cathy was always the top student from the beginning. After a half hour of discussion and healing of feelings I apologized and said I would not use her name or anyone else's name in class for examples again. From then on I brought in pictures of people cut out from magazines and introduced lead-ins with them. Lesson learned here is to play it safe when it comes to presenting lesson plan lead-ins, even if you think they may be positive examples; use pictures of people (from magazines or other sources) and not real students to make your point. You can't always be sure of student sensitivities in your lessons, regardless of how many times you tell students that you're only presenting example sentences.—P.D.

Overall, new E.S.L. teachers will soon discover that detailed planning is the best way to teach dynamic, effective, and efficient lessons that can be carried over from school to school. As you gain more experience with lesson planning and discover which approaches work best for your students, planning time will become less time consuming. The biggest toil in being a teacher of any subject is the preparation time spent on lesson planning. The more efficient you are in lesson planning, the more freedom you'll have in claiming personal time for yourself at school and at home. Here is a filing tip for new teachers: File your lesson plans away under topics (Eg. Simple Present, Simple Past, Articles, etc.) and not under time periods (Eg. Week 1 Day 3). This filing method allows you to conveniently utilize your lesson plans again and again with each new academic term or with each new school that you work for by making your filing system adaptable to wherever you teach. Whatever planning method you choose for your lessons, always put yourself in the shoes of your students and ask yourself how you would like to be taught by your teacher.

CHAPTER 6:

Grammar 1—Form, Meaning, and Use—Shifting Gears

> **In This Chapter**
>
> > Strategy considerations
>
> > Closed lips
>
> > Form, meaning, and use
>
> > Teaching Progression I
>
> > Form to meaning
>
> > Meaning to form
>
> > Teaching Progression II
>
> > Effective grammar lessons

If the highlights of your childhood don't include exciting grammar lessons with an equally excited and enthusiastic teacher, then you probably had painful experiences. The word "grammar" often evokes feelings equal to watching your little cousin Bobby conduct personal hygiene at the dinner table. You may have thought that if you're going to teach grammar to students who may loathe the mere sound of the topic, how are you going to convince them that grammar can be enjoyable and painless? Clever E.S.L. teachers must have a strategy for introducing grammar in a way that communicates to the students that they need and will greatly benefit from the material that's being taught. If the grammar is introduced in the most ideal fashion, students will be grateful to have learned such useful information to take with them into the world.

Strategy Considerations

Considerations on your students' background must be made when planning a grammar strategy. A great article written by Miriam R. Eisenstein, *Grammatical Explanations in E.S.L.: Teach the Student, Not the Method* describes the different teaching methodologies related to grammar and how they relate to various student backgrounds. In Eisenstein's article, studies have shown that unlike children, adult learners benefit from grammar lessons that are consciously presented with rules and structure patterns (Krashen and Seliger, 1975). On the other hand, she points out that children (pre-adolescents) best acquire a second language through interaction with second language speakers rather than through conscious or formal instruction (Hale and Budar, 1970, Dulay and Burt, 1973). When teaching adults, E.S.L. teachers must consider their students' educational and cultural backgrounds. Adults often have a preconceived idea of what is the best way for them to learn a new language. Some students may come from cultures that tend to present grammar rules outright at the beginning of a lesson rather than rely on induction.

Grammar explanations can be verbally presented by the teacher, a book, resource charts, or inferred by the students. The timing of grammar explanations can be made either at the beginning of the lesson following controlled practice or after an inferred presentation of the targeted grammar point. If you have students who are more familiar with an orderly presentation of language, then grammar explanations at the beginning of a lesson would be your best bet; however, if you prefer to hold back the grammar explanations until after students have practiced the targeted rule or structure, you will present many advantages for the students. Students are given a sense of control during the practice and have less fear of making incorrect deductions of the targeted language point. Students become rewarded for logical deduction from initial confusion or ambiguity.

Closed Lips

Should teachers explain the grammar rule or should students be elicited for an explanation? Ideally, it's best for students to have a sense of pride when they figure out a grammar explanation; however, the cultural background of students should be considered when teachers expect a certain level of participation in the class. Some students may not feel comfortable in grammar elicitations and avoid expressing themselves while others openly share any guesses on new structures. Even though you may have the urge to yell out, "Speak to me!!" to your silent students, their reluctance to orally participate in class likely origi-nates deep in their culture. It's best not to force or coerce the students to behave in a manner that goes against what they've been brought up with. An uncom-fortable learning environment for the students minimizes the potential of lan-guage acquisition. Quiet students should be free to keep their lips closed.

Form

Whatever strategy you employ in your presentation, you need to know the form of a grammar point. The form refers to a "formula" that governs the grammar rule and its accompanying mechanics; it describes how the grammar structure is formed and how it is used. If you're teaching the present progres-sive (also known as the present continuous in some books), the formula you would use and write down on the board would be:
SUBJECT + *To Be* + **VERB-*ing***. When providing the form of a grammar les-son, ensure you provide and elicit example sentences from the students.

SUBJECT + *To Be* + VERB-ing +.........
I	am	watching	t.v.
You	are	cooking	my dinner.
He/she/it	is	drinking	water.
They	are	working	in the house.
We	are	divorcing	tomorrow.

The skeleton of the present progressive requires the orderly combination of the subject, the conjugated verb *To Be*, and the—*ing* form of a verb. By under-standing this format, students can manipulate the form and substitute other verbs or subjects to talk about other meanings using the same structural pat-tern.

Meaning

After introducing the form of a grammar point, you need to provide the meaning of it. What does the new grammar structure mean? For the present progressive, you can communicate its use to your students with the use of timelines on the board (see Chapter 7). By using timelines, you can visually show students that the present progressive refers to actions that are now in progress or in progress at a particular time. If you were introducing a lesson on expressions of quantity, such as, *a tube* of toothpaste, *a slice* of cake, or *a cup* of coffee, you can explain what these expressions of quantity are with visual or real examples of a tube, a cut piece of cheese, an empty cup, etc. Students can visually see the expressions that are associated with the use of quantity and would thus retain the knowledge better graphically than through written form. Grammar classes that introduce as many physical or demonstrative examples to students provide stimulating learning environments and improve retention.

> If a student's senses are stimulated through physical or visual contact with items that act as teaching tools, students acquire the target language more effectively and with more retention in an atmosphere of amusement.

One precaution to make when introducing form and meaning is the focus you put on them. According to Jim Scrivener's *Learning Teaching*, students can be confused with a name of a verb tense and its meaning. For example, the present progressive tense makes reference to an action that can be associated to the present (with some connotations to the past) and the future, but a student may see the label, *present* progressive, as just referring to the present and not the future. Likewise when a teacher presents the present perfect tense. A student may be confused with the label, *present* perfect, when it makes reference to a situation originating in the past. A teacher must ensure that form and meaning are clearly separated in the teaching progression.

Use

Now that you've introduced the form and meaning of a grammar point, students need to know how to use it through context. Context refers to provocative situations that result in the language being used. For example, a cooking show that shows a chef describing his/her actions in progress may be a good demonstration for the present progressive. Story telling, role playing or dialoguing are also great activities that teachers can employ for introducing a grammar point. The student's own world provides teachers with a rich source of contexts to present language material. Not only do students know how to grasp new language material, they need to know when and why the new language point needs to be used. Students should have the opportunity to practice its use in the context of the student's environment (the classroom and the school), the world outside the school (situational or functional events), and in purely fictional or possibly real simulations. The more real the context, the bigger the message you send to the students of its relevancy in their lives.

Teaching Progression I

Once you have some background considerations made, where do you begin the grammar teaching progression? Some teachers prefer to present the form of a grammar point first, and the meaning of it second. This kind of progression would be suitable for students who prefer grammar explanations at the beginning of a sentence. If you have students who learn a language better by inferring the meaning before a grammar explanation is presented, you would present the meaning of a grammar point first, then the form of it second.

Form to Meaning

A classic example of this kind of form-to-meaning teaching progression involves a quick presentation. An example lesson on *should have* can be presented by verbally saying an example sentence, such as, *I failed the test this morning; I should have studied last night.* The students would repeat the model sentence and make substitution sentences before they have any idea of what *should have* means. Many course textbooks have the form-to-meaning format but this teaching method has a draw back as it doesn't engage the teacher with the students' understanding of the material. This method normally sees teachers writing on the board, verbally explaining the language point, writing the rules, and assigning students to do written exercises. Teachers do most of the talking while students concentrate on their textbooks and have minimal involvement in the lesson. This traditional form of teaching can cause students to be easily confused or withdrawn in their learning experience.

Meaning to Form

On the opposite end of the form-to-meaning teaching methodology is the meaning-to-form format. A classic example of this kind of meaning-to-form teaching progression involves a lead-in with a situational presentation. A teacher can use resources, such as flash cards, physical examples/demonstrations, anecdotes, pictures, or narratives, to create a situation. To ensure understanding, the teacher can ask students comprehensive questions on the situation. Never ask, "Do you understand?" After asking concept questions, the teacher can make sentences that lead towards the target language by targeting the meaning. For example the sentences: *Bill played basketball in the past; now, Bill doesn't play basketball; Mr. Brown smoked in the past; now Mr. Brown doesn't smoke,* can be presented to prepare the students for the need of a new language point to state an action that no longer is being done in the present but was done in the past. After that, the teacher asks students further concept questions to check comprehension (*Did Bill play basketball in the past? Does he play basketball now? Did Mr. Brown smoke in the past? Does Mr. Brown smoke now?*). When the understanding is clear with the students, the teacher can either elicit or model the new information: *Bill <u>used to</u> play basketball. Mr. Brown <u>used to</u> smoke.* Next, the teacher can drill the class and check for pronunciation, rhythm, and sentence stress. Finally, the teacher can elicit further sentences with the new target language.

Concept Questions = Comprehensive Questions

Never ask, "Do you understand?" A student's understanding may be different from what they should understand. Concept questions are made in the preparation stage of a lesson. The purpose of concept questions is to check a student's understanding of the information presented in the teaching progression. When formulating concept questions, the target structure must not appear in them. They should be kept simple and relevant. Verbally asking 2-4 questions and checking their responses on the board are sufficient enough to check a student's understanding of each concept. To really verify their understanding you can write the concept questions on the board and write down responses as you receive them. To determine what the appropriate concept questions are, turn the target structure into 2-4 statements. Then, turn the statements in to questions to ask the students.

For example, if you're introducing the present perfect tense:

Bob has worked in the factory for 5 years.

This sentence means:

a)   Bob started working in the factory 5 years ago

b)   Bob still works in the factory.

You can change these sentences to concept questions

a)   When did Bob work there?

b)   Does Bob work in the factory now?

While Jim watched the news, Jane went to bed.

This sentence means:

a)   Jim watched the news

b)   Jane went to sleep

c)   Jane went to bed in the middle of dinner.

You can change these sentences to concept questions

a) Did Jim start watching the news before Jane went to bed?

b) Did Jim stop watching the news before Jane went to bed?

c) Did Jane go to bed in the middle of the news?

Teaching Progression II

Whether you begin your grammar lesson by presenting form or meaning first, you need to move on to the next stage of the teaching progression. The next stage involves controlled and less controlled practice. Controlled practice is guided practice with the assistance of the teacher, a book, worksheets or oral exercises. The emphasis is accuracy, which involves being as correct as possible in using the grammar point. Less controlled practice involves doing activities with less guided practice on the grammar point. The emphasis is communicative fluency, which involves using the grammar point as much as possible in speech without having to worry too much on accuracy. After completing the less controlled practice, students may engage in free practice where students can begin using the new grammar point naturally.

Planning Effective Grammar Lessons

Since students have different learning styles, the decision to approach your teaching with presenting form or meaning first will lie on what works best for your students based on their previous learning experiences. The 4 keys stages in introducing a new grammar point in your lessons are:

1) **Introduce** the target language with authentic context that is relevant to the student's world.

2) **Elicit, explain** or **show** the meaning of the language point and demonstrate its form. Go over pronunciation points related to the target language

3) **Practice** the target language with teacher-guided activities that allow students to manipulate and use its form. Grammar exercises that are written or orally done with restricted use of the target language are commonly presented in this teacher-guided stage.

4) **Practice** the target language with student-centered activities that encourage students to fluently use the new language interactively.

Possible Step-by-Step Grammar Teaching Progression

1) Establish a context with a narrative, an anecdote, pictures, objects, etc.

2) Ask comprehensive/concept questions

3) Make new sentences that lead towards the target language

4) Ask comprehensive/concept questions

5) Elicit or model the target language

6) Explain the target language

7) Demonstrate the pronunciation, rhythm, and sentence stress

8) Begin controlled practice

9) Begin less controlled practice

References

Eisenstein, Miriam. "Grammatical Explanations in E.S.L.: Teach the Student, Not the Method". *TESL Talk*. Toronto: Citizenship Development Branch.

Scrivener, Jim (1994). *Learning Teaching*. Oxford: Heinemann.

CHAPTER 7:

Grammar 2-Verb Tenses and Timelines—Turning the Corner

> **In This Chapter**
>
> > Parts of speech
>
> > Overview of verb tenses
>
> > Problem areas in verb tenses
>
> > Board work for verb tenses
>
> > Timelines
>
> > Grammar levels

What is the difference between *I did* and *I have done*?
When do we use *the*?
What is the structure after *I wish*?
When do we use *will* versus *going to* for the future?

If you are not sure of the answers to such questions—questions you'll encounter in teaching E.S.L.—then it is time to brush up on your grammar. It can't be overstated that E.S.L. teachers should KNOW THEIR GRAMMAR. If you don't know your grammar inside-out, then at least prepare yourself before your lessons by studying the rules and usage of the particular grammar point you're planning to introduce before you step into the classroom. Non-western students with some E.S.L. experience know their grammar and often put us to shame with their knowledge. You will be asked questions related to grammar and if you don't know the answer, ooops! If you're ever caught in the uncomfortable situation of not knowing the answer to a student's grammar question, you can always reply, "I'll get back to you later" (if students don't know the phrasal verb *get back*, you can say "I'll have an answer for you in the next class"). English grammar is a subject that can be mastered with patience and a reasonable amount of application. It is the art of using our language-apparatus to express thought clearly and emphatically.

Learning a language is first and foremost a question of learning its grammar. We learn a language sitting on our parent's knees and listening to their stories on how they trekked miles through the snow to get to school when they were youngsters. When we listen to these stories, we don't learn the rules of grammar; through mimicking, repetition, revision, and putting grammar into practice, we can become fluent in any language. A child has no idea what a verb or noun is until he reaches elementary school. At this very moment, you have an excellent command of English grammar. This is an operational command that functions below the threshold of awareness. As you speak, you automatically select—with little conscious thought or effort—the precise forms and arrangements of words that signal the meaning you wish to express. Grammar is the treatment of connected words for the expression of thought. It is not needed for disconnected words like *run, help, no, yes, later, now*, etc. Grammar applies to words when they are arranged in a sequential order to express thought.

Parts of Speech

You probably recall grimacing as a kid when you were in English class learning the dreaded parts of speech. Back then, you didn't realize how important they were in identifying and organizing sentence structure as you do now. If students are familiar with the parts of speech, teachers can guide students in making their own corrections. For example, if a student says, "I need chair"; a teacher can reply, "That sentence needs an article". Upon hearing the teacher's remark, the students can then recognize that he needs to change the sentence by plugging in an article. Utilizing parts of speech can also aid in the presentation of grammar lessons. If for example you were presenting linking verbs (stative verbs of perception such as sound, taste, smell, etc.), you can stress that the part of speech required to follow them are adjectives. The students can then figure out the formula that *linking verbs + adjectives* make a good sentence.

Here are the nine parts of speech:

Adjectives: These words describe nouns and pronouns and answers the questions that begin with *how many, what kind* and *which* one. Adjectives can take different forms such as the *-ing* form, the passive form, the comparative form

and the regular form. They usually precede nouns. Example adjectives are underlined in the sentence:
The blue car drove past the lonely man.

Adverbs: These words modify verbs, other adverbs, or adjectives. Adverbs usually end in -*ly* and can precede or follow verbs. Example adverbs are underlined in the sentence:
The student walked slowly into the classroom while the teacher looked angrily at him.

Articles: These small words introduce nouns. They consist of *a/an/the*. Many E.S.L. students, even advanced ones, tend to have problems with articles.

Conjunctions: These words connect independent thought or phrases together to make a sentence. There are coordinate conjunctions called FANBOYS (*for, and, nor, but, or, yet, so*) which connect independent sentences together, or subordinate conjunctions which connect phrases or clauses together to show a relationship between ideas in a sentence.

Interjection: These words express emotion or surprise with the use of an exclamation mark:!

Nouns: These words describe people, places, or things. They can be classified as proper nouns (specified nouns such as *Betty, Joe, Vancouver, Singapore, etc.*) or common nouns (non-specific nouns such as *child, man, table, chair, etc.*)

Prepositions: These words describe relationships with time, place, actions or situations and help connect nouns and pronouns to make a sentence:
After the earthquake, the people went inside the emergency shelter for protection.

Pronoun: These words replace the use of nouns in a sentence. Example pronouns are *I, you, he, she, it, we, they, me, him, her, them,* etc.

Verbs: These are action words or non-action (stative) words. Many E.S.L. students get confused with the use of non-action verbs that don't take on the progressive tense. Non-action verbs describe states or conditions that exist such as *love, like, hate, seem, appear, believe,* etc.

Verb Tense

To liven up a party, you can ask people, "How many tenses are there in English? Three, ten, sixteen, twenty-one or more? And what are they?" If people start walking away from you, then they just don't know how to get excited about the English language. The answer is twelve. These topics, of course, are what E.S.L.

teachers should know by heart. E.S.L. teachers should be familiar with the names of all verb tenses, their functions, and how and when they are used.

What is the *tense* of the verb in each of the following sentences? What is the *time* reference?

a)   The annual Vancouver Car Show opens next week.

b)   Experimental Plane Flies

The first sentence is in the *simple present* tense (sometimes called the *present simple* too) with future reference or factual information. The second sentence is the simple present tense with a past reference. You may see the second sentence more commonly in a headline of a newspaper rather than in everyday speech.

<u>Extra Practice: Present Tense</u>

Identify all the examples of the simple present tense in this text:

Bill admires his hero, Lucy. Lucy is a rock star and he listens to her ballads every day when he comes home from school. He imagines meeting his hero one day and telling her how much her music has impacted him. He feels thrilled when Lucy's hit songs are playing on his favorite radio station. He remarked to his friend, "Her music drives me crazy!" Her world concert tour begins in Vancouver tomorrow night. He is anxious to see her.

Can you find examples in the above text of the following uses of the simple present?

1.   to talk about factual information

2.   to talk about habitual information

3.   to talk about linking adjectives

4.   to talk about state of being

Overview of Tenses

Classification/Timeline	Example Sentence	Explanation
Simple Present x x x x x x past now future	I <u>want</u> to teach English overseas.	verbs used to express facts, habits, states, conditions and perceptions
Simple Past x past now future	I <u>taught</u> English last year.	verbs used to express a completed action in the past
Simple Future x past now future x past now future	I am <u>going to teach</u> English this year. I <u>will teach</u> English this year.	"going to" expresses a pre-planned event or a prediction "will" expresses a plan for the future, a spontaneous event, an assurance of a particular action and a refusal (in the negative form)
Present Continuous/Progressive past now future past now future	I <u>am teaching</u> English this afternoon.	an action taking place at or around the moment of speaking or a pre-planned action in the future
Past Continuous/Progressive x x past (pm) now future	I <u>was teaching</u> English this afternoon.	an action in progress at a point in the past
Future Continuous/Progressive x x past now (a.m.) future	Don't call me in the morning because <u>I will be teaching</u> English. Don't call me in the morning because I <u>am going to be</u> teaching.	an action in progress at a definite time in the future

Classification/Timeline	Example Sentence	Explanation
Present Perfect x ——— x past ◄——————► now future 5 years	I <u>have taught</u> English for 5 years.	an action which occurred in the past and is evident in the present
Past Perfect x x past study teach now future	I <u>had studied</u> for my TESOL before I began my teaching career.	the earlier of two actions from the past
Future Perfect x x past now start finish future (Feb 14) (Mar 14)	By this time next month, I <u>will have completed</u> my TESOL course.	an action in the future that will be completed before another action in the future
Present Perfect Continuous/ Progressive ∿→ x x past study now future	I <u>have been studying</u> hard for my TESOL.	an activity which started in the past and continues now
Past Perfect Continuous/Progressive ∿| x past sleep come now future 3 hours	I <u>had been sleeping</u> for 3 hours when my mother came. I <u>had been smoking</u> for 5 years when I quit.	an activity that was in progress in the past before it was interrupted by another action; or repeated actions before another time in the past; the emphasis is on the duration
Future Perfect Continuous/Progressive ∿→ x x past now future	By 10:00 pm I <u>will have been sleeping</u> for 5 hours.	an activity in progress that happens before another activity in the future; emphasis is on the duration

* The continuous tense is also called the progressive tense

Like most native speakers, you know how to make grammatically correct sentences but you may not be consciously aware as to why they are correct or what rules they follow. How can you familiarize yourself with verb tenses before you step into a grammar class? Here we have a chart on some potential problems you may encounter when presenting them in class:

Verb Tense	When To Use	Potential Problem Areas
Simple Present	1) facts (She is in the school) 2) habits (She never drinks beer) 3) linking verbs (The food smells nice) 4) non-action verbs (I believe in God)	- conjugation of the *To Be* verb versus all other verbs - *he/she/it* affirmative tenses require an -*s* at the end
Simple Past	1) completed actions in the past	- differentiating regular and irregular simple past verb forms - the simple past verb forms may not be the same as the past participle forms that are seen in the present perfect
Simple Future	1) actions in the future that are planned, predicted, promised spontaneous, or declarative.	- when to use "going to" and "will"
Present Progressive	1) actions in progress at the time of speaking or a planned action in the future 2) simple present uses certain clue words to indicate facts and habits (ex. everyday, Mondays, annually, always, sometimes, never, etc.) 3) present progressive uses certain clue words to indicate actions in progress or the future (ex. at the moment, now, this evening, this month, etc.)	- when to use the simple past versus the present progressive - is also called present continuous in some grammar books - non-action or stative verbs that don't take on the progressive tense - often used with subordinate clauses

Verb Tense	When To Use	Potential Problem Areas
Past Progressive	1) an action that was in progress in the past	- adding a simple past sentence to make a complex sentence
Future Progressive	1) an action in progress at a definite point in the future	- used to emphasize duration of a future action (*ex. I will be teaching the whole day*)
Present Perfect	1) an action that was initiated in the past and is evident in in the present; the time it occurred isn't important.	- the name of this tense may confuse students into thinking it is a present tense - needs the present form of *To Have* as an auxiliary. - the use of contractions with *To Have* may be confused with the contraction of *To Be*
Past Perfect	1) a past action that happened before another past action	- confusion with present perfect
Future Perfect	1) an action that is completed before another action in the future	- doesn't always begin in the future due to the emphasis on duration (ex. Jane and Jim will have been together for 20 years.)
Present Perfect Progressive	1) an action that began in the past and continues in the present	- sometimes is used for a finished action if it was recently completed or if you want to emphasize the duration (ex. "I've been going out of my mind looking for that ring!")

Verb Tense	When To Use	Potential Problem Areas
Past Perfect Progressive	1) an action that was in progress in the past before it was interrupted 2) repeated past actions before another time in the past	- can be used with *since* and *for* - meaning can be similar to past progressive action but the progressive action in past perfect progressive usually stops with the interruption - used in reported speech when a quote is in the past progressive - not used with a specified frequency of time
Future Perfect Progressive	1) puts emphasis on a long duration of an action before a second action in the future 2) the action may be a habit	- the action may begin at any time before the second future action (even in the past). - often used with simple present subordinate clauses

When teaching verbs, you have to go through a process in which all aspects of a verb tense is covered. The introduction of a new verb tense will involve the basic affirmative sentence, and progresses to the negative sentence. After the negative sentence, you teach how to form *yes/no* questions, and finally you teach how to form *wh*-questions. Your board work should be orderly and neat. Since verb tenses can take some time for students to grasp, it's best to teach a verb tense in manageable chunks.

For a one-week lesson on a new verb tense, you can spend the first day on introducing affirmative sentences, negative sentences, and *yes/no* questions. The second day can be spent on further practice of the first day material. The third day can introduce how to make and practice *wh*-questions. The fourth day can be spent with further practice in making and answering *wh*-questions. Finally the fifth day can be spent reviewing the week's material. Your students should gradually see a build up in board work of the verb tense so that on the fourth and fifth day the board will have a comprehensive display showing the heading of what's been taught: affirmative and negative sentences, models of *yes/no* questions, accompanying short and long answers, *wh*-questions and accompanying answers.

Here is an example of board work for a lesson comparing the simple present tense of *To Be* with other verbs in the simple present such as the verb *To Eat*:

To Be	negative	To Eat	negative
	not		do/does not + MAIN VERB

To Be — negative — not

I	am a student. (I'm)
You	are a teacher. (You're/you're not)
He/she/it	is happy. (he's/he isn't)
They	are in Canada. (they're/they're not)
We	are in Vancouver. (We're/we aren't)

To Eat — negative — do/does not + MAIN VERB

I	eat rice.
You	eat pudding.
He/she/it	eats
They	eat salad.
We	eat beans.

do: I, you, they, we   do not = don't
does: he, she, it   does not = doesn't

Yes/No Question*
To Be + SUBJECT + ...?

Are	you	a student?
Is	she	happy?

Yes, I am. No, I'm not.
Yes, I'm a student. No, I'm not a student.
Yes, she is. No, she isn't.
Yes, she is happy. No, she isn't happy.

Yes/No Question
Do/Does + SUBJECT + MAIN VERB + ...?

Do	you	eat	rice?
Does	he	eat	meat?

Yes, I do. No, I don't.
Yes, I eat rice. No, I don't eat rice.
Yes, he does. No, he doesn't.
Yes, he eats meat. No, he doesn't eat meat.

Wh-Questions **

QUESTION + To Be + SUBJECT + ...?
WORD

Why rice?	are	you happy?
Where	is	she?

Wh-Questions **

QUESTION + do/does + SUBJECT + MAIN + ...?
WORD   VERB

When	do	you	eat
What	does	he	eat?

I'm happy because it's sunny.
She is in the store.

I eat rice in the evening.
He eats hamburgers.

* You can use the presented example affirmative sentences to create yes/no questions (remember, when the answer starts with *I*, the subject in the question is *you*; when the answer starts with *you*, the subject in the question is *I*)
** It is sometimes difficult to come up with a wide range of wh-questions with the given affirmative sentences so you may want to combine other example wh-questions that are not guided by the presented affirmative examples.

When introducing verb tenses, teachers should use a tool called a timeline to visually express the use of the tenses. Timelines and diagrams can be very useful ways for provoking discussion and understanding verb tenses. Interesting discussion areas may come up. For example, is the sentence, *She works in a salon,* represented as a series of repeated actions or as a permanent state? There are several different ways of representing verb forms. For an excellent discussion, see Michael Lewis' *The English Verb* for diagrams in Chapter 21 of his book. Since timelines are visual tools, they will aid in understanding the different uses of verb tenses. When should timelines be presented? They should be presented to clarify and reinforce the meaning and use of a verb tense at the end of the presentation stage.

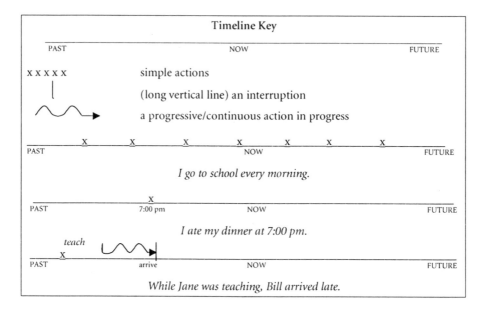

Sentences, Clauses, and Phrases

What defines the above terms? It's important to distinguish between the 3 so as not to confuse your students when presenting sentences of varying complexity.

Sentence: A group of words that contain a subject and a predicate (verb)

Clause: A clause is basically a sentence. A clause can be dependent or independent in thought. A dependent clause needs the independent clause to have a complete thought whereas an independent clause can stand alone as a complete thought.

Phrase: A group of words that looks like a sentence but there is no subject or a verb.

So now that you have the framework of how grammar lessons are conducted, the last point to know is how to organize your lesson into a lesson plan. Keep in mind that a grammar lesson that introduces new material should follow this progression:

1) Introduce the grammar point with authentic context.

2) Elicit/Produce the target language and the meaning with the use of concept questions and/or other aids such as drawings, graphics, etc.

3) Go over pronunciation details of the target language and produce organized boar work.

4) Conduct controlled (teacher-guided) practice.

5) Initiate less controlled (student-centered) practice.

6) If you have time, follow-up with a short closing activity to the lesson.

Check out the example grammar lesson introducing the simple past of *To Be* in the Course Planning section.

Brainstorming for Fun

As you begin your teaching career, you will find that it can get harder and harder to brainstorm creative ways to present your material in the presentation stage of your lessons. There are many good grammar idea books to help you and as you acquire further practice in churning out lesson plans, your creative mind will go into full swing. The important thing to keep in mind is to have fun with your students. Learning doesn't have to be boring with dull presentations and flat exercises. Spice up your classes with board games, competitive activities, dynamic conversations, challenging crossword puzzles, and so forth. When you have fun in the class, time flies and students forget they're "in school" and you may forget you're "at work".

Recommended Reading List

A. Grammar Reference Books

Azar, Betty Schrampfer. (2000). *Chartbook: A Reference Grammar.* New York: Pearson Education

Eastwood, John. (1994). *Oxford Guide to English Grammar.* Oxford: Oxford University Press.

Halliday, Michael.A.K. (1994). *An Introduction to Functional Grammar, second edition.* New York: Hodder Headline PLC

Haslem, John A. Jr. (Ed.). (1998). *Webster's New World Notebook Grammar & Punctuation Guide.* New York: Simon & Schuster.

Swan, Michael. (1995). *Practical English Usage,* second edition. Oxford: Oxford University Press.

B. Grammar Textbooks

Azar, Betty Schrampfer. (1995). *Basic English Grammar, second edition.* New York: Pearson Education. (Beginners)

Azar, Betty Schrampfer. (1992). *Fundamentals of English Grammar, second edition.* New Jersey: Prentice-Hall Regents. (Intermediate)

Azar, Betty Schrampfer. (1999). *Understanding and Using English Grammar, third edition.* New York: Pearson Education. (High Intermediate to Advanced)

Hartmann, Pamela, Zarian, Annette, & Esparza, Patricia. (1998). *Tense Situations: Tenses in Contrast and Context.* Orlando: Harcourt Brace & Company. (High Intermediate)

Maurer, Jay. (2000). *Focus On Grammar: An Advanced Course for Reference and Practice, second edition.* New York: Longman. (Advanced)

C. Grammar Teaching Ideas

Aitken, Rosemary (1992). *Teaching Tenses.* Walton-on-Thames: Nelson.

Forsyth, Will & Lavender, Sue. (1994). *Grammar Activities 1: Intermediate.* Oxford: Heinemann

Forsyth, Will & Lavender, Sue. (1995). *Grammar Activities 2: Upper Intermediate.* Oxford: Heinemann

Klepinger, Lawrence. (1999). *Where the Action is: An Easy E.S.L. Approach to Pure Regular Verbs.* New York: Barron's

Watcyn-Jones, Peter. (1995). *Grammar Games and Activities for Teachers.* London: Penguin Books

Woodward, Suzanne W. (1997). *Fun With Grammar: Communicative Activities for the Azar Grammar Series.* New Jersey: Prentice-Hall Regents.

CHAPTER 8:

An Example Grammar Analysis: Modals and Stative Verbs—The Neighborhood Streets

---

In This Chapter

> Modal Analysis

> Modals versus Auxiliaries

> Form

> Meaning

> Use

> Pronunciation

> Verbs of Being and Condition

Modals and Auxiliaries

Harry can teach English. Harry may go to many countries. Harry will travel extensively. Harry shall enjoy a great teaching career. What do all of these sentences have in common? Besides having the same subject, these sentences contain special words called modal auxiliaries (or *modals*). Modals are words that change the meanings of verbs that follow them. Modals can express ability, possibility, preference, prediction, suggestion, past habit or ability, permission, requests, necessity, obligation, warnings, deduction, expectation or prohibition.

A Class By Itself

How do you teach modal verbs? Since modals have special distinguishing characteristics, they are best taught by grouping them into categories. Presenting modals in groups allows students to understand the varying degrees of meaning involved. For instance, there are varying degrees of certainty with the modals of *will, might, may, could*, etc. There are varying degrees of necessity with the modals of *should, might, had better, have to, must*, etc. There are varying degrees of possibility with the modals of *may, might, could, should, will*, and so forth. There are also some words that share some of the characteristics of modals but may not be considered "true modals". Words such as *ought, had better, need, used to, have to, need*, or *dare* can be called semi-modals. Following the basic strategy of examining the form, meaning, and use of a grammar point, which in this case is modals, you'll be prepared to tackle modals from all directions. Emphasis on pronunciation should be covered as well. If you analyze all of these areas of learning, you'll never stumble over any student's questions on modals. It's a great feeling to confidently leave a class knowing that you were able to answer any question in "the book".

Form

What structural rules govern the use of basic modals?

1) Modals don't conjugate with a subject > Jane <u>mights</u> help us.
2) Modals don't have preceding auxiliary verbs in questions > <u>Does</u> Jane can help us?
3) Modals don't have preceding auxiliary verbs in negative statements > Jane <u>doesn't</u> can help you.
4) Modals don't have an infinitive form > <u>To</u> can/<u>To</u> may
5) Modals precede base form verbs > Jane and John can teach English.
6) Modals don't have past participles following them > Jane must <u>taught</u> English.
7) Modals can't double up in a sentence > Jane <u>must can</u> teach English.
8) Modals don't have an—*ed* ending for the past form > Jane <u>musted</u> teach English.

Meaning

How are modal verbs different from auxiliary verbs? Let's look at some example sentences:

Modal Verbs	Auxiliary Verbs
He _can_ play basketball. (This sentence expresses an ability)	He _is_ playing basketball. (This sentence expresses an action in progress.
He _might_ go to the party tomorrow. (This sentence expresses a possibility)	_Did_ he go to the party last night? (This sentence asks a question about the past.)
She _must_ pay her taxes to the government. (This sentence expresses a necessity)	She _has_ paid her taxes to the government. (This sentence suggests a completed past action.)

Keep in mind that some modals, such as _could_ or _should_, have more than one meaning:

➢ Betty _could_ teach English in a couple of months. (This sentence expresses a future possibility)

➢ When Betty was young, she _could_ run fast. (This sentence expresses a past ability)

➢ Betty _should_ teach English. (This sentence expresses a suggestion)

➢ Betty _should_ be teaching by now. (This sentence expresses an expectation)

➢ Betty _should_ have bought this book. (This sentence expresses a suggestion from the past)

In addition, some modals may have different meanings in their past forms. Consider these examples:

> Jane would like an apple (a present or future wish)	> Jane would have liked an apple (a past unfulfilled wish)
> Jane is supposed to teach English (A present or future expectation)	> Jane was supposed to teach English (A past unfulfilled expectation)
> Jane could talk to the students (A present suggestion)	> Jane could have talked to the students (A past possibility)

All in all, by recognizing the structure patterns and their accompanying definitions, teachers can fully distinguish the various meanings that modals bring.

Use

The key to using modals is to identify the concepts that govern their use. Identifying concepts such as permission, prediction, deduction, ability, possibility, suggestion, and others can lead students in how to use the correct modal form. Teachers can create worksheets with matching exercises. For example, sentences containing modals can be listed on one side of the paper and a list of concepts can be made on the other side. Students can then match the modal sentences with the correct identifying concept. For example, the sentence, *You must not spit on the floor*, would be matched with the concept of prohibition. These kinds of concept identification worksheets are very useful in assisting students in grasping the different meanings of modals. An example concept identification worksheet is included at the end of this chapter. Another example worksheet that teachers can create involves conversing in small groups. Students can be arranged in groups of 4. Teachers can give each group a list of qualities under a certain category. For example under the category of *Good Neighbor*, have students list all the different qualities they wish seek in having a good neighbor.

➢   is quiet

➢   is sociable

➢   mows his yard

➢   doesn't mow your flowers

➢   does/doesn't have pets

➢   doesn't allow his dog to fertilize your yard

➢   etc.

Students would then discuss in their small groups what the 5 most important qualities of a good neighbor are. They may even add some suggestions of their own. In their discussions, students would be required to use modals in their speech. This is a fun activity that students tend to enjoy. An example conversational exercise of this type is included at the end of this chapter.

Pronunciation

When teaching modals, E.S.L. students often have trouble hearing the subtle contrasting sounds between *can* and *can't*. Intuitive teachers such as yourself can inform students that in affirmative sentences, *can* is unstressed but the verb that follows is stressed. In Use sentence stress symbols or capitalization to demonstrate stress on the board:

O ₒ ₒ   O   O   ₒ
Harry can teach English.

HARry can TEACH ENGlish
(capitalization)

In negative sentences, *can't* is stressed and the verb that follows is stressed as well. Use sentence stress symbols to demonstrate on the board:

O ₒ ₒ O   O
Jeremy can't swim.

JERemy CAN'T SWIM.
(capitalization)

Further detailed information on how to use sentence stress symbols is covered in the pronunciation chapters of this book.

Verbs We Take For Granted

A common problem area that often stumbles E.S.L. students is the introduction of stative (or sometimes called *non-action*) verbs. Many students have problems deciphering the difference of how to use stative verbs compared with progressive verbs. Stative verbs express states of conditions or situations, but not actions. They can express possession (have, own, possess, belong), perception (taste, smell, hear, feel, etc), emotion (love, hate, like, dislike, care, etc.), mental states (believe, know, understand, guess, etc.), appearance (look, resemble, seem, sound, etc) or wants (desire, need, prefer, wish, etc.). Stative verbs are used primarily in the simple present tense; however, some can actually be used in the progressive tense as well. For example, *smell* can be stative or progressive. In the stative use, *smell* links a noun to an adjective, much like the *be* verb.

The flower *smells* nice (the verb links flower to nice)

In the progressive use, *smell* describes the action of a subject:

The girl *is smelling* the flower (a physical action is made)

Stative verbs that act as a planned action or an action with a purpose can be used progressively in sentences. In all other cases, stative verbs are used in the simple present.

The best time to introduce stative verbs is after the simple present is learned and again when students are learning the present progressive so that they understand which stative verbs can and can't be used in the progressive tense. Example exercises that make students choose between simple present and present progressive verbs are good practice in understanding stative verbs. Editing exercises, which allow students to make corrections in error-contained passages, are good practice as well. Be prepared to spend extra time with students on how to use and differentiate stative verbs with their progressive counterparts.

WORKSHEET 1: MODAL CONCEPT COMPREHENSION

Match the sentences with modals on the left to the correct concept list on right. The sentences may have more than one answer.

1) Joan and Bob used to smoke. (_____)

2) The children must go home after school. (_____)

3) Would she be mad if I didn't go to the party? (_____)

4) Those birds ought to fly south in the winter. (_____)

5) Sarah might be interested in the offer. (_____)

6) We could go to the movies tomorrow. (_____)

7) Can the dog go outside? (_____)

8) My son would rather go to the baseball game. (_____)

9) The Jeffersons will be here at noon. (_____)

10) People must not commit violence against others. (_____)

11) Jane had better study for tomorrow's test. (_____)

12) Yes, you may go to the washroom. (_____)

13) Harry should do well in his new career. (_____)

14) Of course, you can borrow my car anytime. (_____)

15) Birds can't drive cars. (_____)

16) George might have eaten the cake. (_____)

17) We would always go to the store for candy everyday. (_____)

18) I'll meet you at the airport at 12:00. (_____)

19) When I was young, I could run fast. (_____)

20) The cake must be from Italy. (_____)

a) possibility

b) expectation

c) suggestion

d) obligation

e) advisability

f) deduction about the present

g) formal permission

h) informal permission

i) preference

j) habit in the past

k) informal request

l) inability

m) deduction about the future

n) warning

o) assurance

p) past ability

q) prohibition

r) deduction about the past

KEY: 1-j, 2-d, 3-m, 4-c/e, 5-m, 6-a, 7-k, 8-I, 9-b, 10-q, 11-n, 12-g, 13-b, 14-h, 15-l, 16-r, 17-j, 18-o, 19-p, 20-f

WORKSHEET 2: MODAL CONVERSATION EXERCISE

PART I:

What qualities does a good neighbor have? Listed below are some example qualities of a good neighbor. In groups of 3, decide which are the 5 most important qualities of a good neighbor. You may add more suggestions to the list. Please use modals in your conversation and express why these qualities are important or not important.

A good neighbor...............

- ➢ is quiet
- ➢ is sociable
- ➢ mows his yard
- ➢ doesn't mow your flowers
- ➢ does/doesn't have pets
- ➢ doesn't allow his dog to fertilize your yard
- ➢ is helpful around the house
- ➢ is intelligent
- ➢ is not too intelligent
- ➢ has a sense of humor
- ➢ doesn't have a sick sense of humor
- ➢ is good with children
- ➢ doesn't have 10 children under 8 years old

PART II:

What qualities make a good marriage? In groups of 4, appoint a secretary to represent your group and decide which are the 10 most important qualities of a good marriage. Please use modals in your conversation and express why these qualities are important or not important.

CHAPTER 9:

Teaching Vocabulary & Reading— Parallel Parking

In This Chapter

> Vocabulary exploration

> Sight words

> Word lists

> Procedure for word introduction

> Schema Theory

> Manipulating reading passages

> Barrett's Taxonomy

> SQ3R

> Stages of a reading lesson

Vocabulary refers to the words of a language. What do you know when you know a word? To know a word is to know its meaning and function. Students can run into problems with vocabulary because words can have more than one meaning, or words can have similar sounds to another word with a different meaning (homonyms) or words can be confused with metaphorical meaning, and so forth.

> **How many words do E.S.L. students know in English?**
>
> Intermediate level students know about 1000–3000 words.
> Advanced level students know about 3500–4000 words
> Grade 12 native English graduates know about 50,000 words
> Native English university graduates know about 100,000–200,000 words
> Sleeping students know 1 word = Zzzzzzz....

Knowing a word means being able to do certain tasks with it. What are those tasks?

➢ Understanding a word when it's written and spoken. (ex. an eggplant is a vegetable and has nothing to do with an egg)

➢ Recalling a word when you need it.

➢ Using a word with the correct meaning.

➢ Knowing a synonym or two.

➢ Using a word in a grammatically correct way (ex. **pro**duce [noun] versus pro**duce** [verb]).

➢ Pronouncing a word correctly.

➢ Knowing what other words you can use it with. (ex. think <u>about</u>, think <u>over</u>).

➢ Spelling a word correctly.

➢ Using it in the correct context (ex. The popular meaning of *gay* has changed over the years).

➢ Knowing whether a word has positive or negative associations (ex. the word *kid* may have a negative context depending on how it is used in a sentence)

How many words should English teachers introduce students to in their lessons? It is easy for teachers to frustrate students with too much vocabulary in their lessons. Try to limit the number of new words for each lesson to five to ten. Any amount over ten begins to frustrate students.

When you're teaching the vocabulary component of a grammar lesson, you may want to check for the students' knowledge of 150 of the most frequently used words in English:

a, about, after, again, all, also, an, and, are, as, asked, at, back, be, because, been, before, beside, between, big, but, by, came, can, come, could, did, do, does, don't, down, during, even, far, few, first, for, from, general, get, go, going, good, government, had, has, have, he, her, here, him, himself, his, house, how, however, I, I'm, if, in, into, is, it, just, keep, know, less, like, little, look, long, made, make, man, many, me, might, more, most, much, Mr., Mrs., my, never, next, no, not, now, number, of, old, on, one, or, other, our, out, over, own, part, people, place, play, put, right, said, same, saw, see, she, should, so, some, small, still, such, take, that, the, their, then, there, these, they, think, this, three, time, to, too, two, up, under, us, used, very, was, water, way, we, well, went, what, when, where, which, will, with, without, would, you, your.

It would be beneficial to you and your students to go over some of the most frequently used words in the English language to aid in comprehension production in all language skills. A word list that you may wish to go over contains sight words. Sight words are instantly recognizable words that students are familiar with. Although students can recognize the words, they may not necessarily be able to sound the words out. Sight words can be categorized by function. Can you guess what function these sight words are often seen?

name/surname/given name/initial/maiden name
Mr./Mrs./Ms./Miss
sex/male/female
marital status/married/separated/divorced/single/common law
date/month/year/birth date/date of birth/place of birth/country of birth
address/street/present address/mailing address/postal code/zip code/city/province/state
telephone number/telephone
citizenship/American/Canadian/Australian/British/landed immigrant
age/height/weight
Social Security Number/Social Insurance Number
health plan number/medical card no.
driver's license number
doctor's name/dentist's name

occupation/job/employer/place of employment/part-time/full-time/temporary
first language, if not English
years of schooling/last school attended/location of school
high school/college/vocational school/university/other
certificate/program completed

If you guessed the function of the above sight words are to fill out forms, you're correct!

The Vocabulary Machine

There are various ways to increase your student's vocabulary. One way is through the study of root words, prefixes and suffixes. When a student understands the meaning of these parts of a word, doors begin to open in the understanding of a whole series of words that use the same word part. There are many good vocabulary books that do in-depth studies of roots, prefixes and suffixes.

Another way to expand vocabulary knowledge is through the making of word lists. Word lists can be categorized under a variety of headings. Below are some example headings:

A. Word Sources
  ➤ Teachers and students can make lists of words that are derived from foreign languages such as *frankfurter* (German), *burlesque* (French), *maize* (Spanish), etc.

B. Word Environments
  ➤ Lists of words can be made by analyzing different places or environments. For example environments such as in the office (*stapler, computer, printer, fax, etc*), in the hospital (*orderly, nurse's aide, specialist, needle, etc.*) and in the school (*principal, student counselor, transcript, etc.*)

C. Compound Words
  ➤ Lists of words made by putting together two words to form one can be created. Words such as *highway, newspaper, bookcase, baseball*, etc.

D. Slang Words
  ➤ Lists of words made from slang expressions can be created. Words such as *blurb, has-been, redneck, gadget, etc.*

E. English In Other Places
  ➤ Lists of words that have different meanings or uses in other parts of the English speaking world. Words such as *push-chair*(Britain) versus

stroller (North America); *lorry* (Britain) versus *truck* (North American); *sack* (America) versus *bag* (Canada); etc.

F. Nouns-Adjectives

  ➢ Lists of nouns can be made with accompanying adjectives that may describe the nouns can be created. Words such as *nightmare—scary, threatening, sleepless, etc.*

G. Synonyms, Homonyms, Antonyms

  ➢ Lists of these specialized words can be created. Synonyms are words with the same general meaning, homonyms are words with the same pronunciation but with different spelling and meaning, and antonyms are words with opposite meanings.

H. Prefixes, Suffixes

  ➢ Lists of words that are formed by prefixes or suffixes to a root word. Words such as *misguided, phonograph, biography, etc.* In addition, lists of words that begin with a common prefix or suffix can be made, such as—*logy* suffix: *biology, anthropology, psychology, geology*)

When do you teach vocabulary? Are there certain appropriate times when a teacher presents new vocabulary? How about at a party when you'd like to make new friends...or repel old ones? New words should be taught as pre-teaching items before reading exercises; as tools to expand writing tasks; as fluency aids in listening and speaking activities; and for preparatory purposes for specialized study in proficiency exams such as TOEFL, TOEIC, and the LPI. The most predominant area where vocabulary teaching comes into play will be in reading classes.

Expressing Meaning

When a teacher is asked a vocabulary question regarding meaning, it's important to consider the following in your answer:

➢ Use simple language so the student can understand you.

➢ Determine what the most common meaning of a word is (if there is more than 1 meaning) and explain that meaning.

➢ Provide a physical description of a word, or the emotions related to it.

➢ Provide an example sentence with its context.

When a low intermediate student asks, "What does *embarrassed* mean?" you can answer by explaining in simple language:

- "Embarrassed" is an adjective to describe a feeling. You feel uncomfortable. When you have this feeling, your face sometimes becomes red. Here is an example sentence: *I was embarrassed when my boyfriend visited me because my house was very dirty.* [The teacher can then physically show facial expressions imitating embarrassment.]

Procedure for Vocabulary Introduction

1. Elicit
   Try to elicit the meaning from the students before explaining or modeling it.

2. Model
   If students fail to generate the meaning of a word, model the word's meaning through gestures, facial expressions, body language, context situations, and other such clues.

3. Drill
   Practice the pronunciation of the vocabulary with the correct stress.

4. Check for Understanding
   Ask concept questions that ensure student understanding of the new word.

5. Practice
   Begin activities in which students would have to practice identifying and using the new vocabulary with written exercises (such as matching words with pictures, doing crosswords, matching word parts, etc.), oral activities, and reading activities involving searching for the new words.

<u>Extra Practice: Checking for Understanding</u>

In the previous chapter, you learned how to check for understanding by asking concept questions. Devise some concept questions to check and clarify the meaning of these words:

luggage
tourist
shark
surf board
island

Extra Practice: Teacher—Student Interaction With New Vocabulary

Teachers say things without realizing how students interpret. What are the problems with these utterances made by teachers?

> *Funny* means *humorous.*
> Does everyone know what *eggplant* is? Good.
> What does *patient* mean?

Extra Practice: Explaining Meaning

Imagine you have a class of low intermediate students who would like to ask you the meaning of the following words. How would you explain it to them?

1. poetry	2. play (noun)	3. physical	4. lock (noun)
5. fiction	6. novel	7. stadium	8. sign (noun/verb)
9. speech	10. aerobics	11. ballad	12. tropical

Reading Relevancy

If you weren't one of those ace readers in high school, like Barbara Bookworm, join the rest of us. How do you motivate students to read for the purpose of improving their language skills? Students have to be encouraged to read as much as possible, including "the funnies" in newspapers. Reading theory has many variations. If you were teaching Betty, the E.S.L. student, the best process in teaching reading to Betty is to strive for a balance between Betty's background knowledge of a textbook's contents and the cultural background of Betty herself. By obtaining this balance, language comprehension can be optimally approached.

> *A few years ago, while tutoring a student from India, I asked her to read a story from a textbook about a man gardening in his yard. The original purpose of the exercise was to identify the verb tenses and their utilizations in the passage. After reading the article, her enthusiasm in the session increased noticeably due to the topic of the passage. My student was an avid gardener and spent many hours tending to her yard. She fully related to this man's hobby and her full attention was easily observed. Her identity of the verb tenses became secondary to the ease of how she personally related herself to the man in the article. Thus my student's personal interest in gardening and the general knowledge of gardening itself facilitated the reading session.*

When I was six years old, I recall being a slow reader compared to my book-worm classmates. I attributed this trait to being my inability to decode language at a comparable rate to my peers. I found that familiar or relevant reading eases and motivates my comprehension far more than a topic that did not interest me at all. For example, as a ten year old, reading about the adventures of Alley the Alligator I was fascinated with Alley as he became my imaginary reptilian friend wherever I went. As I got older, Alley's influence wore off on me as my reading interests expanded from reading about the construction of Hearst Castle in San Simeon, California to the latest engineering feats in Popular Science magazine.—P.D.

For second-language students, a teacher has to ensure that what their students read is relevant to their lives and accommodates their different cultural backgrounds. According to educational psychologist R.C. Anderson's "Schema Theory", failure in reading comprehension is when the reader's background knowledge isn't addressed; whether it be from the reader's lack of knowing enough grammar to understand the structure of the text or the reader's lack of knowledge of the contents of the text. The more familiar the content is for the reader, the easier the recall; thus comprehension depends crucially on the reader's ability to relate information from the text to previously acquired background knowledge. In order to facilitate the combination of students' varied cultural backgrounds, teachers can minimize reading difficulties and maximize comprehension by manipulating the text (changing the language or content) and/or the reader (by providing background information and previewing topics). Only by striving for a balance between the students' background knowledge of a text and the background knowledge of the students' themselves can language comprehension be optimally approached.

Teachers or schools can purchase some good quality novels specially suited for an E.S.L. audience. Penguin Longman Publishing sells a wide selection of Penguin Readers, classified under appropriate E.S.L. levels in their catalogue, such as Charles Dickens' *Oliver Twist*, Gustave Flaubert's *Madame Bovary*, Leo Tolstoy's *Anna Karenina*, E.M. Forster's *A Room With a View*, Wilkie Collins' *The Moonstone*, Boris Pasternak's *Dr. Zhivago*, Thomas Hardy's *The Mayor of Casterbridge*, etc.

Manipulating the Text

You've researched a pile of articles to find "the right one" for your reading class and you've discovered that the topic is great but the structure may be too advanced to understand for your beginner E.S.L. students. What should you do? You need to simplify the article to accommodate your students' language level by re-writing it. How? Here are some simple rules for text manipulation:

1)   Find the main idea and ruthlessly chop out chunks of information that is not related to the main idea or is irrelevant

2)   Keep sentences short by using simple and compound sentences only

3)   Keep paragraphs short

4)   Use the active voice (*Tom built the house*) rather than the passive voice (*The house was built by Tom*)

5)   Use concrete words (avoid metaphors, similes, idioms, and slang)

The ultimate format for beginner and high-beginner students can be found in the popular Canadian E.S.L. newspaper, *The Westcoast Reader*. You can find many interesting articles printed in a large typeset and with pictures, maps, graphs, and other visuals. It's a small newspaper printed in an easy-to-handle tabloid format. By observing this style of writing and presentation, you can have a good idea of what level of writing would be required to achieve the readable standards of a beginner E.S.L. level.

Extra Practice: Newspaper Manipulation

Choose an article from a local newspaper. Read the article and note any verb tenses that a beginner E.S.L. student probably wouldn't be familiar with. Clip the article and re-write it in a format that a beginner E.S.L. student would be able to understand by following the simple rules of text manipulation.

E.S.L. LEVELS versus GRADE SCHOOL LANGUAGE LEVELS

The following E.S.L. reading levels in comparison with grade school language levels are approximations only.

Low Beginner = Level 1 = Grade 1
High Beginner = Level 2 = Grade 2
Low Intermediate = Level 3 = Grades 2–3
High Intermediate = Level 4 = Grades 3–4
Low Advanced = Level 5 = Grades 4–6
High Advanced = Level 6 = Grades 6 +

Barrett's Taxonomy

In order to track how your students are processing information in their reading activities, there is a scale of comprehension called Barrett's Taxonomy, which was introduced at a conference in 1968 and cited in Alderson & Urquhart's *Reading in a Foreign Language* (1984). When designing activities, keep in mind what level of processing you wish your students to engage in. Low level processing only demands literal comprehension while high-level processing shows a student's appreciation for the material and may evoke an emotional response as new insight in life is gained. By using Barrett's scale of comprehension below, you can ensure a balance between all 5 levels.

a) Literal (lowest level of processing)
   - recognizing and recalling facts, detail, main ideas and events and the main players of a reading passage
   - the most common type of question students would find on tests
b) Sequential
   - being able to reorganize the information in a reading passage in a different way from the original
c) Inferential
   - being able to read "between the lines"
   - responding to information that isn't directly given
d) Evaluation
   - giving opinions and input on the reading material
   - being able to answer evaluative questions on the material demonstrates a high level of comprehension
e) Appreciation (highest level of processing)
   - gaining new insight in a student's life
   - applying information from the reading material to new situations can evoke an emotional response

Example Activities Following Barrett's Taxonomy

Literal: Since this is the most common question students would encounter on a reading test, a variety of activities can be conducted on the literal comprehension level. A good exercise to practice literal comprehension is to conduct oral quizzes that require students to quickly scan a reading passage for factual information. In small groups of four to five students, one student in each group has a list of questions with answers that are found in a reading passage. The other members of the group have their reading passages face down on the table. The list holder of the group reads out a question from his list. He repeats the question and then signals a "Go" to the students. When the students hear "Go", that signals them they can flip over their passages and begin to search for the answer. The first person who finds the answer says it aloud and gets a point if it's correct. This activity is a great scanning activity for students to practice their test-taking skills.

> If you read a story of a cat stuck in a tree, an example literal question would be: Where was the cat?

Sequential. Jigsaw reading activities are great for testing students' reorganization skills. Jigsaws are reading tasks where parts of a reading passage are given to small groups. Each small group is given a different part of the passage to read and discuss amongst themselves. Members of each group become "experts" in their particular passage and take notes related to their passage of study. Afterwards, teachers separate and reform them so that a representative from each of the previous groups is put together. Now all of the groups have an "expert" in each of the different parts of a passage. In the new groups, members are to "teach" each other what they've learned and work together to understand the passage as a whole. Jigsaws can also be done outside of a sequential activity. Teachers may even incorporate picture sequences as well. Another sequential activity can have the teacher write a list of events from a text in the incorrect order and have students determine the correct sequence on the board.

> Using the same cat story, an example sequential exercise would be to chronologically determine the sequence of events that resulted in the cat being in the tree.

Inferential. This comprehension skill requires a high level of processing. Students without practice will usually just look for literal answers in a text thus they would be deprived of the essential skill of "reading between the lines." Inferential exercises can have students predict the outcome of certain parts of a passage, especially at its pivotal points. Students can make their predictions based on clues in the text and share them with their classmates.

> An example inferential question would be: Will the cat climb the tree again?

<u>Evaluation.</u> Exercises that explore opposite stances characterize the testing of this level. Evaluation exercises can involve the expression of opinions. Students can be assembled in groups to form a common opinion—either positive or negative. Teachers can then have opposing groups debate each other by having them express their opinions aloud and countering the opinions of the other side. Teachers can also assign students to study traits of similarities and differences in a passage for evaluation.

> An example evaluation question would be: The cat had a good reason to climb the tree because it wanted to…(fill-in-the-blank). Explain if you agree or disagree with this statement.

<u>Appreciation.</u> This is considered as the highest level of reading comprehension processing. Acquiring class feedback of the passage by asking, "What are your thoughts on this story?", "Did you like the story?", "Explain why or why not." An example appreciation exercise can be to have students share a personal story that has a relation to the theme of the passage. If a story described a person's experience with bullying, then students can perhaps be put together in groups to share their personal experiences with bullying or share knowledge of someone they know who has experienced it.

> An example appreciation question would be: Have you or anyone you know witnessed an animal rescue? Which animals would you classify as pets and non-pets and why?

SQ3R

Here is another thought-provoking question you can ask at a party: What does SQ3R mean? The answer: Survey-Question-Read-Respond-Review. What is SQ3R? It is a method of reading lessons or absorbing written information in a directed format by helping you comprehend written material and improve recall.

Step 1: *Survey* implies skimming over the passage, checking the table of contents, looking over any graphics, maps, statistics, unknown vocabulary, headings and first sentences, and so forth to have a general idea on the organization of the content and a general sense of what to expect.

Step 2: *Question* implies asking students to question what they're going to read based on the provided title, heading, subheadings, graphics, charts, etc. Students can ask themselves what question their assigned passage is going to answer in the end. This type of questioning actively involves the reader in the comprehension process.

Step 3: *Read* implies reading a passage together with the class in short sections at a time and asking comprehensive questions along the way.

Step 4: *Respond* (and sometimes called the *Recite* stage) implies testing for the students' recall of the passage. A teacher can test recall by asking small groups to take turns recalling the important events in a passage, or assigning a sequential ordering exercise.

Step 5: *Review* implies reviewing the passage by re-reading it, taking notes, or discussing the passage with other readers.

Stages of a Reading Lesson

There are basically three parts to a reading lesson: the pre-reading stage, the reading stage, and the post reading stage. Unless a reading passage is very short, a lesson plan may take more than one class to complete.

The Pre-Reading Stage prepares students for the reading passage by checking for the students' background information and piquing student interest. New vocabulary from the passage can be introduced and learned. An exploration of visuals associated with the passage can be done with the students.

The Reading Stage is when SQ3R can begin. A survey of the chapters and table of contents is useful to gain familiarity, in addition to the headlines, subheadings, and other features that can evoke guesses on content. Predictions and questions can be made of the passage before the reading takes place. As reading takes place, testing for literal, sequential and inferential comprehension can be done as short segments of a passage are read. Afterwards, students can participate in exercises that test their comprehension of the reading by working in small groups. Teachers can then implement review exercises that require note-taking, group discussions, or role-plays.

The Post-Reading Stage requires teachers to expand and exploit the passage with various activities such as role-plays, dramas, oral reports, writing exercises, etc. Even grammar exercises can be designed, such as changing the content of a passage to direct or indirect speech, changing the structure of adjective or adverb clauses, changing the passive into the active voice or vice versa, changing verb tenses, and so forth. See the Course Planning section for an example reading lesson that follows the three stages of pre-reading, reading, and post-reading.

Skimming vs. Scanning

Is there a difference between skimming and scanning? Yes. It's important for students to develop these skills in order to sway them away from reading passages word for word.

Skimming involves finding the theme, main ideas, inferences, value comparisons, character traits, and other information finding tasks without actually reading the passage word for word. Skimming is useful when reading a large passage must be done quickly. Key areas of a passage for skimming are the introductory and concluding paragraphs, the first sentences of body paragraphs, words of opinion and statistical facts.

Scanning involves looking for specific information that has been given, such as finding how old a person is, matching newspaper headlines with topics, checking dates, and other information specific location tasks. A good activity for students would be to distribute a general interest article from a newspaper and have students skim and scan for specific information from it within set time limits.

So when designing lesson plans for your reading classes, there are several things to keep in mind: vocabulary needs, students' background, any necessary text manipulation, Barrett's Taxonomy, SQ3R, and the three stages of a reading lesson. By working under this framework, you have the seeds to create a dynamic reading program.

References

Alderson, Charles J. & Urquhart, A.H. (1984). *Reading in a Foreign Language.* Harlow: Longman

Recommended Reading List

A. Reading Reference Books

Allen, Virginia French. (1983). *Techniques in Teaching Vocabulary.* New York: Oxford University Press.

Dobbs, Carrie. (1989). *Reading for a Reason.* Toronto: Prentice-Hall

Fry, Edward Bernard, Kress, Jacqueline E. & Fountoukidis, Dona Lee. (1993). *The Reading Teacher's Book of Lists,* third edition. New Jersey: Prentice Hall.

Gairns, Ruth & Redman, Stuart. (1990). *Working With Words.* New York: Cambridge University Press.

Gunderson, L. (1991). *E.S.L. Literacy Instruction: A Guidebook to Theory and Practice.* New Jersey: Prentice Hall.

B. Reading Resources

Ackert, Patricia. (1999). *Cause and Effect,* third edition. Boston: Heinle (Intermediate)

Applied Research and Evaluation Services. (1995). *Reading Your Way Into English and Into Canada.* Vancouver: University of British Columbia. (Advanced)

Fry, Edward B. (1995). *Reading Drills,* second edition. Chicago: Jamestown Publications. (Intermediate)

Heyer, Sandra. (1997). *More True Stories,* second edition. New York: Longman (High Beginner)

Heyer, Sandra. (1992). *Even More True Stories,* second edition. New York: Longman (Intermediate)

Heyer, Sandra. (1994). *Easy True Stories.* New York: Longman. (Low Beginner)

Hoppenrath, Christine & Royal, Wendy. (1997). *The World Around Us.* Toronto: Harcourt Brace (Advanced)

Smith, Lorraine C. & Mare, Nancy Nici. (1996). *Themes for Today.* Boston: Heinle (Beginner)

Smith, Lorraine C. & Mare, Nancy Nici. (1996). *Topics for Today,* second edition. Boston: Heinle. (Advanced)

Smith, Lorraine C. & Mare, Nancy Nici. (1996). *Issues for Today,* second edition. Boston: Heinle (Intermediate)

Smith, Lorraine C. & Mare, Nancy Nici. (1999*). Insights for Today*, second edition. Boston: Heinle (High Beginner)

CHAPTER 10:

Teaching Writing—Hill Parking

In This Chapter
> Essential writing skills
> Process Writing
> Lesson plan progressions
> Cursive writing
> Common sentence errors
> Ideal essay outlines
> Editing symbols
> Sample writing activities

Freedom from censorship has been a never-ending quest for writers since the documentation of history. Controversial subjects, written by bold authors who wanted to communicate thoughts that didn't conform to conventional thinking, were often avoided by society or looked upon with shame. Even images conjured up public uproars. Ask Larry Flynt. Although there aren't as many public book-burnings now as there were in the past, censorship still exists in one form or another; either through strategic editing by publishing houses, limited distributorship of written works, banned sales in targeted regions, concerned parents who don't want their children exposed to material deemed inappropriate or even death threats from extremists who want to kill authors they don't agree with. The famous proverb, "The pen is mightier than the sword" implies that profound changes in the world can happen through written works. One does not always have to rely on physical might to influence public opinion. During times of war, cleverly written propaganda can deeply influence public opinion more than any physical demonstration of power. Writing is an immeasurable source of power that can affect worldwide audiences. How can teachers relay the value of writing to students who think writing classes are as exciting as listening to Aunt Martha doing a karaoke performance?

In order for writing classes to be looked upon with more eager anticipation than a karaoke recital, teachers must present students with a comprehensive plan that allows students to clearly see their writing skills progress at a steady pace. A good writing class involves studying various writing skill essentials. Topics in a writing class should explore:

➢ the contrasts between written and spoken English

➢ grammar and mechanics

➢ parts of speech

➢ sentence structure

➢ recognizing common sentence errors

➢ writing styles (narrative, descriptive, personal, etc.)

➢ transition words and sentence combining

➢ variations in sentence patterns and word order

➢ connecting paragraphs

➢ the process writing approach

Higher level E.S.L. students should also be introduced to:

➢ English literature

➢ academic research papers

➢ referencing

➢ plagiarism

There are many useful activities to draw upon to stimulate writing classes. Teachers may utilize writing games and resources such as a daily newspaper, community brochures, books filled with colorful pictures, and so forth to make their writing classes more interesting. Sample student work can be reproduced (with the student's permission) on a transparency and projected on an overhead for class discussions or shown as models. Students can also be given sentence-combining exercises to practice making sentences of varying complexity. If students have particular problems in mechanics, they should be given exercises that give them practice in their areas of weakness. While students are writing, the teacher should circulate the class to provide suggestions. The chief plan in academic writing involves the process writing approach. There are 7 steps in process writing.

Process Writing

STEP 1: The Pre-writing Stage

Students brainstorm ideas for a topic by doing activities that explore it. These activities may involve oral discussions with classmates; listing words, phrases, or ideas that are associated with the topic; clustering ideas under categories about the topic; webbing (making a spider-web design that connect words together by association), free-writing a topic (writing non-stop about the topic for a certain period of time); or simply reading a relevant article that helps a student gain more knowledge about a topic.

STEP 2: The Planning Stage

Upon completion of Step 1, students should have enough information to organize and label it into categories. The assembly of categories is necessary to generate a thesis. In this step, students can decide which information from Step 1 is relevant or irrelevant to their categorization. Once the categories are determined, students decide which categories have the most supporting information and focus on them. If given a topic, students would then select only the information that is relevant to it. After this process, students can then proceed to make an outline of their paper.

Making an outline, particularly a detailed one, can be a time-consuming process; however, once an outline has been made, students have jumped over the biggest hurdle in the writing process and are already finished half the assignment. The more details an outline has, the easier it will be for the student to write his paper. Ensure the students understand the formula:

Detailed Outline = Easy Writing Experience

When an outline has strong detailed support, a student tends not to experience moments of "writer's block" because his ideas are already laid out in a definitive plan with relevant details and strong support. A well-written paper usually has a well-written outline. An example outline format can be found at the end of this chapter. When making an outline, ensure that the outline's main points and supporting details have parallel grammar structures. Although an outline doesn't have to contain grammatically correct sentences, the written structure should be parallel throughout to make the actual writing process of transferring the information on paper easier. For example, if you're writing a paragraph on 3 factors that support Vancouver being known for having excellent recreational facilities, which would you write, outline A or B?

A. Vancouver is well known for its excellent recreational facilities
  1. Whistler Mountain
  2. Fishing in some lakes
  3. You can go camping throughout most of the year.
B. Vancouver is well known for its excellent recreational facilities.
  1. Water parks
  2. Ski hills
  3. Hiking trails

If you chose B, you've advanced to the championship round of Outlining Excellence. Why B? The supporting points are not grammatically correct sentences but they're parallel in structure because they're all nouns. Outline A has a smorgasbord of grammar in their supporting points. The first point names a specific landmark, the second point is a phrase that uses a progressive verb and the last point is a complete sentence. All 3 points in outline A are not structurally the same as they are in B. Outline A would be better written if you changed the points to either all specific landmarks, all phrases in the progressive tense, or all complete sentences. As long as the points are structurally parallel within a body paragraph, they don't necessarily have to structurally match up with the points of the other body paragraphs.

When making an outline, a student should keep in mind the basic framework involved in making an introduction, a body paragraph, and a conclusion. An introduction has 3 parts. It starts with a "hook" that grabs a reader's attention, continues with some background information, and ends with a thesis statement. A "hook" can be an interesting or emotional comment about a topic, a shocking statistic, a question, an unusual fact, a descriptive example, an analogy, a "catching" statement, a quotation or dialogue, or a dramatic description of a real or unreal event related to the topic. For example, a topic on nuclear power plants can begin with an interesting or emotional comment about the controversy of using nuclear energy, or it can begin with a dramatic description of a scene of an accident at a nuclear power plant (perhaps Chernobyl?). The next few sentences will expose some interesting background information about the topic while narrowing the topic's focus. The last sentence of the introduction will be the thesis. Keep in mind that a thesis must have a topic and a controlling idea. The controlling idea is what the writer wants to say about the topic. It shouldn't be too general or too narrow for the student to expand on in the paper. The controlling idea introduces the paper's subtopics or makes an implication of subtopics.

There is usually a minimum of 3 body paragraphs in a well-developed paper. The body paragraphs are the subtopics of the controlling idea. If there are 3 reasons why nuclear power plants should not be used as energy sources, then there should be 3 body paragraphs to cover each reason. Each body paragraph begins with a topic sentence (which would be one of the three subtopics of the thesis' controlling idea) and usually has a minimum of 3 supporting sentences. Each supporting sentence validates the topic sentence. Supporting sentences may include relevant supporting details (such as statistics, expert analysis, relevant quotations, or anecdotes) that further validate the topic sentence. The end of a body paragraph has a concluding sentence. A concluding sentence can either be a summary or a paraphrase of the topic sentence or a concluding personal comment by the writer.

Like the introduction, the conclusion also has 3 parts. The first part echoes the thesis and the second part can add a personal comment from the writer, a summary of the paper, advice on a situation, a quotation, an anecdote, or an evaluation. The last part can provide a concluding description from the introduction's opening, a statement of irony, humor, or any kind of final thought that does not introduce a new idea. The goal is to wrap-up the ideas of the paper and to leave the reader to reflect upon them. A possible final thought to a paper about nuclear energy could be a question posed to the reader to think about whether the hazards of using nuclear energy outweigh its benefits to the world. Graphic and point-form outlines are presented at the end of this chapter.

STEP 3: The First Draft

Now the moment of truth arrives. The student begins to write his paper following the ideas laid out in the outline. Informal essays are written for a wider audience and may not need as many revisions as formal ones before the final draft is made. On the other hand, in academic writing, research papers written in formal English, may use information from other sources, and experience various stages of re-writing. Formal essays usually don't use *I* or *We* and usually use the passive voice; however, in some circumstances the teacher may require the active voice to be used for some topics. Students should not be too concerned with grammar and mechanics in the first draft. The central focus is on the student's ability to organize and logically communicate his/her thoughts.

STEP 4: Editing For Coherence and Unity

After the first draft is complete, the first editing process begins. When checking for coherence, the editor checks the paper for smooth transitions between sentences and paragraphs. Coherence can be achieved with the repetition of key nouns, the use of pronouns in strategic positions, the use of parallel structure, transition signals, and the logical linking of ideas. When checking for unity, the editor checks to see that all of the sentences discuss only the topic of their particular paragraphs. Supporting sentences in each paragraph must have relevant information that validates their corresponding topic sentences. Any deviation of support from the topic sentence will make a paragraph less unified in its structure. This first editing stage can be done with fellow students.

Editing a peer's piece of writing is called peer-editing. When initiating the peer-editing stage, it's important to communicate its usefulness to students. Some students may see peer-editing as unbeneficial to

learning and may prefer teachers to do all the editing. Peer-editing allows students to identify each other's strengths and weaknesses in their writing skills while being less reliant on the teacher. When students experience peer-editing, they become more empowered, and more objective in their writing and may even acquire organizational ideas from each other. Students also are more actively involved and take added responsibility for their writing when they edit each other's work. Although peer-editing enables students to be less reliant on teachers, teachers should take the time to read the student's first draft. When commenting on a student's writing, a teacher should praise the student on the positive points of his writing first before making suggestions on improvements. E.S.L. students need more detailed comments on their writing other than "Good work!" or "Needs improvement". Teachers must indicate specifically what was good, what exactly needed improving, or what exactly should students be cautious of in their writing.

Teachers should meet with individual students to comment and give advice on assignments. Such meetings are called conferencing. Conferencing provides a student a chance to discuss the strengths and weaknesses of his writing (such as the first draft) with the teacher. Teachers should remind students that academic progress rests on the student's shoulders and not the teacher's. When teachers are going over writing errors, they can prompt students for the corrections with hints or general error identification rather than provide the actual corrections themselves. During conferencing, the other students in the class can be assigned exercises or work on their assignments while the teacher meets with each individual. A teacher can inform students that if they wish to record a conference with a tape recorder they may do so.

In addition, it's always a good idea for students (and the teacher) to utilize a checklist for the editing process. Teachers can make a checklist that asks editors to check for the various areas that coherence and unity demands in a piece of writing. The checklist may ask editors, "Does the introduction contain a *hook*?", "Does the paper have a well-defined thesis?", "Do all the paragraphs have strong supporting sentences?", and so forth. It's best that teachers model an example of how to use the checklist with an example well-written passage and a poorly-written one and respond to them with a copy of a checklist for each on an over-head projector for comparison. By seeing the detail you put in the responses to each checklist, students will have an idea of what is expected of them as editors to their classmate's writing. Teachers should always have this stage of editing repeated twice by having students exchange papers with different partners so that each student can acquire a second opinion on their writing. An example checklist for coherence and unity is included at the end of this chapter.

STEP 5: The Second Draft

After the first editing process is complete, the student rewrites the paper by applying the editing suggestions for coherence and unity. The student's original outline may have to be modified to match the revised essay. In their papers, students may have to reorganize their paragraphs, add more concrete support, provide more detailed explanations, change words or sentences, and make other revisions to satisfy the requirements for coherence and unity.

STEP 6: Editing For Grammar and Mechanics

The second stage of the editing process begins with a check for punctuation, spelling and grammar. Correction symbols can be utilized to simplify this proofreading stage. When peer editors or teachers are proofreading, they should use the symbols to identify the errors rather than make the corrections for the writers. Another checklist can be provided for this second editing stage. The checklist may ask editors to analyze what kinds of errors are made: punctuation, sentence structure, capitalization, articles, vocabulary, etc. An example checklist is included at the end of this chapter. Ensure that students have been given plenty of practice on identifying the 10 most common sentence errors writers make. A list of these errors is at the end of this chapter. Teachers may pair students up for proofreading or set up stations for proofreading. Various stations can be assigned to check for particular details in students' papers. For example, Station 1 can check for punctuation; Station 2 can check for run-on sentences; Station 3 can check for subject-verb agreement, etc. Teachers may also elect to have another conferencing session with students for this editing stage. Particular grammar problems can be dealt with by asking students to refer to specific sections in a grammar book if one is used as a reference.

<u>STEP 7: The Final Draft</u>

The finish line is just up ahead at this stage. can now write the final draft of their essays by applying the proofreading corrections of the previous step. In this stage, students must ensure that their final drafts follow the formats that their teachers expect them to use. Universities may adopt formats that follow guidelines from the American Psychological Association (APA), Modern Language Association (MLA), Turabian, Campbell,  Chicago Manual of Style, Oxford, Ballou, and Slade among others. Teachers and students can follow these guidelines by referring to a writer's reference book or obtaining information from the internet. These formats demand specific layouts, citations and referencing.

Lesson Plan Progression

Prior to commencing the 7-step writing process, it's best for teachers to provide a topic of general interest that flows smoothly into the writing activities. How do you introduce or create interest in a writing topic among your students? The first day should not involve the writing process itself, rather, a day should be spent exploring the topic by acquiring the students' background knowledge of it and gauging their personal viewpoints. By asking students what they personally know about the topic, teachers help engage students in the learning process by providing a context. The day can be spent exploring the topic with listening, speaking and reading exercises to get students to start thinking and talking about the topic. The first day provides a smooth transition to the next day's writing process. After a day of topic introduction, students can begin stage 1 of the process writing cycle. Throughout the week, realistically plan how long it would take to complete each stage and assign steps for homework, if necessary, to complete the writing process in a reasonable amount of time. An example writing unit can be seen in the Course Planning section of this book.

Other Possible Writing Activities

Students should begin their writing skills as early as possible. Beginner writers can be introduced to controlled writing activities such as being asked to rewrite a paragraph by changing specific pieces of information, or completing half-finished stories. Teachers can also present a series of questions for students to answer in paragraph form. Other more guided writing activities can include introducing sentences with missing pieces of information, providing opening sentences for a paragraph to be completed, and writing assignments that require a sense of order such as recipe writing. Beginning students may utilize these controlled writing exercises as models for their own compositions.

Intermediate students may advance to exploring descriptive and narrative writing on personal experiences. The writing can incorporate the students' senses of smell, sight, sound, touch, and taste. Newspapers, magazines, cartoons, pictures, and other physical objects can be used to initiate writing topics. Opinions on various topics can begin to be expressed. At this level, students should be encouraged to keep a personal journal to practice their writing everyday. Students can write their personal thoughts on their school day or daily activities. Journaling helps students improve their writing skills; however, journals should not be marked by teachers. Other kinds of useful activities that may be introduced are personal and business letter writing. Teachers can introduce the proper formats and language expected from both categories. Autobiographies, incomplete stories, chain stories, new vocabulary and other writing components can be used to brainstorm writing activities.

Higher-level students should be introduced to the process of writing academic papers. Writing academic papers need not be a painful experience. From the 7 step writing process, learning how to reference, avoiding plagiarism, learning error identification to incorporating proper English usage, students should be prepared for the demands academic writing requires in universities.

> One day in China, I asked students to do a writing assignment on the increasing crime rate in the cities. Most students responded by using the word "crime" as a verb "to crime" and as a noun "crimers". After a while, one begins to understand "Chinglish" and "Konglish".
> —R.R.

The Fancy Style

E.S.L. students in many countries sigh when they see cursive writing. To them, cursive writing is a big effort in deciphering a kind of "chicken scratch". It's always good to introduce students in the intermediate level this alternative writing style. Teachers can utilize worksheets and an overhead projector to introduce each cursive letter of the alphabet. An overhead projector with a magnification function can enable teachers to demonstrate how each cursive letter is formed and joined with other letters. Wall charts that show each cursive letter are also useful. Students can be assigned to practice their cursive writing by making letters, greeting cards, proverbs, songs, etc. Although it's a good idea to familiarize students with cursive writing, it's best not to overly emphasize it too much in the course.

Throughout a writing course, students should feel more comfortable with participating in the peer revision and editing processes as long as they fully understand the advantages of it. A focus towards writing an organized essay to clearly expressing their opinions and ideas rather than writing an essay that's grammatically and mechanically perfect would help in students' writing skills. If their thoughts can be organized in a logical and clear manner with relevant information, their grammar and mechanical language skills would improve alongside their writing creativity. Corrections in writing don't significantly increase writing skills; instead, practice alone would enhance skills. Writing is not a first draft process but a series of processes where in each stage, a piece of writing becomes more creative and complex and comes closer to its communicative potential. In order to maximize the learning potential in students, heed the formula:

```
Student Attitude = Student Achievement
```

A positive classroom atmosphere must therefore be produced and maintained by the teacher for students to reach their writing potential. In the end, students should feel comfortable in writing their thoughts on paper (whether or not it involves a controversial subject) as much as they do in expressing them verbally.

CHECKLIST FOR PEER-EDITING
COHERENCE AND UNITY

In the space provided, answer the following questions and comment on your classmate's writing. Offer suggestions in areas where improvement is needed. You should also include positive feedback for areas done well.

INTRODUCTION

❏ Does the introduction have 3 parts (the "hook", background information, and a thesis?)

❏ Does the "hook" grab your attention?

❏ Is there sufficient background information that would interest you to read further?
If no, why not?

❏ Is the thesis clear and defined?

BODY PARAGRAPHS

❏ Do the body paragraphs have topic sentences in the first line? Which paragraph(s) does not have a clearly stated topic sentence in the first line?

❏ Do the body paragraphs have relevant supporting sentences? Which paragraph(s) does not have sufficient supporting sentences?

❏ What kind of support is used? Statistics, expert opinions, facts, etc?

❏ Are the supporting details valid enough to give "power" to the supporting sentences? If no, why not?

❏ Do the body paragraphs repeat key nouns and use pronouns in strategic positions? Which paragraph(s) needs improvement in this area?

❑ Do the body paragraphs use parallel structure and enough transition signals to provide a smooth flow of information? Which paragraph(s) needs improvement in this area?

❑ Do the body paragraphs have a logical linking of ideas? Which body paragraph(s) needs improvement in this area?

❑ What kind of organization do the body paragraphs offer? Chronological, sequential, cause and effect, basic idea groupings, etc.?

❑ Do all of the sentences focus on the topic of their particular paragraphs? Which paragraph(s) does not have this unity?

❑ Do the body paragraphs have a concluding sentence in the last line? Which paragraph(s) does not?

CONCLUSION

❑ Does the first part of the conclusion echo the thesis in the introduction?
❑ Does the writer offer an evaluation, advice, a suggestion, a summary, a quotation or an anecdote in the second part of the conclusion? Which one(s)?

❑ Does the last part of the conclusion provide a concluding description from the introduction's opening, a statement of irony, humor, or any kind of final thought that does not introduce a new idea?

❑ Are you left with a feeling of reflection after reading this material? How?

CHECKLIST FOR PEER-EDITING
GRAMMAR AND MECHANICS

In the space provided, check your classmate's writing for correct usage of the following areas. Use the Editing Symbols in parentheses to indicate problem areas.

- ❑ Subject-verb agreement (sv)
- ❑ Pronoun use (pron)
- ❑ Punctuation (p)
- ❑ Capitalization (cap)
- ❑ Parallel structure (‖)
- ❑ Sentence fragments (frag)
- ❑ Run-on sentences (run)
- ❑ Misplaced modifiers (mm)
- ❑ Dangling modifiers (dm)
- ❑ Unnecessary word (X)
- ❑ Adjective/adverb use (adj/adv)
- ❑ Articles (art)
- ❑ Word form (wf)
- ❑ Missing words (mw)
- ❑ Spelling (sp)
- ❑ Conjunctions (conj)
- ❑ Preposition use (prep)
- ❑ Wrong words (ww)
- ❑ Wrong word order (∿)
- ❑ Transition (T)
- ❑ Paragraph (¶)

COMMON SENTENCE ERRORS

1) SENTENCE FRAGMENT

➤ A sentence fragment pretends to be a sentence but it does not have either:

- - a subject
- - a verb
- - an independent clause
- - a complete thought

I've been here for several hours. Waiting for the train.   (incorrect)
I've been here for several hours waiting for the train.   (correct)

2) RUN-ON SENTENCE

➤ A run-on sentence occurs when 2 or more independent clauses are combined without appropriate separating punctuation or connecting words.

By day the cats sleep at night they hunt mice.   (incorrect)
By day the cats sleep. At night they hunt mice.   (correct)

By day the cats sleep, at night they hunt mice.   (incorrect)
By day the cats sleep, and a night they hunt mice.   (correct)
By day the cats sleep; at night they hunt mice.   (correct)

3) MISPLACED MODIFIER

➤ A misplaced modifier occurs when a clause or a phrase is modifying the incorrect noun.

I was really lucky to get a great photograph of the race car <u>with Bob's camera.</u>
        (incorrect)
(the race car doesn't have Bob's camera)

I was really lucky to get a great photograph <u>with Bob's camera</u>, of the race car.
        (correct)

4) DANGLING MODIFIER

➤ A modifier that opens a sentence must be followed immediately by the word it is meant to describe.

While reading the book, my dog sat next to me on the couch.   (incorrect)
(the dog doesn't read books)

While reading the book, *I* was approached on the couch by my dog. (correct)

Swimming in the river, the abandoned car was found by Jack.   (incorrect)
(a car doesn't swim)

Swimming in the river, Jack found the abandoned car.   (correct)

5) FAULTY REFERENCE OF A PRONOUN

➤ a faulty reference of a pronoun occurs when an incorrect pronoun is used to refer a noun in the sentence

If you happen to own a top-of-the-line computer, you can use <u>them</u> to go on the internet, send e-mail, or play games.   (incorrect)

If you happen to own a top-of-the-line computer, you can use it to go on the internet, send e-mail, or play games.   (correct)

6) FAULTY SUBJECT—VERB AGREEMENT

➤ A verb must agree in person and in number with its subject

Studies <u>shows</u> that fewer people are smoking cigarettes now.   (incorrect)

Recent statistics <u>show</u> that fewer people are smoking cigarettes now. (correct)

Physics <u>are</u> my favourite subject.   (incorrect)

(*Physics* is the name of **one** subject. *Statistics* is also the name of **one** subject)

Physics <u>is</u> my favourite subject.   (correct)

7) FAULTY PARALLEL STRUCTURE

➤ Words in a series should be parallel (or balanced) by having the same grammatical form.

George and Martha are considerate, generous, and <u>have good manners.</u> (incorrect)

George and Martha are considerate, generous, and <u>well-mannered.</u> (correct)

8) REDUNDANCIES

➤ A sentence with redundant words such as unnecessary conjunctions and virtual synonyms.

<u>Although</u> Tina paid a lot of money for her new motorcycle, <u>but</u> she says it was really worth it.   (incorrect)
(you must omit *although* or omit *but*)

Although Tina paid a lot of money for her new snowboard, she says it was really worth it.   (correct)

We saw a movie last night that was dull and boring.   (**redundancy**)
(*dull* and *boring* are virtual synonyms to each other)

9) FAULTY ADJECTIVE/ADVERB

➤ Adjectives instead of adverbs are incorrectly used in sentences

He swims <u>good</u>.   (**incorrect**)

(*good* is an adjective)

He swims <u>well</u>.   (**correct**)

Sam needs a haircut <u>bad.</u>   (**incorrect**)

(*bad* is an adjective)

Sam needs a haircut <u>badly.</u>   (**correct**)

I laugh <u>loud</u> when I watch that show.   (**incorrect**)

(*loud* is an adjective)

I laugh <u>loudly</u> when I watch that show. (**correct**)

10) CONFUSING WORDS

➤ **E.S.L. students sometimes confuse the usage of homonyms and other words.** Below is an example list of homonyms that may confuse E.S.L. students:

Homonyms

acts-ax	ad-add
aid-aide	allowed-aloud
all ready-already	bare-bear
be-bee	cents-scents-sense
course-coarse	cue-queue
dam-damn	foul-fowl
hear-here	hole-whole
its-it's	knew-new
lends-lens	know-no
one-won	pair-pare-pear
passed-past	peak-peek-pique
plain-plane	principal-principle
rest-wrest	rite-wright-write-right
review-revue	scene-seen

than-then
thrown-throne
time-thyme
verses-versus
warn-worn
weight-wait
whether-weather

their-they're-there
through-threw
to-too-two
walk-wok
wear-where
we'll-wheel

Other:

accept—except
affect-effect
among-between
fewer-less
foreground-background
know-learn
none-any
much-many

IDEAL ESSAY

Introduction

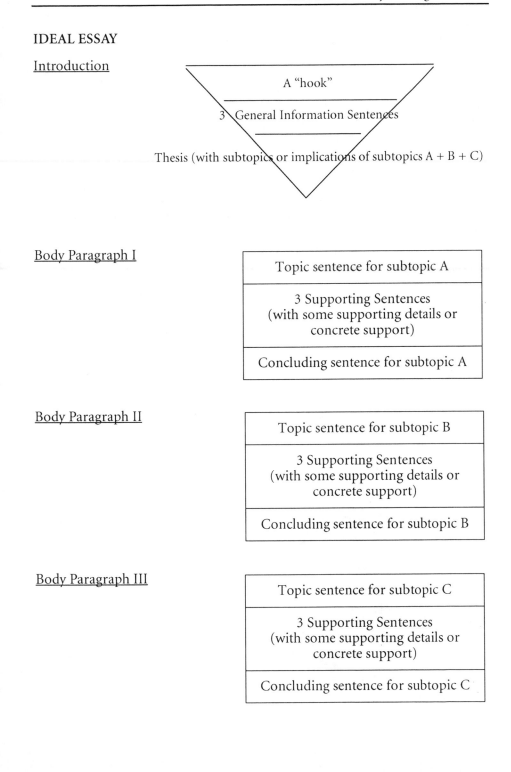

A "hook"

3 General Information Sentences

Thesis (with subtopics or implications of subtopics A + B + C)

Body Paragraph I

Topic sentence for subtopic A

3 Supporting Sentences
(with some supporting details or
concrete support)

Concluding sentence for subtopic A

Body Paragraph II

Topic sentence for subtopic B

3 Supporting Sentences
(with some supporting details or
concrete support)

Concluding sentence for subtopic B

Body Paragraph III

Topic sentence for subtopic C

3 Supporting Sentences
(with some supporting details or
concrete support)

Concluding sentence for subtopic C

Conclusion

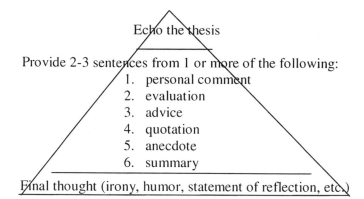

Echo the thesis

Provide 2-3 sentences from 1 or more of the following:
1. personal comment
2. evaluation
3. advice
4. quotation
5. anecdote
6. summary

Final thought (irony, humor, statement of reflection, etc.)

EXAMPLE ESSAY OUTLINE FORMAT

I.   Introduction:

   A.   Hook:

   B.   General Information Sentences:

Thesis statement:

_____

_____

_____

II. Body

   A.   Topic sentence for sub-topic 1

      1.   Supporting sentence

         a.   Supporting Detail

         b.   Supporting Detail

         c.   Supporting Detail

      2.   Supporting Sentence

         a.   Supporting Detail

         b.   Supporting Detail

         c.   Supporting Detail

      3.   Supporting Sentence

         a.   Supporting Detail

         b.   Supporting Detail

      c. Supporting Detail

B. Topic sentence for sub-topic 2

   1. Supporting sentence

      a. Supporting Detail

      b. Supporting Detail

      c. Supporting Detail

   2. Supporting Sentence

      a. Supporting Detail

      b. Supporting Detail

      c. Supporting Detail

   3. Supporting Sentence

      a. Supporting Detail

      b. Supporting Detail

      c. Supporting Detail

C. Topic sentence for sub-topic 3

   1. Supporting sentence

      a. Supporting Detail

      b. Supporting Detail

      c. Supporting Detail

   2. Supporting Sentence

      a. Supporting Detail

      b. Supporting Detail

      c. Supporting Detail

   3. Supporting Sentence

      a. Supporting Detail

      b. Supporting Detail

      c. Supporting Detail

III. Conclusion

A. Echo thesis:

B. Comment, advice, evaluation, etc.:

C. Final thought:

> ➤ This outline has a total of 5 paragraphs: an introductory paragraph, 3 body paragraphs, and a concluding paragraph.

> ➤ The number of supporting details for each paragraph will vary.

References

Hoppenrath, Christine & Royal, Wendy. (1997). *The World Around Us.* Toronto: Harcourt Brace & Company

Recommended Reading List

A. Writing Reference Books

Best, Michael, Tucker, John, Oliver, Neil, Palmer, Erin, Lyne, Steve, & Neufeldt, Audrey.(1997). *A Writer's Guide.* Victoria: University of Victoria.

Hacker, Diana. (2001). *A Canadian Writer's Reference.* Ontario: Nelson Thomson Learning.

Krashen, S. (1984). *Writing: Research, Theory and Applications.* Oxford: Pergamon Press.

Ling, Sue & Rothschild, Dennie. (1991). *Interactive Composing: Techniques in Process Writing for E.S.L. Students.* Vancouver: Vancouver Community College.

White, Ron & Arndt, Valerie. (1991). *Process Writing.* Harlow: Longman

B. Writing Resources

Blanchard, Karen & Root, Christine. (1998). *Get Ready to Write.* New York: Pearson Education. (Beginner)

Blanchard, Karen & Root, Christine. (1994). *Ready to Write*, second edition. New York: Addison-Wesley Publishing. (Low Intermediate)

Blanchard, Karen & Root, Christine. (1997). *Ready to Write More.* New York: Longman. (High Intermediate)

Carver, Tina Kasloff, Fotinos, Sandra Douglas, Olson & Christie Kay. (1982). *A Writing Book: English in Everyday Life.* New Jersey: Prentice Hall Regents. (Beginner)

Gray-Richards, Barbara. (1984). *Composition: Writing Academic English for Students of English As A Second Language.* Vancouver: Vancouver Community College.

Hadfield, Charles & Hadfield, Jill. (1990). *Writing Games.* Walton-on-Thames: Thomas Nelson and Sons

Klepinger, Lawrence. (1993). *Write English Right.* New York: Barron's

Langan, John & Winstanley, Sharon. (2000). *College Writing Skills with Readings*, second edition. Toronto: McGraw-Hill Ryerson.

Oshima, Alice & Hogue, Ann. (1999). *Writing Academic English*, third edition. New York: Pearson Education (advanced)

Oshima, Alice & Hogue, Ann. (1997). *Introduction to Academic Writing*, second edition. New York: Longman (intermediate)

Spencer, Carolyn M. & Arbon, Beverly. (1996). *Foundations of Writing.* Lincolnwood: National Textbook Company.

CHAPTER 11:

Phonology & the Phonetic Alphabet— Downtown Ahead

In This Chapter

> Language profiling

> Development of a pronunciation program

> The phonetic alphabet

> Two-stage teaching progression

> Drilling

> Lesson tips and tools

If you won a free trip to the Amazon, would you bring your high heel shoes, silk evening gown and tiara when you go trekking in the jungle? If you answered yes, please send a photo to us so that we may hang it in our office under our "Avid Reader's Wall". If you wouldn't venture to the jungles of the Amazon unprepared knowledge-wise, why would you go into a pronunciation class without knowing the mechanics and fundamentals of English sounds? Preparation for pronunciation classes is the key to speaking success.

Pronunciation difficulties with E.S.L. students during speech often come with the unfamiliar positions required of tongue placement; insufficient airflow in the larynx, oral or nasal cavities; incorrect lip movement; or a combination of these factors. To anticipate potential pronunciation problems, E.S.L. teachers can investigate the language profile of their students with the use of linguistic research. Much like a detective, you'll look into the background of all suspects, in this case the native languages of your eager students, before conducting an investigation (lesson planning) and ultimately making your final conclusion (the lesson itself).

A good language profile book on potential pronunciation problems with students of 13 different languages was put together by Charles E. Killam and Bruce Watson in *Thirteen Language Profiles: A Practical Application of Contrastive Analysis for Teachers of E.S.L.*. It explains in simple terms based on contrastive analysis why students from particular language groups have trouble with English verb conjugations, consonant pairs, vowels, intonation, stress, etc. For example, Arabic students may have problems with consonant clusters due to the fact that in the Arabic language, vowel sounds are usually inserted between consonants. The word *smoke* may be pronounced *esmoke* or *books* may be pronounced *bookes* (Killam & Watson, p.8). Meanwhile, Punjabi students aren't familiar with the *w* or *y* sounds or unstressed *r* sounds due to their non-existence in the Punjabi language (Killam & Watson, p.74-75). If you have a class of Japanese students, they may have problems with the unfamiliar "th" sound. Even languages that use the Roman alphabet such as Spanish, Danish, or Swedish, will have conflicting pronunciation problems with English. Then there's your North American teenager who will adopt trendy accents or imitate their favorite hero from the "hood" and say sentences that sound like a foreign language even though English is his mother tongue.

When the famous Polish linguist, Doctor Ludovic L. Zamenhof developed the universal language of Esperanto in the late 19th century, he ensured a simplistic straight forward correspondence of sound and spelling. He realized that in order to allow his universal language to be easily understood by the general world population he had to devise a simple spelling system that didn't allow much room for sound-spelling contradictions like you see in English. To achieve a simplistic sound to spelling correspondence with English, you will need the assistance of a phonetic alphabet. The principles of phonology involve learning a symbolic system of sound representation and at the same time deciphering English sound patterns. There are many components to teaching pronunciation using phonological approaches. Included in these components are an understanding of joining sounds (such as sentence reduction, blending, contractions, etc.), word stress and intonation, sentence stress and intonation, rhythm and pitch, speech volume and speed, general non-verbal features (pauses, eye contact, facial expressions, and body language) and odd speech expressions (*uh-huh, uh-uh, shhh, ho-hum, whoo-ee, duh, phew,* etc.).

Teaching the English sound system can be divided into two categories. The first fundamental category that should be taught is segmentals. Segmentals involve the teaching of consonants, vowels, diphthongs (two vowels sounds in a syllable), digraphs (two letters paired up to form one sound), and clusters (consonant sounds that are pronounced together in words or through the blending of words) and enlists the aid of a phonetic alphabet. The second fundamental category is called suprasegmentals. Suprasegmentals involve teaching anything that has to do with putting words together to pronounce a sentence (syllables, rhythm, stress, reduction, linking, etc.). This book will look at both categories in this pronunciation unit.

Pronunciation: From Birth to Retirement

Teaching pronunciation has different elements to choose from. In a restaurant, you may wish to sample all the categories a menu has to offer from appetizer to dessert; in pronunciation class, you will wish to cover the basic elements of pronunciation from phonemes (the smallest element of a sound) to non-verbal gestures. The evolutionary stages of a comprehensive pronunciation program will cover all aspects of segmentals and suprasegmentals. The length of time you spend in each stage will depend on how advanced your students are in pronunciation.

Evolutionary Stages of a Pronunciation Program:

Birth:	Segmental focus on vowels, consonants, diphthongs, digraphs, clusters
Secondary School:	Connecting sounds together, linking, blending, contractions, sound reductions and changes, etc.
University:	Suprasegmental focus on syllables, word and sentence stress, content/function words, rhythm, the "music" of English, etc.
Yuppy Years:	Intonation, expressions, phrases, etc.
Middle Age:	Voice speed, volume, pitch, non-standard expressions (*gee, phew, yup,*…), etc.

Retirement: General non-verbal features (pauses, eye contact, facial expressions, and body language)

The Phonetic Alphabet

When we were barely able to walk, our young sponge-like minds started to hear and absorb the fundamental sounds of English. As all fluent English speakers know, not all of the sounds seem to agree with the actual spelling of words. For example, how do you get the basic *s* sound from the spelling of "ps" as in the word *psychology*? Where does the *f* sound come from when you have "ph" in *photography*? Why do some letters in a word act as silencers? Now comes the $99,000 question: how do you translate the actual sounding of words to E.S.L. students when not all letters in a word may correspond to their basic alphabetical sounds? Pronunciation teachers of E.S.L. can tackle this problem with the introduction of a phonetic alphabet. A phonetic alphabet is a notation system that matches a symbol with a sound. Many E.S.L. students and almost all foreign dictionaries use some form of a phonetic alphabet system.

Example difficulties of corresponding symbols with sound:

> 1-Letter sounds with modifications: <u>c</u>are, <u>c</u>itation, <u>c</u>al<u>c</u>ium

> 2-Letter sounds: <u>ch</u>aos, <u>sc</u>issors, <u>ch</u>lorine, <u>ch</u>ute, <u>sc</u>ience

> 3-Silent sounds: wa<u>l</u>k, fragi<u>le</u>, <u>th</u>yme, be<u>au</u>ty

---

There are various phonetic alphabets that teachers can consult when designing pronunciation lessons. One well-known alphabet is the IPA (International Phonetic Alphabet) developed by the oldest organization for phoneticians, the International Phonetic Association. Many phonetic alphabets use many familiar Roman letters to correspond to sounds and a few non-English symbols for others such as:

æ	back	ə	the	ʊ	book
ŋ	ring	ʃ	shy	ɔ	off
ɛ	hen	θ	path	ʒ	pleasure
ʌ	cut	ð	clothes		

In this book, we'll refer to the following phonetic alphabet below :

Vowels			Consonants		
a	on	[an]	d	today	[tuwdey]
æ	bat	[bæt]	t	tea	[tiy]
ɛ	men	[mɛn]	b	baby	[beybiy]
ɪ	kit	[kɪt]	p	pot	[pat]
ɔ	off	[ɔf]	k	cake	[keyk]
ʌ	bus	[bʌs]	f	feel	[fiyl]
ʊ	put	[pʊt]	g	goat	[gowt]
ə	about	[əbawt]	v	van	[væn]
iy	read	[riyd]	θ	think	[θɪnk]
ey	train	[treyn]	ð	this	[ðɪs]
uw	too	[tuw]	s	sell	[sɛl]
ow	toe	[tow]	z	zoo	[zuw]
ir	fear	[fir]	dʒ	join	[dʒoyn]
er	lear	[ber]	m	man	[mæn]
ur	more	[mur]	n	no	[now]
or	wore	[wor]	ŋ	ring	[rɪŋ]
ər	bird	[bərd]	l	like	[layk]
			ʃ	sheep	[ʃiyp]
Diphthongs			tʃ	cheese	[tʃiyz]
			y	yes	[yɛs]
ay	guy	[gay]	w	week	[wiyk]
aw	now	[naw]	ʒ	vision	[vɪʒən]
oy	groin	[groyn]	h	he	[hiy]
			r	run	[rʌn]

Please always keep in mind that the phonetic alphabet consist of SYMBOLS FOR SOUNDS and <u>are not letters</u>!

Segmental Sound Inventory

When you're at a party where people are engaged in trivia, you can impress them with your statistical knowledge of the English sound system. Although if people start moving away from you, you'll know when to change topics. English has 24 consonant sounds and 20 vowel sounds ranging from the simple to the complex. Vowel phonetic symbols rarely match its English spelling due to the fact that vowel sounds out-number vowel letters. Vowel sounds differ from consonants with the flow of air stream from the lungs to the mouth and with tongue height as the air flows out. The wider you open your mouth, the closer you get to a vowel sound. A screaming baby will emphasize a vowel sound to you in the middle of a night. Different English accents, such as British English, American southern English, Canadian Maritimes English, Newfoundland English, and so forth, originate from vowel differences rather than from consonant differences.

Sound articulation is further classified into categories that describe airflow in the oral or nasal cavity when producing consonants. English has 8 fricatives (airflow that's partially obstructed with the convergence of the tongue or lips to the upper mouth), 2 affricates (immediate stops in airflow following a fricative), 3 nasals (airflow controlled in the nasal passages), 6 stops (completely obstructed air flow), 2 semi-vowels (two vowel sounds that create one syllable such as /oy/ are called diphthongs), and 2 liquids (lateral air flow in the mouth with relaxed lips). Affricates differ from fricatives by the stopping of airflow. Affricates require immediate stops in airflow following a fricative; for example, <u>church</u>, rather than the incorrect fricative pronunciation <u>shursh</u>). Single sounds that are formed with pairs of letters such as *ph* in *photo* are referred to as digraphs.

Approach

With so many variables to consider when teaching pronunciation, where do you start? The best way to approach pronunciation classes is to ensure a solid elementary sound framework is built upon, which would focus on segmentals. One approach can be to start off with short vowel sounds and building from there. While keeping in mind that English consonant sounds are already shared by many other languages, you should devise your first approach to teaching contrastive vowel sounds using short one-syllable words (*B<u>o</u>b c<u>a</u>n* *run*). Next you can progress to consonant pairs (*Frank plants grass*), and then move on to long sounding vowel words (*Paul swims fast*). Afterwards, you can introduce more complex sounds such as digraphs (*Philip shops for fudge over there*), r-influences with vowels (*Carl's sister loves purple*), and diphthongs.

Diphthongs are 3 different complex vowel sounds that join vowels to the semi-vowel sounds of /y/ or /w/ to produce the phonetic sounds of /ay/, /aw/, and /oy/ (*shy, house, joy*). American southern English speakers sometimes drop the semi-vowel part of diphthongs, particularly before consonants. According to Peter Avery and Susan Ehrlich in *Teaching American English Pronunciation*, other sounds that involve the joining of semi-vowels such as /iy/ (*tea*), /ey/ (*play*), /ow/ (*no*), and /uw/ (*too*) should not be considered as diphthongs due to the reduction of tongue movement in their pronunciations. After building a solid foundation in segmentals, the pronunciation class can move forward to the more complex practice of forming sentences by studying the suprasegmental sound system. Lower level E.S.L. students will soon discover in their study of suprasegmentals that their low-speed listening and speaking skills will not get them far in the real world of fast-pace spoken English. With diligent practice of suprasegmentals, pronunciation teachers can conclude their course by teaching general non-verbal features and odd verbal expressions of English.

Two Stage Process

When designing a pronunciation lesson, teachers have to utilize the 4-Ps: Planning, Perception, Production, and Prediction. The first stage of a pronunciation lesson involves planning and the second stage involves the actual teaching of the lesson through perception, controlled practice and less controlled practice of the target sound.

Stage 1 (Planning Stage)
In this stage, teachers need to investigate what the student needs. How? Listen to his speech and take note of what sound substitutions he makes. You can also research a pronunciation profile of your student's language group from a specialized pronunciation textbook to give you an idea of common pronunciation problems you may expect. The objective of the planning stage is to teach only what the student  needs. In order to do that, you have to play detective and prepare yourself by

familiarizing yourself with the backgrounds of your students and the mechanics of sounds and sound patterns.

Once you determine the articulation of a targeted sound, decide what tools are required to relay this information to your student in non-technical terms. Pre-plan your non-technical articulation instructions to your student. You may use helpful tools to assist you in your lesson. Tools you may use could be visuals of words that reinforce a sound, rubber bands to stretch to emphasize long and short sounds, a tissue to hold in front of the mouth when pronouncing stops to visually show the required puffs of air, cross-section diagrams of the oral cavity to show tongue and teeth movement, drawings of how the lips should be shaped, mirrors for students to see how they're moving their mouth, tape recorders to record student feedback, etc. When you have the tools, the non-technical language for articulation, and the knowledge of what to expect and anticipate from your student, you only need to brainstorm vocabulary suitable to your lesson theme and pronunciation point. Keep in mind that if you focus on vocabulary that your students already know, they can concentrate more on creating the target sound rather than focus on the meaning of the words.

Upon completing the necessary planning, teachers can progress to the application stage: the teaching of targeted sounds.

Stage 2 (Teaching Stage)
The teaching stage raises awareness of a pronunciation point with demonstrations of how and when a pronunciation point is encountered. This part focuses on the **perception** of the target sound. It isn't enough for the teacher to ask the student to listen to the target sound and ask him to repeat it. When the student repeats it, he's using only his perception of the sound and is frustrated when his teacher says, "No, no, no. It's not *DABLE*, it's *TABLE*." Since many English sounds don't correspond to sounds in some foreign languages, teachers have to initially train their students to LISTEN and DISTINGUISH the target sound rather than dive into trying to reproduce them. Only the art of listening and distinguishing is initially needed for now. Perception can be introduced with listening exercises that require students to discriminately listen for the target sound and provide feedback. Word pairs called minimal pairs (two words that sound similar to each other with the exception of the target sound being in one of them) can be said aloud for students to distinguish the target sound. The target sound in minimal pairs can be placed in the beginning, middle, or end part of a word. Target sounds at the beginning of a word are said to be in the initial position (eg. /l/ = light /b/ = bite). Target sounds in the middle of a word (eg. /l/ = wallow /b/ = wobble) are said to be

in the medial position. Target sounds at the end of a word (eg. /l/ = Bill /b/ = bib) are said to be in the final position. When it comes time to showing students the articulation of the target sound, use non-technical language in your explanation accompanied by tools such as a diagram of the oral cavity, lip drawings, mirrors, tissue, rubber bands, etc (see the *Tips and Tools* section). It is also helpful to include common and uncommon spelling patterns associated with the target sound. The teacher may now allow students to begin perception practice with pre-planned vocabulary (ideally words the students are already familiar with in meaning) and minimal pair drilling (see the section below on this kind of drilling).

The next step in the teaching stage is implementing controlled practice. Here, the students get to further practice reproducing the target sound. Activities in this production stage will begin with controlled activities such as minimal sentences (a sentence is given with two minimal pair answers possible), cued dialogues with the target sounds contained in them, audio recording activities, pronunciation bingo, etc. Teachers can gradually progress to less controlled practice with activities such as information gap exercises (1 student has information that another student needs and vice versa), vocabulary brainstorming, cued dialogues, problem-solving exercises, etc. Afterwards teachers can apply freer tasks with role plays, improvised dialogues with target vocabulary, story telling, etc.

The last step in the teaching stage involves having students produce the target sound with less controlled practice involving **new contexts** and **new vocabulary**. Teachers would have to pre-plan new vocabulary and exercises with new contexts to challenge their students. This less controlled practice helps students reinforce the pronunciation point through their own conscious awareness.

Minimal Pair Drilling

The initial drill for pronunciation lessons should engage the minimal pair drill. If you recall a few pages ago, a minimal pair is two words that sound similar to each other with the exception of the target sound being in one of them. Minimal pair drills or activities involve one person uttering a word and the listener pointing to the correct word he heard. If you are conducting this drill with your class, you should refer to the following procedure:

1) The teacher should point to the target word and say it (the student simply listens)

2) The teacher then says a target word and the student listens and identifies the correct word from a given list.

3) Next, the teacher points to a word and the student says it.

4) The learner chooses to say a word from a list and the teacher identifies the correct word.

5) Afterwards, the teacher can pair students up and have one student say a word from a list and another student identifying it.

Tips and Tools

Before we explore some useful pronunciation tools let's present some pre-lesson planning tips. When planning a pronunciation lesson, ask yourself some of the following questions:

❑ Does the set-up of the student tables and chairs facilitate your lesson?

❑ How will you group students and conduct any group changes? (In a class with multinational students, it's best to not have any students from the same native language grouped together)

❑ Where will you be standing in the classroom during communicative practice? (Will you be standing too far away to listen for errors?)

❑ How will you provide correction?

   a) Immediate Correction
      Are you standing in a position where you can listen and provide immediate corrective feedback?

   b) Cued Correction
      Do you have any pronunciation tools to point to and to cue students for self-correction? What question cues can you provide to aid self-correction?

   c) Delayed Correction
      When do you step into a communicative activity between students? What errors will you point to students to after the completion of an uninterrupted communicative activity?

❑ Will students be focused on worksheets, the front board, audio or visual equipment, or charts?

❑ How organized and functional will your board work be at the end of the lesson? Will it look too much like a road map?

❑ How clear are instructions for exercises and activities? Are they specific or generalized? Are you prepared to model the directions? (Instead of telling groups of students "Discuss the pros and cons of capital punishment", assign each student in a group to perform functions such as a secretary to write down ideas, a timer to keep students talking, a specific pro or con person, a presenter, etc.)

❑ How can you check student comprehension of the activity procedure? Would you ask them for a demonstration?

❑ Do your lessons have a variety of multimedia to work with? Are the communicative activities practical for real-life situations?

❑ Does the curriculum provide for guest speakers?

❑ Are there any contact field trip assignments for real-life speaking practice?

With the above questions in mind, teachers will need some helpful tools to reinforce their lesson points. There are a variety of tools ranging from the simplistic (a rubber band to help you teach long vowel sounds) to the more expensive (interactive computer software). The following is a list of useful tools that pronunciation teachers may consider:

a) Dictionaries
   Dictionaries will have pronunciation references for words but may not have references on stress. (Funk & Wagnalls' *Standard Dictionary* has both pronunciation and stress references for words.).

b) Spelling Rule Charts
   Grammar books will have some predictable spelling patterns for certain words

c) Rubber Bands, Straws and Tissue
   Teachers may stretch a rubber band to emphasize the duration of sounds such as the sound duration of long vowels.
   Teachers may softly blow at a tissue with a straw to demonstrate correct airflow.

d) Hand Gestures
   Teachers can develop a system of gestures and signals to indicate syllables, stress, intonation, etc.

e) Audio Equipment
   Does the school have tape recorders, language master machines, or computer speech labs for students to use?
   Are there any televisions, radios, video equipment, or overhead projectors?

f) Visuals
    Do you have phonetic alphabet charts?
    Do you have cross section pictures of vocal tracts to demonstrate tongue positioning and air flow?
    Do you have pictures of mouth and lip shapes for sounds?
    Do you have pictures of words that sound similar for differentiation exercises?
    Do you have small mirrors that students can use to form the correct mouth and lip shapes?

g) Notation System
    What kind of notations do you use to indicate intonation, stress, pitch, linking, etc.?

h) Role Play Props
    Teachers can add realism to role plays or dialogues to enhance communicative activities (such as providing dining props for restaurant dialogues, or consumer articles for making complaints to a store, etc.).

i) Music and Poetry

j) Games

k) Guest Speakers

l) Telephone/Contact Assignments (Assign students to speak with waiters, store clerks, bank tellers, tourist information assistants, restaurant servers, and others to obtain information or make requests.)

In essence, with appropriate pre-lesson planning, pronunciation teachers can create dynamic classroom lessons. Teachers should basically anticipate potential pronunciation problems in their classrooms, provide a symbol-sound correspondence system, follow a pedagogical sequence in teaching segmental to suprasegmental aspects of English all while utilizing the tips and tools of teaching pronunciation.

References

Avery, Peter & Ehrlich, Susan. (1992). *Teaching American English Pronunciation*. Oxford: Oxford University Press.

Killam, Charles E. & Watson, Bruce. (1983). *Thirteen Language Profiles: A Practical Application of Contrastive Analysis for Teachers of E.S.L..* Vancouver: Vancouver Community College.

Recommended Reading List

A. Pronunciation Reference Books

Avery, Peter & Ehrlich, Susan. (1992). *Teaching American English Pronunciation*. Oxford: Oxford University Press.

Celce-Murcia, Marianne, Goodwin, Janet & Brinton, Donna. (1996). *Teaching Pronunciation: A Reference for Teachers of English to Speakers of Other Languages*. Cambridge: Cambridge University Press.

Dauer, Rebecca. (1993). *Accurate English: A Complete Course in Pronunciation*. (New Jersey: Prentice Hall

Funk & Wagnalls Standard Dictionary, second edition. (1993). New York: HarperCollins

Kenworthy, Joanne. (1987). *Teaching English Pronunciation*. Harlow: Longman

Killam, Charles E. & Watson, Bruce. (1983). *Thirteen Language Profiles: A Practical Application of Contrastive Analysis for Teachers of E.S.L.*. Vancouver: Vancouver Community College.

Ladefoged, Peter. (1993). *A Course in Phonetics*, third edition. Fort Worth: Harcourt Brace Jovanovich.

Morley, Joan (Ed.). (1994). *Pronunciation Pedagogy and Theory: New Views, New Directions*. USA: TESOL Publications

Nilsen, D. & Nilsen, A. (1971). *Pronunciation Contrasts in English*. New York: Regents Publishing Company.

B. Pronunciation Resources

Baker, Ann & Goldstein, Sharon. (1990). *Pronunciation Pairs*. Cambridge: Cambridge University Press. (High Beginner-Intermediate)

Chernen, Joann. (2000). *Interactive Pronunciation Games*. Vancouver: Vancouver Community College.

Essig, Janet. (1992). *Practical Pronunciation Prints*. Burnaby, Canada

Gilbert, Judy B. (2001). *Clear Speech From the Start*. Cambridge: Cambridge University Press. (Beginner-High Beginner)

Gilbert, Judy B. (1993). *Clear Speech*, second edition. Cambridge: Cambridge University Press. (Intermediate-High Intermediate)

Grant, Linda. (1993). *Well Said*. Boston: Heinle & Heinle (Advanced)

Hagen, Stacy A. (1988). *Sound Advice*. New Jersey: Prentice Hall Regents. (Intermediate-Advanced)

Hancock, Mark. (1995). *Pronunciation Games*. Cambridge: Cambridge University Press.

Wiley, Kaye. (2002). *Fast Track Phonics*. New York: Pearson Education. (Beginner-High beginner)

Woods, Howard B. (1977). *Intonation*. Ottawa: Public Service Commission.

CHAPTER 12:

Teaching Vowels and Consonants—
Rush Hour

In This Chapter

> The oral cavity

> Consonant articulation

> Consonant error identification

> Vowel articulation

> Vowel error identification

The smallest units of a language are phonemes. The word *hat* has three phonemes: /h/ + /æ/ + /t/. In order to guide your students in how to pronounce words correctly, they should begin their studies with how to pronounce phonemes correctly using the right articulation of airflow, tongue movement, and lip shape. Phonemes comprise of vowels, diphthongs and consonant sounds. As you learned in the previous chapter, there are 20 vowel sounds and 24 consonant sounds ranging from the simple to the complex. E.S.L. students will usually have more problems with vowel sounds rather than with consonants. How do you introduce these basic units of sounds to students? This part is where technical jargon comes into play. In biology class, you had to locate and label parts of a dissected animal; in pronunciation planning, you won't have to do any dissecting but identifying areas of the oral cavity will be necessary. When you study parts of the oral cavity, you will be bombarded with terms that can be confusing to understand. Below is a cross section of the larynx and the vocal tract where sounds are made (see Figure 12.1).

Figure 12.1

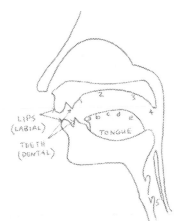

Tongue Parts

a) Tip

b) Blade

c) Front

d) Central

e) Back

Places of Articulation

1) Alveolar (tooth ridge)   2) Alveo-Palatal (hard palate)   3) Velar (soft palate)

4) Uvula   5) Glottis (vocal cords)

Vowel sounds will differ from consonants with air stream flow. Vowel sounds enable air to freely pass through the mouth with little obstruction while consonant sounds involve the narrowing of the air passage to obstruct airflow. The wider you open your mouth, the more a vowel sound comes out. The narrower you open your mouth, the more a consonant sound comes out.

Consonant Error Identification

When you make consonant sounds, there are three areas of articulation that involve the oral cavity: voicing (determining if there's a vibration in the throat when you place your hand over your vocal cords), place of articulation (where the airflow is blocked or narrowed), and manner of articulation (how the air flow is blocked or narrowed). When you can correctly target these three areas, it will be easy for you to identify errors made in articulation and consequently correct them with precision. Let's look at each of the three areas in more detail.

I.   Voicing: Voiced versus Voiceless

This category in forming consonant sounds involves the vocal cords. Hold your hand to your throat, and say "Ah". You should be able to feel a vibration made as the vocal cords (or vocal folds) are engaged. Now, make a prolonged /h/ sound, as if sighing. Notice that there is a clear passage of air passing through the vocal cords, which are wide apart and not vibrating. When there's a vibration present, such as in the /z/ sound, we say that the sound is *voiced*. When there's no vibration present, such as in the /s/ sound, we say that the sound is *voiceless*. The vocal folds that vibrate are folds of tissue that protrude from the mucous membrane and are attached to the larynx (or the voice box). When the folds are pulled together, the passing airflow causes them to vibrate.

II.   Places of Articulation—Part 1: the lips (bilabial, labiodental)

The narrowest point where airflow is obstructed or narrowed is the place of articulation. Locations where the air stream is obstructed can occur with movements in the lips and parts of the tongue. Consonants formed with the convergence of both lips are called *bilabial* articulation and those involving the convergence of one of the lips with the teeth are called or *labiodental* articulation (see Figure 12.2). Bilabial consonant sounds involve *p, b, m,* and *w* while *labiodental* consonant sounds involve *f* and *v.*

Figure 12.2

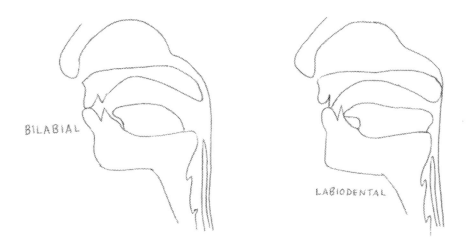

Places of Articulation—Part 2: the tongue (interdental, alveolar, alveopalatal, velar)

The obstruction or narrowing of airflow is made by the parts of the tongue involving its tip, its blade and the back section. There are four places where tongue movement produces a wealth of consonants

1) Contact between the tip of the tongue and the teeth is called *interdental* articulation. Phonemes such as /θ/ or /ð/ are *interdental* because the tip of the tongue is placed between the teeth or at least is in contact with the upper teeth (see Figure 12.3)

Figure 12.3

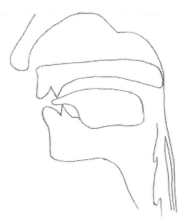

2) Generated sounds involving the tip of the tongue and the area behind the upper teeth (the tooth ridge) is called *alveolar* articulation. The consonants /t/, /d/, /n/, /s/, /z/, /l/, and /r/ are *alveolar* sounds because of the contact or the close proximity of the tip of the tongue to the *alveolar* ridge (see Figure 12.4)

Figure 12.4

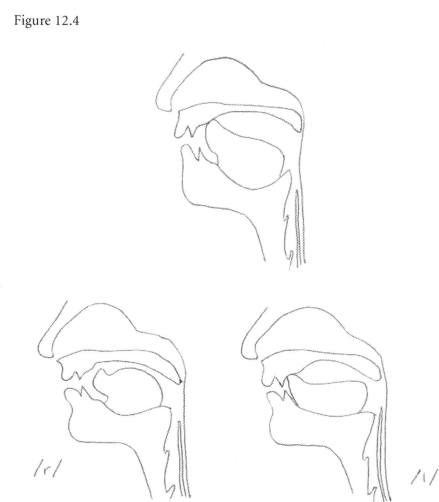

3) Generated sounds involving the blade of the tongue and the hard palate
    are called *alveo-palatal* articulation. The consonants /ʃ/, /ʒ/, /tʃ/, /dʒ/ and
    /y/ are *alveo-palatal* sounds because there is movement of the tongue blade
    towards the hard palate that's behind the alveolar ridge (see Figure 12.5)

Figure 12.5

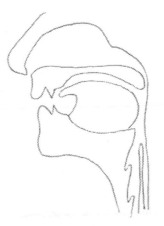

4) Sounds generated with the movement of the back part of the tongue touching the soft palate (velum) is called *velar* articulation. Consonants such as /k/, /g/, /ŋ/ and /w/ are characteristic of *velar* movement (see Figure 12.6). The /h/ on the other hand is produced by the *glottal* area.

Figure 12.6

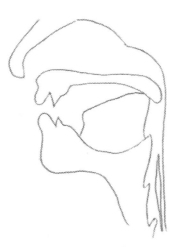

Bilabial: This term refers to the place where airflow is obstructed when both lips converge together. (b, p, m, w)

Labiodental: This term refers to the place where airflow is obstructed when the upper teeth contact the lower lip. (f, v)

Interdental: This term refers to the place where airflow is obstructed when the tip of the tongue is placed between the upper and lower teeth. (θ, ð)

Alveolar: This term refers to the place where airflow is obstructed when the tip of the tongue contacts or converges towards the ridge behind the upper teeth. (d, l, n, r, s, t, z)

Alveo-palatal: This term refers to the place where airflow is obstructed when the blade of the tongue converges with the hard palate region (ʃ, tʃ, ʒ, dʒ, y). The /ʃ/ and /ʒ/ sounds require an accompanying rounding of the lips.

Velar: This term refers to the place where airflow is obstructed when the back of the tongue contacts the soft palate (g, k, ŋ, w)

Glottal: This term refers to the place where airflow is originates at the glottis. (h)

III. Manner of Articulation: stops, fricatives, affricates, nasals, liquids, semi-vowels

Now that you have gained a newfound appreciation of the oral cavity, the third key element in making consonant sounds involves the manner in which air flow is obstructed to form the sounds.

1. *Fricatives* are partial obstructions in the air stream due to the approach of the lip or tongue to the upper part of the mouth. The airflow is narrowed but not completely blocked.

2. *Affricates* are a combination of a fricative and a stop. The pronunciation of affricates begins as a fricative but is finalized as a stop. The phonemes /tʃ/ and /dʒ/ are characteristic affricates.

3. *Nasals* involve sounds generated by the flow of air through the nasal passages. The obstruction of air is done by the tongue touching some part of the upper mouth.

4. *Stops* (sometimes called "plosives" in some textbooks) are complete obstructions in the air stream due to contact between the upper mouth and the

tongue or lips. Compare the stops involved with /p/ and /t/. The phoneme /p/ is a stop because the lips are closed together while /t/ is a stop because the tip of the tongue touching the alveolar ridge obstructs the flow of air.

5. *Liquids* involve a "fluid" motion of air through the mouth. They involve the phonemes /l/ and /r/. Students from Japan in particular often substitute /r/ for /l/ sounds in words such as *river* versus *liver*, or *red* versus *lead*. Correction can be made by informing students that /l/ is made with the tip of the tongue contacting the alveolar ridge whereas the /r/ is made with the tip of the tongue curled back in the mouth and not contacting any area of the mouth.

6. *Glides or Semi-Vowels* are sounds that are produced with a widening of the mouth (which is characteristic of vowels) and with little friction in the air stream. The phonemes /w/ and /y/ are characteristic semi-vowels. The back of the tongue converges towards the soft palate for /w/ while the blade of the tongue converges towards the hard palate for /y/.

Summary of the Science of Consonants

Step 1: Determine Voicing	
Voiceless	**Voiced**
f fan [fæn] ————————	v van [væn]
k kite [kayt] ————————	g gate [geyt]
p pit [pɪt] ————————	b boy [boy]
s sit [sɪt] ————————	z zoo [zuw]
ʃ she [ʃiy] ————————	ʒ vision [vɪʒən]
tʃ cheese [tʃiyz] ————————	dʒ jump [dʒʌmp]
t tape [teyp] ————————	d dog [dag]
θ thing [θɪŋ] ————————	ð then [ðɛn]
	l lip [lɪp]
	m man [mæn]
	n nap [næp]
	ŋ ring [rɪŋ]
	r rak [reyk]
	w week [wiyk]
	y you [yuw]

Step 2: Determine Place of Articulation

Bilabial:	Both lips converge together (b, p, m, w)
Labiodental:	Upper teeth contact the lower lip (f, v)
Interdental:	Tip of the tongue is placed between the teeth (θ, ð)
Alveolar:	Tip of the tongue contacts or converges towards the ridge behind the upper teeth (d, l, n, r, s, t, z)
Alveo-Palatal:	The blade of the tongue converges with the hard palate (ʃ, tʃ, ʒ, dʒ, y) The /ʃ/ and /ʒ/ sounds require a rounding of the lips.
Velar:	The back of the tongue contacts the soft palate (g, k, ŋ, w)
Glottal:	Airflow streams out from the glottis with tongue in a resting position (h)

Step 3: Determine Manner of Articulation

Fricatives:	airflow that is narrowed but allows a continual sound to be emitted (f, h, v, ʃ, ʒ, θ, ð, s, z)
Affricates:	fricatives with a downward movement of the tongue and mouth creating a final stop (tʃ, dʒ)
Nasals:	nasal passages are open (m, n, ŋ)
Stops:	puffs of air that involve the complete blockage of airflow (p, b, t, d, k, g)
Liquids:	air that flows laterally along the sides of the tongue (r, l) liquid retroflex (tip of tongue is curled up) = /r/ liquid lateral (air flows laterally at the sides) = /l/
Glides or Semi-Vowels:	involve the widening of the mouth and little friction in the air stream (w, y)

SEGMENTALS: <u>consonant sounds</u>

MANNER OF ARTICULATION		PLACE OF ARTICULATION						
		BILABIAL (2 lips)	LABIO-DENTAL (lip & teeth)	INTER-DENTAL (btwn teeth)	ALVEOLAR (tooth ridge)	ALVEO-PALATAL (behind alveolar)	VELAR (soft palate)	(GLOTTAL) (vocal folds)
FRICATIVES	vcls		f	θ	s	ʃ		(h)
	vcd.		v	ð	z	ʒ		
AFFICATES	vcls					tʃ		
	vcd.					dʒ		
NASALS		m			n		ŋ	
STOPS	vcls	p			t		k	
	vcd.	b			d		g	
LIQUID-RETROFLEX					r			
LIQUID-LATERAL					l			
GLIDES		w				y	w	

vcls. = voiceless
vcd. = voiced

* CRITERIA for describing consonants: 1) <u>Voicing</u>—is there vibration in the throat?
2) <u>Place of articulation</u>—where is the sound occurring? (location of airflow obstruction)
3) <u>Manner of articulation</u>—how is the air flow coming out?

Now that your brain has been bombarded with all these technical terms, is it necessary to teach them to your students? No. These terms are necessary only for you to understand and pinpoint how to correct your students' pronunciation problems. If you know the parts of the mouth and the manipulations required of the tongue, lips and airflow to produce a sound, it will be easier for you to precisely target the areas of the mouth that need correcting rather than blindly repeating to a student, "No, no, Betty. It's _three_ not _free!_". It makes more common sense to train Betty how she should be moving her mouth and tongue and controlling her airflow in order to make the necessary _th_ sound. Correcting for consonant pronunciation is a matter of determining if the correction is needed in the location of where airflow is narrowed, in the manner in which it's narrowed or in the voicing. When you cover these three areas and teach Betty how to move her mouth in simple non-technical terms, you will begin to hurdle pronunciation obstacles as quickly as a monsoon wind in the tropics.

Correcting Pronunciation of Consonants

Now that we know how to classify consonants under voicing, place of articulation and manner of articulation, we can provide technical descriptions for them. If you were to teach the /p/ sound, you would determine the three classifying characteristics.

/p/ = voiceless, bilabial, stop

The above technical description of the /p/ being a voiceless bilabial stop can be translated into non-technical language: The /p/ requires no vibration in the throat, a convergence of both lips (bilabial) and a puff of air. Which description would you give the student? Life would be easier if you chose the later description rather than the former. You would probably need to pre-teach the words _convergence_ and _puff_ or use other simpler words that have the same meaning. The technical descriptions are more for the teacher to target problem pronunciation areas. How would you technically describe the /b/ sound?

/b/ = voiced, bilabial, stop

As you can see, the articulation is similar to the /p/ sound except for the voicing. If a Cantonese student was saying _big_ instead of _pig_, how would a teacher correct the student? Since the target sound of /p/ is voiceless and the error sound of /b/ is voiced, a teacher would have to demonstrate the need for the vocal cords to relax and not vibrate in the utterance. Error correction can be accurately targeted when you can identify the 3 main characteristics of consonant sounds and compare which area(s) is (are) different from the target sound.

How would you correct a student if he was saying *sink* instead of *think*? First, determine the target sound and the error sound:

target sound = think = /θ/
error sound = sink = /s/

/θ/ (target)	/s/ (error)
voiceless	voiceless
interdental	alveolar
fricative	fricative

What is the articulation difference between the error and target sounds? You can see that the only place of difference is in the place of articulation, thus this is an error of *place*. The student is mistakenly placing the tip of his tongue towards the alveolar region (the tooth ridge). The teacher can inform the student (with the aid of visuals) what he is mistakenly doing with his tongue and then tell him to place his tongue between the teeth or just behind the teeth instead. Thus, by utilizing the classification process of voicing, place of articulation and manner of articulation, teachers are able to specifically target consonant problems and relay targeted corrective action.

As you can see, you will be exposed to a lot of technical jargon with how sounds are made, the notation process of stress and intonation, the organization of sound categories, and so forth; however, the key isn't to transfer this technical jargon to students. They don't need to know this technical side. What they need to know is non-technical information that consciously brings self-awareness in their speech utterances.

Vowel Error Identification

When you speak English to someone from a distant land and you notice a slight accent whether it is a foreign or domestic one, the accent is likely due to the differences in vowel pronunciation. Vowels differ from consonants by their need for a wide opening of the mouth and an unobstructed airflow. Babies are good at vowel sounds. Vowel variations depend on certain movements of the tongue with the mouth. There are four characteristics in articulating vowel utterances:

a)   The frontward or backward movement of the tongue

b) The height of the tongue inside the mouth

c) The involvement of firm or loose facial muscles (compare the tenseness of *wheat* with the laxness of *wit*)

d) The rounding or relaxing of the lips

The higher the tongue's position in the mouth, the more the mouth is in a closed position. Below is an illustration that shows the frontward and backward tongue movements and the corresponding vowel utterances with each tongue position (see Figure 12.7).

Figure 12.7.

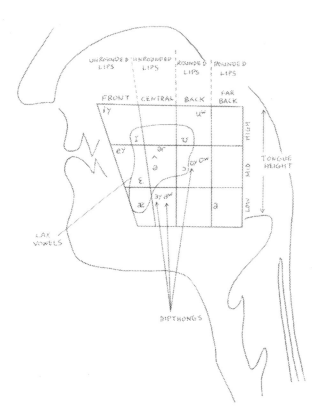

Corresponding vowel utterances with tongue positioning

Tongue Forward/Backward Movement

When describing tongue height, speakers have to differentiate which part of the tongue requires any necessary raising. Take /iy/ and /uw/ for example. Both require a rise in tongue height but for /iy/, the front part of the tongue is raised while /uw/ is made with the back part of the tongue raised. A sound such as /iy/ would be considered a *high front vowel* while /uw/ would be a *high back vowel*. Similarly /a/ and /æ/ are low vowels but they utilize different parts of the tongue. The back part of the tongue that is held low produces /a/ and the front part of the tongue that is held low is /æ/. Thus, /a/ is considered a *low front vowel* while /æ/ is a *low back vowel*. Vowels that aren't sensitive to tongue height see the tongue more at its resting position. The sound /ʌ/ and /ə/ are in this category.

Tongue Height

According to Figure 12.7, a word with the /iy/ sound such as in *wheat* would require a high tongue height while the /æ/ sound such as in *cat* would require a low tongue. As you begin with the /iy/ sound and progress to /ɪ/, /ey/, /ɛ/ and /æ/ you'll notice that your tongue gradually starts to drop. The vowels of /iy/, /ɪ/, /uw/, and /ʊ/ are *high vowels* because the tongue is at a high position from its resting place, while /ey/, /ɛ/, /ʌ/, /ow/, /ɔ/ and /ə/ are *mid vowels* because the tongue is in a middle position of the mouth. The *low vowel* of /æ/ and /a/ are low vowels due to the tongue being at its resting position.

Tense/Lax Facial Muscles

Tension in the facial muscles plays a role in differentiating vowels. When facial muscles require extra tension during articulation such as in the /iy/, /ey/, /ow/ and /uw/ sounds, we say they are *tense vowels*. Here is a list of vowels that require extra muscle tension and their lax counterparts.

Tense Vowels   and   Their Lax Counterparts
- /ow/ — /ɔ/
- /iy/ — /ɪ/
- /ey/ — /ɛ/
- /uw/ — /ʊ/

Lip Rounding/Relaxing

Another variable in vowel production is the shaping of the lips. The rounding of the lips involve the back vowels of /uw/, /ʌ/, /ow/ and /ɔ/. The lips are unrounded for /iy/, /ey/, /ɪ/, /ɛ/, /æ/, /ə/, /a/ and /ʊ/.

Correcting Pronunciation of Vowels

Now that you have a grasp of he four characteristics of vowels we can describe them with more articulation precision. If you were to teach the /iy/ sound, you would determine the four classifying characteristics:

/iy/ = front, high, tense, unrounded.

The above technical description of the /iy/ vowel being a front high tense unrounded vowel can be translated into non-technical language: The /iy/ requires the front part of the tongue to be raised high, tense facial muscles, and unrounded lips. You may even add that the mouth is almost closed. The higher the tongue height, the more the mouth is closed. How would you technically describe the /ʌ/ sound?

/ʌ/ = central, mid, lax, rounded

In non-technical terms, you can describe the /ʌ/ vowel as requiring the central part of the tongue to be at mid-height, lax facial muscles, and rounded lips. If a Spanish student was saying *wait* instead of *wet*, how would a teacher correct the student? Since the target sound of /ɛ/ is a front mid lax unrounded vowel and the error sound of /ey/ is a front mid tense unrounded vowel, the only difference in articulation is the tenseness of the facial muscles. The teacher would have to demonstrate the need for the facial muscles to relax and not tense up in the utterance. Error correction can be accurately targeted when you can identify the 4 main characteristics of vowel sounds and compare which area(s) is (are) different from the target sound.

How would you correct an Italian student if he was saying *hot* instead of *hut*? First, determine the target sound and the error sound:

target sound = hut = /ʌ/
error sound = hot = /a/

/ʌ/ (target)	/a/ (error)
central	(far) back
mid	low
lax	*
rounded	rounded

* doesn't require any extra facial tension than normal

What is the articulation difference between the error and target sounds? You can see that the tongue height and muscle laxness are places that differentiate the two sounds. The student should be raising the tongue a little higher and relaxing the facial muscles more to utter the correct /ʌ/ sound. Thus, by utilizing the classification process of determining the four characteristics of vowel articulation, teachers are able to specifically target vowel problems and relay precise corrective action.

Now that you have a relative idea on how consonants and vowels work, you can apply this technical knowledge and transform it into simple but relevant teachings for your students. By understanding the specific articulation areas for different sounds, teachers have the wonderful capacity to play detective by spotting the specific pronunciation deficiencies involved. Use this technical know-how for your own reference and for the benefit of perfecting student pronunciation.

See an example pronunciation lesson plan for students who tend to say *tink* instead of *think* in the Course Planning section of this book.

CHAPTER 13:

Teaching Specialized Sounds—Traffic Precautions

In This Chapter

> Semi-vowels

> Diphthongs

> The /r/ factor

> Consonant clusters

> Correcting clusters with creative additions and deletions

> The /h/ factor

> The most pronounced sound: the schwa

> Notating combined phonemes

> Dictionary phonetics

If you were able to absorb the technical information from the previous chapter, this chapter will be a breeze to flip through. We studied the complex process of what the body goes through in making vowel and consonant sounds; now we're going to study how sounds of a more complex nature are generated. There are several categories of sounds that are neither true vowels nor true consonants; they're in a separate category of specialized sounds that need their own individual attention. Let's start with a term that would be great in scrabble games: diphthongs. Diphthongs are complex vowel sounds that need the assistance of semi-vowels. What are semi-vowels?

Semi-Vowels

Semi-vowels (also known as *glides*) are sounds that are pronounced in a similar fashion as vowels—with a wide opening of the mouth and similar tongue positioning that allows air to flow out with minimum obstruction. The sounds of /y/ and /w/ are classified as semi-vowels because of its close association with vowels. These two sounds of /y/ and /w/ tend to form the latter part of a vowel syllable.

Diphthongs

Diphthongs are complex vowel sounds comprised of a vowel and a semi-vowel put together to form one sound. In order to generate the sounds of diphthongs, there is more tongue movement involved compared to their vowel counterparts. There are three diphthongs in English: /aw/, /ay/ and /oy/ as in *now*, *lie*, and *boy*. Although the tense vowels of /iy/, /ey/, /uw/, and /ow/ have the same vowel + semi-vowel format of a diphthong, they are not categorized as such due to the lack of tongue movement involved.

The /r/ Influence

When you join the consonant /r/ with a vowel, what you get is a blended sound that combines the lax central vowel of /ə/ and /r/ to form /ər/. Vowels such as /iy/, /ɪ/, /ey/, /ɛ/, /ʌ/, /a/, /æ/, /uw/, and /ʊ/ combined with /r/ form the blended sound /ər/ or as in *her*. The vowel /ow/ + /r/ combine to form the blended sound /or/ as in *bored*. Note that the /or/ sound drops the /w/ influence of /ow/. Diphthongs and /r/ combined together form sounds that can be one or two syllables. The combination of /ay/ + /r/ forms /ayr/ or /ayər/ as in *shire* (1 syllable) or *shyer* (2 syllables). The combination of /aw/ + /r/ forms /awr/ or /awər/ as in *flour* (1 syllable) or *flower* (2 syllables). The combination of /oy/ + /r/ forms /oyr/ or /oyər/ as in *lawyer* (two syllables)

Consonant Clusters

Since the word *cluster* means group, the term *consonant cluster* must mean a group of consonants. In this case, the group that we're referring to is generally 2-3 consonants grouped together to form a sound. In the previous chapter, we learned that one of the characteristics of forming consonant sounds is the way in which airflow is obstructed in the mouth (manner of articulation). Consonant clusters can be categorized with their manners of articulation and placements in a word. If the consonant cluster is at the beginning of a word, it's in the initial location—at the end of a word, it's in the final location. Here are some example initial and final position consonant clusters:

Initial two-consonant clusters that begin with fricatives: fl (fling), fr (fraught), θr (throat), ʃr (shrink), sp (spew), etc.

Clusters that begin with nasals: my (mute), ny (numerical)

Initial two-consonant clusters that begin with stops: bl (black), br (brown), dr (drain), gr (green), kl (class), ky (Kyoto), pl (please), pr (proud), tr (tree), etc.

Clusters that begin with /h/: hy (human)

Initial three-consonant clusters: skr (scream), skw (squish), spl (splint), spr (sprout), str (straw), spy (spew), etc.

Final two-consonant clusters that begin with a fricative or stops: ft (left), sp (gasp), st (must), etc.

Final two-consonant clusters that begin with a stop: dz (ads), ks (wax), kt (lacked), ts (hits), pt (wept), etc.

Final two-consonant clusters that begin with nasals: mp (hemp), nd (wand), ns (fence), nt (can't), etc.

Final two-consonant clusters that begin with a liquid: lp (kelp), lθ (health), lt (hilt), lk (milk), rb (barb), rtʃ(church), rd (shard), rk (pork), rt (heart), rv (swerve), etc.

Final three-consonant clusters: kst (next), lts (halts), rts (quartz), rld (curled), mps (mumps), etc.

Some students find it difficult to pronounce consonant clusters so they plug in vowels between the consonants or drop one of the consonants. Some languages such as Cantonese, Vietnamese and Japanese don't use consonant clusters so students from these backgrounds will probably have difficulty with them. Peter Avery and Susan Ehrlich point out in *Teaching American English Pronunciation* that the Spanish don't employ initial consonant clusters that begin with /s/ so they substitute /ə/ to initiate these clusters (*estreet* instead of *street*). Teachers can focus on correcting the problem by lengthening the /s/ sound in *street* to the point where the added /ə/ could be faded out. The authors also mention that Arabic students tend to plug in vowels in three syllable clusters such as saying /estr/ instead of /str/. The word street would be mispronounced *sitreet* or *istreet*. Teachers can correct the problem by using two words to assist in deleting the unnecessary vowel, such as *this treat*. Arabic students can combine the two words to *thistreat* and gradually drop the *thi* from *this street*.

The deletion of consonants in a consonant cluster is a common way for learners to deal with its pronunciation. Native English speakers do the same in natural speech when sentences are said with a whole series of sound reductions (*don't* becomes *do' no*; *want to* becomes *wanna*). Asian languages such as Cantonese or Vietnamese use the CVC (consonant-vowel-consonant) word pattern in the place of CCVC of CVCC as in *poud* instead of *proud* and *poke* instead of *pork*.

When correcting cluster difficulties, don't worry about the inappropriateness of its correction in terms of being proper English. By simplifying pronunciations with creative adding or deletion of vowels or consonants in mispronounced clusters, teachers can eventually lead their students to the targeted sound.

The Charging Train Technique

If your Arabic student was saying *esmoke* instead of *smoke*, how would you correct him? His error involves an unnecessary vowel sound being added to a consonant cluster. Your strategy will require some creative thinking by incorporating a process of gradual deletion of the unnecessary initial vowel sound. How? Since the error sound involves the consonant cluster, you can break up the word by breaking up the cluster to create two nonsensical words:

> *tess moke.*

Practice with the student saying these two words separately several times. Next, focus on the first word (tess) by dropping the t so that you are practicing *ess*. Practice saying the two words "ess" "moke" separately.

> *ess moke*

Afterwards, focus on the *ess* and drop the *e* so that you are just practicing the *s* phoneme and the word "moke". You can incorporate the "Charging Train" technique by slowly practicing with the student in saying "sssss" and "moke", "sssss" and "moke", "sssss" and "moke". Make it sound like two separate words at first like this:

> *ss   moke*

Show the student a cut-up picture of a train slowly turning its wheels as you slowly say "sssss" and "moke" with the student. Then show the student that the train is starting to pick up speed and at the same time slowly pick up the speed of the pronunciation of "sssss" and "moke". Next, show that the train is going pretty fast and as a result, gradually say "sssss" and "moke" faster and faster until together the student seems to join the two "words" to create the targeted cluster of *sm* to pronounce *smoke*

Let's look at another method of using creative adding and deletion to correct pronunciation problems with clusters. If your student was saying *theory* instead of *three,* there is an unnecessary /ir/ sound in the medial position. Here we have a problem with the student giving a CVCV (consonant-vowel-consonant-vowel) sound when it should be a CCV sound for *three* /θriʸ/. You can divide the word into the words:

> *the   ree*

Practice the two words several times. Focus on *the* and gradually drop the *e* so that you're practicing the /θ/ phoneme with the second word of *ree*:

> *th   ree*

Use the "Charging Train" technique to practice these two "words". Slowly start the train on its travels as you slowly start the pronunciation engine. As the train picks up speed, so does the speed of pronunciation of the two "words". At full speed, the student should be starting to combine the two "words" into one word with the targeted *thr* cluster.

That Special /h/

When you make the /h/ sound it's similar to a sound you would make when you would exhale your breath on a hot day. The /h/ is a voiceless consonant that requires certain positioning of the tongue depending on the proceeding vowel that follows it. Note the position of the tongue when you combine /h/ with the vowels /iy/ (heal), /æ/ (hat), /uw/ (hoop), and /a/ (hop).

The Schwa /ə/ = A weak "Uh"

The most common vowel sound in English is the schwa /ə/ as in *about*. You can hear the schwa (including the high schwa) in about 35% in all vocabulary made in English speech (Woods, 1983). The schwa is used with many spellings (a, e, i, o, u, y, and other combinations) and as a marker for vowel sounds in unstressed syllables. In fact, the schwa is what generally gives native English speakers an Anglo-accent when other foreign languages are spoken. To generate the schwa sound, the tongue, lips, and jaw are very relaxed and little air and energy is exerted to produce this "uh" sound. Note the spellings below that utilize the schwa sound:

A = announce   E = elevator   I = stencil   O = complete
U = subsist   Y = electrolysis

Notating Combined Phonemes

We've studied symbols in a phonetic alphabet as representing single distinct sounds that when combined together make words. Some phonetic sounds are represented by one character (/θ/ for *th*), or two characters (/iy/ for *ee* as in *see*). When you have a word that requires pronunciation of single characters from a phonetic alphabet, you can translate it phonologically using the required symbols:

hat = hæt   Canada = kænædə   dog = dɔg   Fred = frɛd

If you are phonologically translating a word that requires phonetic symbols that use two Roman letters such as /aw/, /oy/, /iy/, and so forth, it's best to make it into "one" by superscripting the second letter so that you have a^w, o^y, i^y, and so forth when you are doing a translation. See the following examples:

June = dʒu^{w}n   shower = ʃa^{w}ər   meal = mi^{y}l   shake = ʃe^{y}k

Dictionary Notations

Phonetic symbols vary from dictionary to dictionary. Generally dictionaries will have a pronunciation key in the front section to refer to. When using a dictionary for pronunciation, teachers should inform students how information is presented so that pronunciation referencing can be easy.

1. Syllables
   ➤ Words with syllables are notated with a space, a dot, or a hyphen. (help ful, help•ful, help-ful)
2. Stress
   ➤ Words with major stress are notated with a boldface mark (′) in front of, behind or above the stressed syllable (′help-ful).
   ➤ Words with major stress can also be notated with capitalization (HELP-ful).
   ➤ Words with minor stress are notated with a lighter mark (′) or a low-positioned mark (,) (′help-,ful).
   ➤ Words with minor stress can also be notated with lower case letters as in (proDUCE) (verb form).
3) Long and short vowel indicators
   ➤ Words with long vowels have macrons (ā) above them (bōwling = ′bow-lŋ).
   ➤ Words with short vowels have breves (ă) above them, no markings at all, or specialized phonetic symbols associated with them.

Teachers can incorporate special dictionary reference exercises with students to help familiarize them with pronunciation notation systems. Example exercises can be to have students make phonological translations of a list of words on their own using a dictionary's phonetic symbols; have them work in groups to devise a list of hard-to-pronounce words that they've encountered in a class, an assignment, a discussion, or a recent debate; or perhaps have pronunciation games in which teams would challenge each other on phonological translations.

References

Avery, Peter & Ehrlich, Susan. (1992). *Teaching American English Pronunciation*. Oxford: Oxford University Press.

Woods, H. (1983). *Vowel Dimensions*. Ottawa: Public Service Commission.

CHAPTER 14:

Teaching Suprasegmentals— Dodging Traffic

After increasing the volume of your brain cells from learning all the technical jargon of the previous chapters, you have arrived at the point where the technicality slows down and the fun turns a corner with the other branch of pronunciation: suprasegmentals. If learning segmentals was the science of correctly pronouncing phonemes, learning suprasegmentals takes that knowledge a step further by applying it to words to link and produce native-sounding sentences. As a teacher, your job is to take your unconscious speaking skills and transform them to conscious awareness so your students can learn how to speak with native-like skill. Suprasegmentals consist of the following elements: syllable awareness, word stress, sentence stress, intonation, linking, pausing, and reduced speech. Improper practice in the suprasegmental aspects of speech can lead to misunderstandings in a person's tone of voice, attitude, personality, or emotional state. The grammar of a sentence may be correct but the manner of its delivery is equally important to convey the correct meaning and emotions of a message to listeners.

Syllables and Your Handy Chin

The elementary step in introducing suprasegmentals begins with a basic understanding of what syllables are. Syllables are units of uninterrupted sound. They can be whole words or comprise of parts of a word and they must have just one vowel sound (but any number of consonant sounds). *Cat* would be one syllable whereas *com-put-er* would be three syllables. The best way to count syllables is with the hand-under-chin routine. Place the back of your hand flat out under your chin and say a word. As you say the word, notice with the back of your hand how many times your chin drops as you say the word. The number of drops will verify how many  syllables are in the word. When a student says a word, they may mispronounce it by skipping a syllable. Teachers can catch this by making sure that as students say a word, their chins drop the required amount of times. You can have fun with this syllable-chin word check.

Further syllable awareness can be taught by any number of methods:

➢ Model and get the students to do the chin routine.

➢ Tap out the syllables in words and get the students to tap as well.

➢ Get students to recognize the difference between vowel sound and the various spellings that can match it.

➢ Get students to recognize that some vowels are silent in pronunciation.

➢ Quiz students on how many syllables there are in any new vocabulary.

➢ Add syllables in some final position grammatical endings such as in contractions and -*ed* endings.

➢ Delete silent letters in the spelling of a word to compare syllable presence and the presence of silent vowels/consonants.

Our definition of what a syllable is may be different from your students'. Your students may have been taught that in their native languages, a syllable is any single word, or it must have a one-consonant-one-vowel sound structure or a word that has no more than one consonant sound. In English, we have a number of words that combine a variety of sounds and are considered one syllable: *you, your, yours, new, news, why, while, white, ray, rain, range, strange, etc.*

Word Stress

After students have mastered the art of distinguishing syllables, teachers can move on to introducing how words with more than one syllable are stressed. There are three kinds of stress—major stress, minor stress, and unstressed (represented by the schwa—/'/). Stressed syllables have longer sounds, higher pitches, and louder volume. The markings of stress can change the meaning of one word even when the spelling remains the same. Compare the meanings of *PROduce* (noun) and *proDUCE* (verb) or *PREsent* (noun/adjective) and *preSENT* (verb). Stress notation can be made in a number of ways:

1) capitalization (TAble)   O o
2) small circles above the syllables (table)
3) underlining (<u>ta</u>ble)
4) bold face lettering (table)
5) accent marks (I = International) (╱ = U.S.)

Make a notation key of the system that you'll be using in class so students can refer to it and be consistent in its use. A notation key can adapt any of the following systems:

SYL•la• ble	<u>syl</u>• la• ble
syl•la• ble	syl•la•ble
	╱
I syl•la• ble	syl•la• ble

If you're using the circle system, make sure that you locate the circle above the stressed vowel of the syllable rather than the central location of the syllable.

O o   O o
Table X   Table √

If students encounter difficulties with distinguishing the number of syllables in a word, you can use markers to indicate their presence as long as they're separated from the stress notations.

Table   Table   Ta·ble

If your students have problems with pronouncing stressed syllables, you can try a notation system to represent the pitch. Pitch means the highness or lowness of a sound You can use lines that rise and fall to visually indicate the rise and fall of pitch. See the examples below:

Ta|ble   Mus i|cian   Engi|neer

Teachers can introduce some predictable patterns that word stress follows:

a)   Abbreviations have major stress on the last letter: R.R.S.<u>P</u>.

b)   Compound nouns usually have major stress on the first word: HIGHway

c)   Numbers with -teen and multiples of ten have major stress: fifTEEN, TWENty

d)   Nouns with two syllables usually have major stress on the first syllable: PROduce

e)   Verbs with two syllables often have major stress on the second syllable: proDUCE

f)   Words with three syllables usually have major stress on the first or second syllables: CUR·i·ous

g)   Major stress is found on the following suffixes of foreign origin: -aire, -esque, -ette, -ee, -eer, -eur, -ique, -oo, -oon,…

h)   Major stress is found on the syllable before these suffixes: -graphy, -grapher, -logy, -logist, -ic, -ical, -ion, -ian, -ity, -ify, -tion…

i)   Major stress is found 2 syllables before *-ate*: TOL er ate

Sentence Stress: Content Words versus Function Words

Like word stress, sentences follow a stress pattern as well. When native English speakers say a sentence, there are certain words in a sentence that are said louder and with more clarity than others. These words carry essential meaning and are called *content words*. Words that are said to be "extra baggage" in a sentence and are said in a weaker voice are called *function words*.

Content words that are stressed in a sentence comprise of:
names: Sally, Betty, Chris, Vancouver, Newfoundland, Volvo,…
nouns: table, chair, pen,…
numbers: eigh<u>teen</u>, <u>for</u>ty, <u>six</u>ty…(numbers with "teen" and multiples of ten)
main verbs: eat, swam, drink, playing,…
adverbs: slowly, loudly, early,…
adjectives: blue, pink, grey,…
question words: why, when, where,…
demonstratives: this, that, these, those
negatives: neither, never, no, not
negative contractions: can't, don't, won't, didn't,…

Function words that are unstressed in a sentence comprise of:
articles: a, an, the
pronouns: I, you, he, she, it, they, we, him, her, them,…
auxiliary verbs: is, was, are, has, have, will, do, does, did,…
conjunctions: FANBOYS, while, after,…
relative pronouns: that, which who,…
prepositions: in, at, on, to, of,…
To Be **verb in all forms**
modals: can, should, may, might,…

A good activity to practice distinguishing content and function words is making telegrams. Explain to the class that you must send a telegram to your friend Peter and present a detailed message on the board:

To: My friend Peter in Toronto
Message: BRAD IS GOING TO ARRIVE AT THE TERMINAL 1 AIRPORT ON FRIDAY AT 3:30 ON NOVEMBER 31ST FROM FRANCE. PLEASE MEET THEM AT THE DEPARTURES' LEVEL AND PICK THEM UP.
Tell students the cost per word for telegrams is expensive and that you don't have much money. Challenge students to translate the message using the least amount of words possible so that you can save money. Attempts can be written on the board and analyzed by the class. The message should eventually be broken down to:

Message: BRAD ARRIVE TERMINAL 1 AIRPORT FRIDAY 3:30 NOV 31 FRANCE. MEET DEPARTURES' LEVEL PICK UP

> Have students focus on the words left out and add them in using a different coloured pen. Tell students how fast (and less clearly pronounced) the omitted words are said in a sentence and how little meaning is lost when they're omitted. Teachers can also use this opportunity to increase student awareness of how vowel reduction and deletions in function words contribute to the ability to produce and understand native English speech.

Content words receive stress in a sentence while function words are usually unstressed (unless the speaker wants to give special attention to it). Even though all content words are stressed in a sentence, there usually is one content word that will have the greatest stress over all the other content words. This "grand-daddy" of all content words in a sentence is the *focus stress* and is usually the last content word in a sentence.

O o O   o O o O o O OO▼
Betty bought a book on how to teach E.S.L.

stressed	O
unstressed	o
focus stress	▼

O o O O o oo   O o ▼ o
David taught English in a school in Thailand.

O   O o O o o o Oo   ▼
John went to Mexico to visit friends.

At times, the focus stress may fall on a content word that may not be the last word in the sentence. If a speaker wants to emphasize a certain piece of information in a sentence, the focus stress will be on that important piece of information rather than on the last content word. Thus focus stress serves to: provide new information, show contrasting information, and to provide special emphasis on a piece of information.

o O   o ▼   o   o   o O o
I bought the black one, not the red one.

o O   o ▼   O o o o   O
I bought the first model of its kind.

Reduced Speech: Sound mutilation

Native English speakers don't exert the effort to say each word with precision in their sentences due to a mutilation of words. This mutilation is called sentence reduction. Native speakers reduce standard English to a natural blended sound by applying unstressed vowels; deleting and blending sounds; and linking and contracting certain parts of a sentence. When teachers introduce the concept of sentence reduction, they have to teach students how important it is to learn this way of natural English speech. Often students will find the process amusing and think it's some kind of joke and tell the teacher they want to return to learning "proper" English. Since your students' past exposure to native English will be limited, you will have to stress to them that learning sentence reduction is important in their quest to listen to and speak more like a native speaker; otherwise they will think that you're exposing them to "uneducated" English. The mutilation follows certain processes:

1) Vowel Reduction (reducing vowels to a schwa)

- Vowels in function words take on the /ə/ sound such as *in to, and, of, for, the, etc.*

- See Chapter 13 under the schwa section for a look at some reduced words using the schwa.

2) Deletion (deleting consonants)

- If the final consonant cluster has a grammar ending (such as phrasal verbs) as the next word, there's no deletion: *passed over* [pæst owvr].

- If you have a final consonant cluster as part of a compound word, the final consonant in the cluster can be deleted: *carton* [kər ɪn].

- If you have a final consonant cluster in a word and the next word begins with a vowel, the consonant usually isn't deleted: *help out* [hɛlp aʷt].

- If you have a final consonant cluster in a word and the next word begins with a consonant, the final consonant in the cluster can be deleted or have its air unreleased. When we say the consonant is unreleased, it means that the parts of the mouth forms the articulation with place and manner but air is not emitted or "puffed" out.
  last call [læs kal] deletion
  last call [læst˥ kal] unreleased stop
  * the symbol for unreleased stop consonants at the end of a word: ˥

- Pronouns and auxiliaries that begin with /h/ and /ð/ will experience this deletion
  He (hiʸ) → 'e /iʸ/   Who did /iʸ/ (he) see?
  Her (hər) → 'er /ər/   I saw /ər/ (her) last week.
  Them (ðɛm) → 'em /əm/
  Of (əv) → 'uh' /ə/
  etc.

3) Contractions (forming contractions where possible)

- Contractions with nouns and pronouns with verb forms of *To Be, To Have*, and *Will* occur in sentence reduction.
  Is/has can have a reduced schwa sound and/or a /z/ sound when they follow vowels, liquids, nasals, and the consonants /b/, /d/, /g/, /ʒ/, /dʒ/, /ŋ/, /ʃ/, /s/, /ð/, /tʃ/, /z/.
  Cash is valuable. [kæʃ əz vælyuʷəbəl]
  The ring's there. [θə rɪŋz θer]
  Is/has is pronounced as /s/ when they are after the voiceless sounds of /f/, /k/, /p/, /t/, /θ/.
  The cake's on the table [θə keʸks an θə teʸbl]

4) Linking Between Word Borders

- Identical consonants C$_1$ + C$_1$ delete one of the consonants and blend the border together as one long consonant.
  Bob⌣Brown is here. [b + b]

  I have a black⌣coat. [k + k]

- C+C (consonant + consonant) word borders tend to have a deleted or an unreleased final consonant:
  She is a good⌣girl. [d + g]

  It's a late⌣day [t + d]

- Glides (semi-vowels) + V blend together with the /w/ or /y/ sounds
  You should go⌣out tonight. [ow + a]

- Glides (semi-vowels) + Semi-Vowel blend together as one long /w/ or /y/ sound
  You should go⌣west on your trip. [ow + w]

- C+V (consonant + vowel) word borders tend to have blended sounds in a sentence:
  She went⌣out. [t + aw]

  I passed⌣up the opportunity. [t + ə]

5) Final Consonant Transformation

  a) Sometimes a word with a final /n/ consonant is transformed into an /m/ consonant sound if the next word begins with a consonant:

I went on   board the ship [n → m]
     \ /
     m

I put it in   Carl's briefcase [n → ŋ]
    \ /
    ŋ

b) Unreleased /t/ in the negative *n't* auxiliary contraction.

They can't do it today. → /nt/ → /nt$^{\intercal}$/

c) High frequency word borders with /t/ and /y/ are normally transformed to /tʃ/ while /d/ and /y/ word borders are normally transformed to /dʒ/

What did   you do? [wat dɪddʒə duw?]
    \ /
    dʒ

Can't   you go tonight? [kæntʃə gow tuwnayt$^{\intercal}$?]
  \ /
  tʃ

6) Frequently mutilated phrases:

going to + BASE VERB = "gonna"	*won't you* = "won'tcha"
going to + (a place) = "goin' ta"	*did you* = "didja"
don't know = "dunno"	*could you* = "couldja"
have to = "hafta"	*can't you* = "can'tcha"
has to = "hasta"	*who did you* = "whoodja"
want + BASE VERB = "wanna"	*might have* = "mighta"

<u>Example notated sentences:</u>

Can I use your car for a week?
ə ə   \ / ər   ər ə
  3

You made a bad left turn a mile back.
ə   ə   ə

Intonation

Intonation refers to the melody or pattern of pitch changes in speech. It con-
veys meaning and expression. It can denote questions, confirmation of information, emotions, lists or groups of items, the conclusion of a dialogue and
personalization of social addresses. Teachers should spend some time in this

area because different pitch patterns over clauses or sentences can produce unintended meanings. There are seven basic intonation patterns.

1. Rising-Falling

   ➢ The most common pattern in English is the final rising-falling intonation.

   ➢ The pattern is used in information (*wh-*) questions, statements, and single-action imperative sentences.

   When do your classes start?   *I think it's going to rain*   *Close the door.*

2. Rising

   ➢ Usually *yes/no* questions require a rising intonation pattern: *Are you a student?*

   ➢ The intonation rise in *yes/no* questions suggests that the speaker genuinely doesn't know the answer.

   ➢ Surprise questions also have this pattern: *You invited <u>who</u> to the party?*

   You did <u>what</u>?

3. "Or" Questions With Two Alternatives

   ➢ There are two types of "or" questions: the open-choice question that requires the listener to answer "yes" or "no" and the closed-choice question that is an information (*wh-*) question.

   ➢ Open choice questions require rising intonation:

   Did you notify his mother or father?

   ➢ Closed choice questions require a rise before "or" and a fall afterwards in intonation:

   Would you like chicken or fish?

4. Tag Questions

   ➢ There are two kinds of tag questions: those that act as *yes/no* questions where the speaker doesn't know the answer:

   John aced the test, didn't he?

   and those that act as confirmation type questions where the speaker just wants to confirm some information or to initiate a conversation:

It's a nice day today, isn't it?

A good activity to practice tag questions is to present students with some T.V. or radio commercials that persuade consumers to buy products. These commercials can be recorded or self-produced by the teachers. Students can then be assembled with partners to make their own commercials using tag questions.

5. Listing
    ➤ When listing or grouping three or more items together, the intonation follows a rising pattern among the listed items but a falling pattern on the very last item:

    I need to buy a toothbrush, tooth paste, soap, shampoo, and mouthwash.

    Would you like a steak, a pork chop, or a hot dog?

    Close the door, open the window, and relax.

6. Social Addresses
    ➤ When you personalize a social address, there is a rising intonation pattern:

    Hi Betty, how's life?   Good morning, Peter.   Hey Tim, what's new?

7. Conditionals
    ➤ When there are conditional sentences, the provisional part follows a rising pattern and the resulting part follows a falling pattern:

    If you don't go to school, you won't learn much.

    Unless he goes to school, he won't learn much.

A variety of activities can be arranged to practice these basic intonation patterns. Teachers can devise a variety of role plays that present real-life situations, such as making a shopping list, creating *yes/no* and information (*wh-*) questions, tag questions, "or" questions, etc.

Reverse Sequencing

A good activity to practice linking and intonation is called "Reverse Sequencing" that builds up a sentence by going backwards. You begin with the last word in a sentence and gradually add words one at a time. This gradual construction helps keep certain intonation linking patterns in a sentence. It works best when you start backward and not forward so you can maintain the original intonation pattern in the sentence and not subject it to distortion. For example, you can introduce the sentence:

I don't think he called the doctor.

You would sequence the sentence backward in this manner:

doctor
the doctor
called the doctor
he called the doctor
think he called the doctor
don't think he called the doctor
I don't think he called the doctor

To increase the speed of pronunciation, you can use "The Charging Train" approach as mentioned in Chapter 13 in which teachers would introduce a pronunciation point and have students practice a sentence very slowly and gradually pick up speed much like a gradually accelerating train. When the train reaches full speed, the students' pronunciation would reach the level of normal speed.

Intonation and Your Feelings

There is a link between your feelings and the intonation expressed in your sentences. It's important to teach students some basic pitch patterns so that they can convey their feelings correctly. Here are some basic pitch patterns:

Very high pitch

> ➢ This pitch communicates fear or surprise: *There's a snake in the house?*

Repeated rising pitches

> ➢ This pattern communicates anxiety or uncertainty:
> *I think the bus arrives at 9:00. Or maybe 10:00. I don't know, actually. I know it arrives sometime in the morning.*

Balanced pitch with variance

> ➤ This pattern communicates well-mannered speech, and interest.

Very low pitch

> ➤ This pitch expresses a threatening attitude or anger.

Very low pitch with no variance

> ➤ This pitch communicates ill-health, fatigue, or lack of interest.

Excessive variation

> ➤ A pitch that repeatedly goes up and down too much expresses impolite behavior, particularly mimicry, and sarcasm.

Strategic Pausing and Linking

Strategically pausing in certain places of a sentence will communicate one meaning but pausing in another place of the same sentence can change the meaning ninety degrees. Consider the examples, *"Betty," said Aunt Wilma, "is going to Church tomorrow."*
Betty said, "Aunt Wilma is going to Church tomorrow."

Teachers can introduce a good activity that presents sentences with the same content but are said with strategic pausing. Upon hearing the sentences, students would have to write down what they hear with correct punctuation placements.

Addresses of location must have appropriate pauses when a series of numbers are involved. Consider the potential problems that would occur if you were to communicate a house address such as: Suite 532—72548 138th Avenue.

To further practice pausing and linking, students can analyze tapes and transcripts of native English speakers and practice imitating and manipulating the dialogues. Dialogues with numbers, quoted speech, passive speech, and words with similar pronunciation to each other when said at different speeds can be included.

Rhythm Targeting

Teachers have to remember that our perception of intonation is unconscious and deeply ingrained; thus students need plenty of time and practice to learn this rhythmic way native English speakers communicate. If students have difficulty with rhythm, teachers can introduce "nonsense syllables". You can replace the syllable in a sentence with a nonsense syllable such as "da" and use it to point out the target rhythm. Here is are some examples of "nonsense syllables in action:

> Did you buy the red one, or the blue one? = Da da da da DA da, da da DA da?
> What time is it? = Da DA da da?
> Hi Betty, how are you? = DA DA-da, da da DA?

Time Allotment

Now that your brain is full of pronunciation tips, ideas, and scientific details, you can apply this information to creating or aiding a pronunciation course. Which should have more emphasis: segmentals or suprasegmentals? The answer: a little more emphasis should be made on the suprasegmental aspect of pronunciation. The features involved with correct stress, intonation, pausing, linking and sentence reduction are the basic principles in communicating thoughts and feeling to people thus it should receive a heavier emphasis than the production of individual sounds. Any pronunciation course should attempt to cover a wide range of features including phonemes and gradually narrow its objective to specific problems that involve suprasegmentals. With this aim in mind, teachers will have the makings of a dynamic comprehensive pronunciation course.

An example of a suprasegmental lesson can be seen in the Course Planning section of this book.

CHAPTER 15:

Diagnostic Profiling in Pronunciation—Looking Ahead

In This Chapter

> Language profiling

> Six areas of analysis

> Elements of a syllabus

Certain non-teaching factors will affect the success of any pronunciation course. The attitudes and expectations of your students will determine which areas of focus need more attention. A student's commitment in improving his pronunciation will depend on personal factors such as those mentioned in Chapter 4 and whether or not he's prepared to immerse himself in the new identity of a new culture. Some students may be in the class to learn ways to speak more fluently rather than with more accuracy or vice versa. Thus it's helpful for teachers to gauge what attitudes and expectations students have in the class when teaching a pronunciation course.

Teachers can prepare themselves for potential pronunciation difficulties by researching common problems among different language groups as mentioned in Chapter 11. The following are examples of good reference books out there for contrastive language analyses: *Thirteen Language Profiles: A Practical Application of Contrastive Analysis for Teachers of E.S.L.* (1983) by Killam and Watson, *Learner English: A Teacher's Guide to Interference and Other Problems*

(1987) by Swan and Smith, and *Teaching American English Pronunciation* (1992) by Avery and Ehrlich. See the recommended reading list at the end of this chapter for more detailed publishing information.

By utilizing contrastive language profiles, you can develop a pronunciation course customized to the dynamics of your classroom. After you've researched the language profile of a target group, not all members of it, unless you have a homogenous group, will experience the same difficulties. Teachers can diagnose areas of difficulties with individual students by conducting pronunciation assessments. There are several ways to gather samplings of a student's pronunciation profile. Speech samples can be collected by conducting in-class surveys that would enable teachers to listen for correct intonation patterns; oral readings which could be taped and checked to find pronunciation areas needing improvement; or spontaneous speech activities requiring students to interview and tape record each other for responses to be later reviewed. Teachers will have to guide the activity by ensuring students select certain questions requiring a variety of stress, rhythm and intonation patterns to be tested.

After gathering speech samples, teachers can now create a diagnostic profile for each student to record strengths and weaknesses and to track progress in areas needing improvement. Teachers can use the profiles to custom design a pronunciation course syllabus tailored to the needs of the students.

Diagnostic Profiling

A diagnostic profile can be divided into six areas:

1) <u>General Communication</u>: This area measures different characteristics of a student's speech from intelligibility, speed, volume, pauses, facial expressions, eye contact, and other aspects.

2) <u>Consonants</u>: This area records performance in producing consonant sounds in words.

3) <u>Vowels</u>: This area records performance in producing individual vowel sounds in words.

4) <u>Stress:</u> This area records whether correct word stress and sentence stress are applied.

5) <u>Intonation</u>: This area records whether proper intonation patterns were used.

6) <u>Linking, Reduction, Sound Transformation</u>: This area records whether certain linking patterns, sound blending, unreleased stops, and sound transformations occur between word borders in a sentence.

The Gourmet Syllabus

After diagnosis, you essentially have the ingredients to make a nice gourmet meal—being your course syllabus. You may wish to ask your restaurant customers (your students) how they would like their meals prepared: with little or no salt; with little or no fat; with little or a lot of sauce; etc. Likewise, pronunciation courses should be tailored to fit the needs of your students. At the same time, teachers have to be aware of the time the restaurant will be open to cook the meal (course length), the general culinary tastes of your clients (the general proficiency of your students), and the amount of meat and vegetables that would be served (the weighing of accuracy versus fluency). The atmosphere of your restaurant should satisfy certain criteria in terms of cleanliness, good service, and ambience to further enhance the culinary (pronunciation) experience. Your syllabus should equally satisfy certain criteria in terms of general speaking habits and segmental and suprasegmental production.

General Communication

Students should be aware of habits that would inhibit their speech such as not looking at their partner's eyes, mumbling words, speaking too softly, etc. Teachers can exaggerate such habits but they would have to be careful not to directly or indirectly project them towards specific students in the class. Examples from video or audiotapes are great sources of presenting bad speaking habits.

> *I have found great examples of bad speaking habits from newscasts featuring sports interviews with certain celebrities after a game. You'll find some good examples of sports celebrities who portray good speech habits and those who look like they're rookies speaking in front of the media for the first time.—P.D.*

Consonants

Teachers can refer to their student profiles to develop priorities for which consonant problems need more attention than others. When prioritizing consonant work, be aware that some consonants are easier to correct than others and that some occur less frequently in day-to-day speech than others. Corrections involving consonants articulated at the front of the mouth (eg. /l/ and /f/) are generally easier to make than corrections articulated from other areas. In addition, certain consonants (eg. /ʒ/) occur less frequently compared to others. Consonant clusters may pose a problem for students and specific positions of them in a word may also be difficult (eg. initial and final positions). Teachers can check for substitution of sounds (such as /b/ for /p/), deletions of sounds (such as final position consonants), general articulation performance (such as appropriate aspiration), and complex articulation with clusters. It's always advisable to start a consonant curriculum with lessons that are likely to pose less of a problem in articulation to build up student confidence before progressing to the more difficult lessons.

Vowels

The first vowel to focus on would probably be the one that is said with the most frequency: the schwa /ə/. Afterwards, teachers can progress to the glides /iy/, /ey/, /ow/ and /uw/, and dipthongs. The most difficult vowels students have trouble with are the lax vowels as they tend to be substituted with their tense counterparts. Teachers can check for substitution of sounds (such as /iy/ for /ɪ/), articulation performance (such as the shaping of the lips), length and stress of vowels and reduction of vowels in unstressed syllables.

Stress

Teachers should also include this essential ingredient in their cooking. Low-level students can focus on stress and rhythm with high frequency words or sight words such as *name, address, telephone number*, etc. Pronunciation clues such as clapping and pitch gestures by teachers would be helpful. Simple sentence patterns and common stress patterns can be introduced. Students should be introduced to the concept of function and content words and identifying focus stress in sentences. More advanced students can experiment with consonant reductions, deletions, assimilation, and linking for rhythm.

Intonation

Every syllabus should include an intonation component for all levels. Low-level students should practice correct pitch with the basic intonation patterns while intermediate and advanced students should practice non-verbal cues in less controlled practice of intonation patterns. Teachers can also introduce the relationship between different pitch ranges and the emotional patterns associated with them.

Linking, Reduction, and Sound Transformation

This area covers the tip of the iceberg in fluency. Since native English speakers don't normally use big pauses between words nor should you with your students. Linking and sound reduction patterns should be introduced early so students can become more familiar with "natural" English. Sound transformations are essential in a pronunciation program as they occur in high frequency expressions. Check out Nina Weinstein's *Whaddaya Say?*

Bottom Line

When considering the above factors, a pronunciation syllabus is most effective when teachers tailor it to the background and needs of the students. Through careful diagnosis and research in language profile variables, teachers will have the recipe for a dynamic pronunciation course. Since the main goal of all pronunciation classes is to attain certain levels of comprehensibility, there should be heavier emphasis on suprasegmentals than on segmentals.

See the Appendix for an example diagnostic pronunciation profile form

Recommended Reading

Avery, Peter & Ehrlich, Susan. (1992). *Teaching American English Pronunciation*. Oxford: Oxford University Press.

Killam, Charles E. & Watson, Bruce. (1983). *Thirteen Language Profiles: A Practical Application of Contrastive Analysis for Teachers of E.S.L..* Vancouver: Vancouver Community College.

Swan, M. & Smith, B. (Eds. (1987). *Learner English: A Teacher's Guide to Interference and Other Problems*. Cambridge: Cambridge University Press.

Weinstein, Nina. (1982). *Whaddaya Say?* New Jersey: Prentice Hall Regents

CHAPTER 16:

Teaching Listening—Closing in on the Highway

In This Chapter

> Precision listening

> Correcting precision listening tasks

> Listening obstacles

> Listening strategies

> Audio use in listening tasks

Regardless of the native language of your students, teachers have to train them to listen for target sounds to help them distinguish incorrect sounds they may be making. Imagine your student is showing you his new car and you engage in a conversation like the one below:

Student: Do you like tis car? Tis is my car.
Teacher: No, you should say, 'This is my car'.
Student: Tis is my car.
Teacher: No, no! Listen. You have to say, 'THIS is my car'.

As you've probably figured out, this conversation is going to go nowhere, unless he's actually showing you *your* car. The student repeated his errors the second time because he wasn't trained to hear the /θ/ sound. If the student has never heard the target sound before, he's going to insist that his /t/ is the right one. Students need to exactly perceive what the sound is and how to listen for it. Even if the teacher provides articulation correction, students who've made the same pronunciation error for years may not automatically adjust their speech. Students need the time to get used to hearing the target sound so they can become more aware of it and realize where correction needs to take place. Self-correcting students would eventually rely less on teachers to catch their errors. Knowing the precise target sound and learning to listen for it is the ultimate goal of precision listening practice.

Target Listening

How do you teach a student what to listen for? Teachers should take the target sound and present it in a way that allows students to compare it to the sound that students think they are hearing. Here are some example steps that you may follow if you were teaching Polish students how to differentiate the confusion between /θ/ and /t/.

A) Demonstrate the articulation of the target sound and the error sound with diagrams and with your mouth. Ask students to verbally signal you by saying "change", "aha", or other words when they hear a change of sound from /θ/ to /t/ as you read them a list of words.

B) Repeat the previous step, but change the word sequencing and cover your mouth so students can hear the sound difference rather than just see the difference. You can alter your tone of voice and add different intonation.

C) Repeat the above two steps but ask students to signal changes in sound from /t/ to /θ/.

D) Begin perception practice activities that allow students to listen to new word utterances from the teacher and to point to the new words that are posted and labeled by number (for referencing) on the board

E) Repeat the previous step but utter the words from behind the students so they can't see your mouth.

F) Practice using the words in simple sentences.

Note that throughout the six steps students were not required to articulate the target sound itself. These steps are purely to train students how to listen for target sounds and not to articulate them. Students have to know what to listen for before they attempt to reproduce the sounds themselves, thus it's best to separate articulation from this listening component. These steps should be gradually built up in time so students aren't overloaded with random occurrences of target sounds in words. Teachers should carefully pre-plan their word choices as students tend to have the most problems with final position sounds, consonants, and consonant clusters.

The prime function of precision listening is to show students how sounds correspond to particular combinations of words. Repetition of words can introduce students to combinations that may sound like one word such as *wanna* in *want to* or *whatcha* in *what are you.* It often helps students to think of these manipulated forms as being one word. Precision listening practice allows students to be aware that different contexts may produce different sound with words.

Although precision listening is important, a whole lot of time should not be spent on it due to its potential for taxing the capabilities of students. Students often don't realize the importance it provides in enabling them to utilize more accurate and sophisticated vocabulary. Teachers have to be persistent in including a precision listening component in their speaking and listening classes.

During IELTS testing (International English Language Testing System) in various parts of China, I would sometimes encounter how just subtle misunderstandings in listening can reveal unexpected responses from candidates, such as:

Examiner: What is the most interesting *part* of your city?
Candidate: The most interesting park is….

Examiner: So you *keep* photographs to remind you of the past?
Candidate: Yes, I take photographs.

Examiner: Do you *wear* a watch?
Candidate: Yes, I like to watch comedy on T.V.

Examiner: Can you tell me your name?
Candidate: That is a hard question.

On one occasion a student was talking about a popular comedy show called Lucky 52. She was talking about how she liked the comedian's smell. I was a bit confused until I realized she meant the comedian's smile. Another student had to speak for two minutes about a personality trait and his focus was on what I heard was his hemorrhoids. I later realized he was trying to say humorous.— R.R.

Needle in a Haystack

How do you correct precision listening tasks? Teachers should not immediately provide the correct answer. Allow students to seek and self-correct themselves first by giving clues to help them discriminate the sounds. If you were playing a tape exercise, don't just rewind and replay the portion of the tape where students have listening
problems. You have to provide specific clues that would help them locate that needle in the haystack. If students missed a word in a taped dialogue between a mother and son, provide a clue by saying the son on the tape said something immediately after he greeted his mother. Students then have a clue as to where in the dialogue a piece of information if missing. If they still have problems, narrow the clue by saying, "It's a question." Then play the tape again. The more you gradually focus in on the clues, the more likely students will be able to self-correct their listening problems.

The Zen of Listening

Listening is not an easy skill for anyone, let alone for foreign-language learners. Some listening skills are easier to grasp than others. We listen for five purposes: gist, specific information, general information, sequence, and opinion. There are some strategies that teachers can encourage students to use in their listening tasks. Students can be reminded of the knowledge they already have about a topic to help predict what vocabulary they may encounter. Students can use visual cues such as facial expressions and body language to predict what is being said. An example activity can be to present the students with a scene from a movie without sound and then have them write about what they think the dialogue was about. This activity is a good way to fixate students on visual clues.

Another way for students to help themselves is to scan for announcements. Key words such as *Congratulations, Attention Ladies and Gentlemen, Happy Anniversary,* etc. are useful predictors of what would be said following these opening lines. Another key tip for students is to recognize conjunctions as markers in a sentence. Conjunctions such as coordinators (FANBOYS: for, and, nor, but, or, yet, so) and subordinators (before, therefore, after, thus, however, etc.) help predict parts of a sentence. The key to using conjunctions is to ensure students know how to use them in the proper sequencing. In addition, non-standard English expressions such as "uh-huh", "really", "is that so", and "oh-oh" convey feedback and are useful in confirming understanding.

Students should also be made aware of babble in speech. Babble is redundant information that is said in the midst of a conversation and isn't important to the main idea that is being conveyed. In Chapter 3 we looked at giving instructions and how easy it is for teachers to include a lot of babble in their instructions that easily confuses students. Thus it's important to have pre-planned, clear and precise instructions in the classroom.

> *During IELTS oral testing in China, I've often noticed how candidates focus on what is said in the last part of a question. For example is you asked, "What are some personality types that are considered typical in your culture?" some candidates would answer focusing on their culture rather than personality types.—R.R.*

Motivation

Once you've found interesting and relevant material (relevant in the students' world) for your lesson plan, the next step is to create a need to listen for information. Teachers can choose a variety of listening activities to create the need for listening. You can distribute comprehension questions, play interactive games, assign video tasks, sing songs, distribute closes (fill-in-the-blank exercises), do dictations, assign sequence activities for reconstructing a story, do picture drawing exercises, share stories with questions and answers, etc. When assigning tasks, you should evaluate each one by asking yourself if:

1) The task demonstrates comprehension.

2) The instructions to accomplish the task are simple.

3) The students have the necessary skills to accomplish this task.

Basic Sequence for Staging an Audio Recording Listening Lesson

a) Provide background information for students as a "Lead-In". This is similar to the pre-reading stage of a reading lesson in which student interest is piqued.

b) Contribute any new information associated with a topic and provide new vocabulary associated with it.

c) Conduct topic exploration activities with vocabulary exercises, prediction making, simple worksheets, etc.

d) Introduce background information for a recording. The recording should be no longer than a couple of minutes in length. Introduce an information-finding exercise based on the recording.

e) Play the recording.

f) Students can discuss the events on the recording with a partner. Teachers should monitor but not correct the students' work nor give non-verbal cues for right and wrong answers. Teachers can provide clues to help the students. Students should come to an agreement with their partners on their findings.

g) Play the recording again. Check for student progress.

h) Play the recording in strategic moments until comprehension is clear. If there are enough copies of the recording, students can control playback with their own machines.

i) Review the task's answers and provide a closing activity to reinforce the lesson's objective. The follow-up may be a focus on vocabulary, grammar, situational or functional approaches to the script. Fluency tasks such as having discussions or role plays can be involved to give learners an opportunity to respond to the theme or content of the tape.

Teachers should use the above basic steps as a guide to help them design lesson plans involving audio recordings.

Teachers will find that teaching listening shouldn't be in isolation. The listening portion is only one part to the essential overall skill of listening and speaking. Listening tasks don't necessarily have to deal with content comprehension. They can involve listening for stressed syllables, content words, target vocabulary, etc. The following chapter on teaching speaking will expand the opportunities that present themselves in a comprehensive listening and speaking course.

See the Course Planning section for an example listening lesson using an audio recording.

CHAPTER 17:

Teaching Speaking—Heading for the On-Ramp

> **In This Chapter**
>
> \> The linguistic development of speech
>
> \> Teaching written versus spoken English
>
> \> Language, message, and interactive functions
>
> \> Steps to effective conversation
>
> \> Guided to student-centered discussions
>
> \> Organizing debates
>
> \> Correcting students
>
> \> Contact assignments
>
> \> Recipes on getting students to talk
>
> \> Fluency activities
>
> \> The world of "Improv"

The Science of Speaking

In most language teaching situations today, there has been a move towards a more oral emphasis in lesson planning. There has been a cyclical progression in response to the increasingly oral nature of human communication in the last 50 years with the advent of the radio, the telephone, the television, the computer, video, films, satellite communication, information technology, voice-commanded software, etc. The fact that your mother may have used a megaphone to wake you up in the mornings to go to school may also be included as advancement in communication technology. Along with these changes, there has been a greater demand from learners who now feel the need for greater oral proficiency in the spoken language.

What is spoken language? By understanding the different characteristics of speech, you can predict the effectiveness of your speaking lessons. Note the following characteristics between spoken and written language:

1) Spoken language is intuitively learned

   When babies are born, they don't enter language classes right away so they can tell their parents when they're thirsty, hungry, or when they need a diaper change. Usually a good scream from them is enough for their needs to be quickly tended to by parents. Children acquire their first language intuitively without a classroom environment, whereas the written form is deliberately taught and learned.

2) Spoken language is less standardized.

   You may already know that there are various dialects of spoken English all over the world. These dialects are from people who fall in the subjective category of native English speakers. An English speaker from New Zealand may have minor difficulties with understanding an English speaker from the Caribbean. On the other hand, writing tends to adopt a universal standard understood by the broader population of speakers from a language group.

3) Spoken language has a faster comprehension rate

   The time it takes to explain how a computer works will be much shorter than the time it would take to write a technical manual on it. Written communication demands more time to produce than spoken communication. Because of the dynamics involved in the rules of writing, production is slower; on the other hand, sometimes reading a piece of written information can produce faster reception than listening to an explanation.

4) Spoken language tends to be less detail-oriented or explicit.

   In real-time speech, the listener may already know some of the information referred to in the conversation. In contrast, written language necessitates more detail and explicitness to communicate clear understanding to readers who may not be familiar with information the text refers to.

5) Spoken language is less dense in content.

Spoken language tends to contain babble and non-standard expressions such as "Uh-huh", "Uh-uh", "Oh my!" "No way!". These expressions don't contribute to the meaning of a sentence, thus they add a lot of redundant content to oral communication. In contrast, written language is more specific and doesn't allow much room for redundancies to occur, thus it is denser in content.

6) Spoken language involves the participants more.

Since spoken language takes place in real-time, input and feedback take place immediately. On the other hand, written language tends to detach the readers from involvement because of the fact a book can be put down at any time by the reader and there is no personal relationship between the writer and the reader (except for personal correspondence).

7) Spoken language has less permanence.

Written information is fixed and stable so the reading can be done at any time. In contrast, spoken information moves in real time and is continually changing in content and expression. The speaker sets the speed of conversation forcing listeners to adjust to it to comprehend what is heard.

8) Spoken language is less organized.

Speakers have to improvise the content of what is said in real-time; thus alterations in content through clarification, questioning, repetition and reorganization of information, and so forth continually shape a conversation. In contrast, written language has the opportunity to be more organized and carefully formulated through the advantage of having more time for composing. Since a writer has more time to convey his thoughts, conformity to rules of grammar and vocabulary is stricter than in speech.

Butterflies in Your Stomach

According to studies, researchers have discovered that there is one fear that people have that is worse than the fear of death: the fear of speaking in public.

At least with death, it may strike you when you least expect it, but with public speaking, you're consciously aware of what is happening to you the moment you initiate the "dreaded" act. Most North American school-goers have experienced public speaking in one form or another by doing classroom presentations, debates on controversial topics, or speeches in an auditorium. Our first oral presentation for most of us would have been the "Show and Tell" presentations when we were six year olds. We all remember the sinking feeling of wanting to crawl in a hole as the time drew closer to our turn to do our performance in the classroom spotlight. Your E.S.L. students will have the same feelings of having butterflies in their stomachs when they are asked to do oral presentations. Added to their "burden" is the fact they would have to speak in a language that isn't their mother tongue. Imagine yourself having the pressure to do an oral presentation on the theory of Plate Tectonics to a class of Swahili As A Second Language students. Although students themselves are the only ones who can control their responses to speaking out in the classroom, E.S.L. teachers are responsible for providing a comfortable atmosphere to facilitate effective discussion by keeping in mind the following considerations.

Step 1: Provide Interesting Topics

As a student, there's nothing more boring in a conversation class when you are forced to talk about a subject that does not seem to have any significance in your life. If you were a 16 year old male E.S.L. student who was into hip hop music, pizza, parties, and stick-thin girls, you wouldn't find yourself engaging too much in your conversation class if the topic of the day was gardening. In order to promote effective conversation, E.S.L. teachers should take the time to discover what interests their students. If you choose a topic that you think is new to them but may spur interest, then you have to initiate the steps to teach them about the topic. Pre-teaching an unfamiliar topic before asking your students to discuss it is essential in maximizing student motivation and participation. You may generally introduce an unfamiliar topic to them the day before a lesson and send them home to think about it or introduce it by preparing an exercise that would allow for further exploration for the next day.

Step 2: The Raison d'Etre

Often during unprepared speaking sessions, students will come to a point where they stop talking and say to you or to their partners, "I don't have anything to say!", or "I'm finished. I can't say anything more." E.S.L. teachers then look at the now-quiet students and conclude that although the conversations were brief, now what? Are the students really finished talking when they have that "there's-no-more-to-say" look?" To ensure on-going and enthusiastic conversation, students need to have a purpose as to why they are discussing the topic. The purpose of a conversation can be to brainstorm ideas to solve a problem or a controversial issue, to generate inspiring theories or concepts, to compare or contrast different opinions, to survey results, etc.

Advice Columnists

E.S.L. teachers must ensure that students have a direction where their conversations are going to lead them. A generalized topic on boyfriend-girlfriend relationships will not go very far unless teachers specify a topic of discussion and give students a purposeful task to accomplish. For example, a teacher can look for letters in an advice column describing relationship problems between couples and clip them out for the students to read. If such letters aren't readily available, a teacher can compose a few for the lesson. Next students can be divided into small groups of four to five students in which each group can be given a letter. Afterwards, each group can be given the task to act as advice columnists to solve the problem specified in their assigned letters by composing a collective response. Since students are given a specific goal in their discussions (to solve a couple's relationship problem stated in their letters) they will likely engage in a more lively and enthusiastic discussion than being given the instructions, "Okay, now let's talk about boyfriend-girlfriend relationships everybody!" Modeling the activities becomes important in getting an activity off the ground.

Step 3: Introduce Conversation Management

Before beginning any speaking activity, teachers should introduce some basic rules of conversation. These rules are necessary to maintain a sense of civil order should there be times when discussions, particularly controversial topics, get out of hand and you have a brawl erupt in the class. You should introduce conversational etiquette with regards to interrupting, respecting a person's opinions, recognizing that everyone has a right to disagree, not monopolizing a conversation, disengaging in a conversation, etc. Teachers can introduce these rules with various listening exercises that demonstrate certain problem areas or role model each behavior for the students and asking for their feedback on how to counteract negative behavior.

Step 4: Present Useful Speech Patterns

When students are given an interesting topic and a task to complete in their discussions, teachers must provide another language tool: useful speech patterns, expressions, vocabulary and gambits. Students have to have the discussion skills to engage in any conversation. For example, if students needed to express their opinions, they should learn the different expressions that embody having opinions, such as, "In my opinion..", "I think...", "I believe....", "Are you kidding?, It seems to me...", etc. Expressions that focus on asking for an opinion, agreeing and disagreeing, clarifying, interrupting, showing interest, adding details to an explanation, persuading, and closing a topic of discussion should be covered. Teachers can elicit and introduce expressions under the above categories and incorporate them in controlled and less controlled practice.

Keep in mind that the above expressions are not enough in the pre-teaching stage. Teachers have to consider what necessary vocabulary and other sentence patterns students need in order to engage in their task-based discussions. Are there any useful idioms that are common with the topic of discussion? If you're going to introduce the topic of capital punishment, do students know what a lethal injection is? Do they know the terms used for serious crimes? In addition, correct pronunciation, intonation and sentence stress of the useful expressions should be covered so that students can use their new expressions confidently and fluently.

Step 5: Group Dynamics

Students feel less intimidated speaking in small groups than they do in a large crowd. It's best to limit the size of group discussions to four to five students per group. The more comfortable the students are in a small group, the more participation you will tend to have from the students. In addition, smaller groups enhance peer-teaching and peer-correcting while the teacher has the chance to roam the classroom to observe and assist individual students who need extra help. During monitoring, teachers can consider using a tape recorder to record students during their discussions and playing the tape back to them for feedback on grammar or pronunciation.

In guided discussions with a worksheet, distribute only one copy to each group rather than individual copies for everyone. Teachers should assign a member of each group to act as the group facilitator to ensure the discussions flow smoothly and everyone in the group is participating. Moreover, it's easier for teachers to harass the group facilitator who is responsible for the group's performance than it would be to harass all the group members for dismal participation. In really vocal groups where everyone seems to be talking all at once, the group facilitator can pass around a *talking stick* (or any object that can act as a *talking stick*) that allows whoever is holding it the right to speak at that moment in time. For groups with shy students, facilitators can distribute an equal amount of poker chips to everyone in the group. During the discussion, whenever a student makes a comment, he/she throws a chip in the center of the table. The goal for these shy students is to discard all of their poker chips, so they are encouraged to actively participate in the discussions.

For controversial topics, some students may not feel comfortable debating a certain side of an issue. In order for students to feel more relaxed and to dissipate the heat that controversial topics generate, teachers can assign opinions to students. When students have an opinion assigned to them, they often feel more at ease and willing to express themselves more without being pressured or concerned about being judged by other classmates for having an opinion that may not be commonplace in the society they're from or currently live in.

There are certain personal factors that may impede the success of your discussions. From personal experience, it seems that the older the students are in your class, the more opinionated they become. Gender and personal relations with other classmates will affect discussion as well. For example, Mr. Suzuki will not disagree with Mr. Hiro, his boss, if they are in the same class together, or young Jimmy may seem reserved in expressing his contrasting opinion openly to an elder in his group. Sometimes students will question why they are talking about certain topics and think such conversations are a waste of time. You may face an uphill battle in getting your students to openly discuss a topic. Consequently, teachers have to remind students that the principle aim of their discussions is to practice speaking and that depending on each student's lifestyles, they may not have the opportunity to practice speaking English outside the classroom.

Step 6: Speaking Goals

E.S.L. teachers have to determine what the object of the lesson is going to be. If the goal is to just get the students talking, then teachers can introduce a controversial topic. If the goal is to improve the students' confidence and fluency in discussion, then teachers won't want to use a controversial topic; a generic topic such as "Which makes a better pet—a dog or a cat?" would be more conducive to the lesson's objective.

From Childhood to Jupiter Island

The first stage in the progression from guided conversations to discussion activities should begin with simple conversations among the students. You can begin these guided conversation activities by introducing positive personal experiences with the students. You can model a narrative by recounting a positive childhood experience to the class and then asking concept questions to check the students' listening comprehension of your story. Before class ends, you can ask students to think about their own specific childhood memories that they can prepare to share with their classmates for the next day. The childhood memory could be a particular holiday time they shared with the family, a particularly memorable birthday, a sporting event, an academic achievement, and so forth. On the next day, you can divide the class into groups of four to five students to share their stories with each other. With each group having a facilitator, ask students to pick "the best" story in their group to share with the others in the class. These kinds of personal discussions are the least intimidating form of conversation you can have.

The second stage in developing students' conversational skills is to test their ability to talk about non-controversial topics, such as "Summer is the best season of the year", "Hockey is more exciting than basketball", "Driving a car is better than riding a motorcycle". You can divide the class in half with one side brainstorming the pros and the other side brainstorming the cons. Afterwards you can regroup the class into small groups of four with two pro-students joining two con-students. Teachers can then ask the groups to share their views by matching their arguments and rebuttals together by filling out a chart that shows the matching opinions and response from each side. Students can later use their charts to practice using new speech patterns or perhaps for a writing assignment.

The third stage in developing students' conversational skills is to test their ability to engage in more controversial topics such as "Marrying in your 30s is better than marrying in your 20s", "Studying art is not as important as studying science", etc. As you move into more controversial topics, you may encounter some cultural biases in student views. To prevent a classroom brawl from breaking out among students due to misunderstandings in cultural differences, you can take preventative measures in the form of cross-cultural exercises. For example, elicit two or three possible questions from students that surround a topic such as marriage customs in Canada. You can prepare some pre-teaching material such as vocabulary related to getting married.

Assemble students in small groups and tell them they are going to visit a country called "Jupiter Island" and they need to research its marriage customs. Each group can draw up a list of questions to ask a Jupiter Islander. Afterwards each group can submit their lists to you for (optional) correction and editing in preparation for guided discussions for the next day. The question list should contain vocabulary learned in the pre-teaching stage of your lesson. You can also choose not to correct the questions and leave the errors in tact for the students to detect and correct the errors themselves. On the next day, you can assemble the students in small groups of four to five students with each group having a facilitator. Give everyone a list of their discussion questions to look over and have each facilitator go over the questions with their group members and make any necessary corrections to them. Review the corrections with the class. If there are a lot of errors, the correction exercise may take up a big chunk of the lesson.

Next, assemble students in groups with each student having a question sheet. Announce that you're going to present a guest from Jupiter Island who would be happy to answer all of their questions. Inform students that they are required to record the responses on their sheets made by the guest. You can then either ask a fellow colleague who will play the part of the visiting guest to enter the classroom or step out of the room yourself, dress up in the native dress of a Jupiter Islander, and play the role of a typical Islander who is eager to answer the students' questions.

> *I performed the above lesson to an intermediate E.S.L. class and at the end of the semester the memory of the friendly "visitor" from Jupiter Island stood out the most.*
> —P.D.

Upon completion of the interview, you can step back into your role as the E.S.L. teacher who "accidentally missed" seeing the foreign guest and ask the students for some feedback on what they've learned. You should give them some time amongst themselves in their groups to share their answers to the question sheet. Students can also be instructed to make a comparison chart with their own culture. Later in the next few days you can instruct the students to apply this kind of cultural research towards other topics and by speaking to "real" people from different cultural backgrounds.

The Limelight

When students have gained vast experience in discussing slightly controversial topics, brainstorming ideas with each other, doing research, and engaging in lively discussions while being active followers of basic conversational rules, they are ready to go to the next level: heavy duty controversial topics. This level is also known as the "Hot Topic" Level involving abortion, capital punishment, child discipline, euthanasia, etc. A great step to presenting hot topics is to introduce the fun world of debates. Following debating rules is a great way to control any potential problems with maintaining classroom order. Debating rules can be extensive so I will present a brief general description here. Debates involve having 2 teams (1 pro-side and 1 con-side) and 1 chairperson who controls the debate. Each team can be comprised of 2 individuals who must present their arguments and think of rebuttals for counterarguments to support their viewpoints. The chairperson acts as a "referee" who ensures presentation time limits are respected, certain behavioral rules are followed and both sides don't physically assault each other.

Rules

➢ debates must not be read from a sheet of paper; however, cue cards are permitted

➢ no audio-video aids are permitted

➢ debates must focus on ideas and not on personal attacks

➢ participants must respect established speaking times and speaking order with the pro-side starting and finishing the debate:
For example, 1st speaker of the pro-side..............................3–5 minutes
1st speaker of the con-side..............................3–5 minutes
2nd speaker of the pro-side..............................3–5 minutes
2nd speaker of the con-side..............................3–5 minutes
1st speaker of the con-side rebuttal.................2–3 minutes
2nd speaker of the pro-side rebuttal...............2–3 minutes
Cross-examination

Debaters must ensure that they research and organize their presentation by providing an introduction, relevant body information, and a conclusion. In other words, there should be a beginning, a middle, and an end. They must focus on the topic at hand, not overuse their arguments and vocabulary, and not stray in to unrelated details. Their speeches must be loud, clear, and full of enthusiasm for the other student observers to hear and rate their presentations.

After the presentations, there may be a time-limited cross-examination by observing students to assist in their evaluations of the debaters. Observing students can be given a ratings form to evaluate the debater's presentations. Debate evaluations can be based on:

a) Research of the topic.................10 points

b) Supporting evidence.................10 points

c) Organization.............................10 points

d) Rebuttal....................................10 points

e) Delivery.....................................10 points

f) Cross examination....................10 points

Point system:
1–5 = poor   6 = weak   7 = satisfactory   8 = good   9 = very good
10 = excellent

Afterwards, all marks are tallied up for each side and calculated to obtain a percentage among all observers. Percentages can be recorded on a chart in a friendly competition to see who were the best debaters. You can even establish debating tournaments as an after-school extracurricular activity. Since a single debate can last a whole lesson, you may have to disperse the presentation times in order to allow for all the students to take their turns at participating. Perhaps every Friday can be designated as Debating Day. Once students are familiar with the rules and regulations surrounding debates, you open a world of creativity and exciting challenges for students to test their conversational skills.

The Tip of The Tongue

When teaching speaking, the most common bad habit that E.S.L. teachers have is speaking too much. Teachers must remember not to monopolize the class time with their own ramblings. Since the main goal in speaking class is to encourage students to speak out, you have to remember to limit *your* speaking time even when explaining a point to the class. If a student doesn't understand a certain point, the teacher can always ask

another member of the class who may know that particular point to explain it to those who don't. If no one can offer an explanation, the teacher can ask other questions such as *yes/no* questions or *wh*-questions that may lead to an explanation. By continually asking students these types of concept questions, you, as a teacher, would be allowing the students rather than yourself do most of the talking. Keep in mind that the longer an explanation is, the less likely students will understand it.

Correcting

When students make errors in their speech, teachers should minimize their involvement in the correction process. As soon as you hear an error from a student, ask the student to repeat what was said in the hope of self-correction, or ask a second student if what the first student said was correct. Hopefully, the second student will pick up the error and say the correction. If the second student doesn't detect the error, then ask a third student, and a forth student until the correction is spotted by someone in the class. Teachers must make sure that they provide minimum input in the learning process and that each input is followed by output from students.

Students sometimes complain that their conversation teachers don't correct them enough in class. During such episodes you can explain to them the goal of the lesson is fluency rather than accuracy and inform them what the differences between the two are. Sometimes when the goal of the lesson is fluency, you wouldn't want to focus too much on correction. The main goal of fluency is to have students speak English as much as possible to get their meaning across without worrying about having perfect English. If the goal is accuracy, then delivering more perfected grammar would be the focus. There would be more correction in a lesson that focuses on accuracy. If you stand in front of the student nodding your head in a "yes" manner to indicate that you understand what the student said but he/she said it with partially correct grammar, you're not doing them a favour. Students must distinctly know through your facial expressions, your gestures, or body language that the sentence they gave was 100% correct, partially correct, or totally incorrect. A sigh from a teacher doesn't communicate anything to the student in terms of knowing if what was said was correct. After a student corrects an error, you should give a consistent indication of approval by saying, "good", "perfect", or some other positive response.

When reading or reiterating sentences, use regular sentence stress patterns as though you were reading them to a native English speaker. A common error in among teachers is over-emphasizing stress points in a sentence. By over-emphasizing these points, teachers are not teaching students how to recognize the regular speech patterns they actually hear in the real world. The ears of your students, regardless of whatever level they are studying at, must be trained to listen to speech patterns at normal speed rather than turtle speed. Over-emphasizing pronunciation points should be done only in the initial learning stage of a lesson; teachers should then quickly move to saying the presented points in the same manner as native speakers would use them in regular conversational speed.

If students make repeated errors of one type or another, you can point out what kind of mistake they are making by classifying the errors. Minimize the correction process by making the appropriate facial expression to indicate there's an error and saying phrases such as, "article", "verb tense", "preposition", "the last part of the sentence", "stress the first syllable" etc. Remember, for each teacher input, there is student output.

Another great way to correct errors is to have peer correction done in class. You can create a list of common errors that students make. It's best to list the number of errors with the same number as students that you have in the class. Assign each student an error to look out for whenever another student makes a presentation to the class. When a speaking student knows that the whole class will be checking his presentation for errors, he becomes more careful at achieving accuracy. Students who are identifying different types of errors can report back their findings after the presentation is finished, rather than interrupt the speaking student.

Contact Assignments

A great way to encourage students to speak is by assigning contact assignments that require students to go outside the class and practice using the new sentences structures they have just learned. Of course, contact assignments are carried out in places where English is the language spoken outside the school. The goals of contact assignments should be limited so students can easily accomplish them and teachers can follow up on them. If the unit of the week was learning how to ask for information, a contact assignment for students could be for them to seek certain information at a local community center. If the unit of the week was entertainment, a contact assignment could be for students to phone a live theatre for box office information. Most importantly, research the rules for your school on taking students outside the classroom for these assignments. Moreover, before initiating a contact assignment you probably would have to explain what it is as students probably may not have had previous experience with doing one. Below are example contact assignment sheets. Students can be assembled in pairs and assigned various nearby places to make contact with people in English. If there is more than one place in the contact assignment, you can divide the students to begin at different locations to encourage small group cooperation.

The following questions can be a series of contact assignments:

The Bay Department Store

Walk to *The Bay* department store.
Ask a store clerk which floor you can find "Ladies Wear" _____

Find the price of *Totes* umbrellas. Ask a store clerk what their return policy is on faulty umbrellas_____

Can you go inside Pacific Center Mall from *The Bay*? How?_____

Is there a book department? Ask a store clerk on their return policy on books.

_____

Ask a store clerk how many years *The Bay* has been in business. _____

The Capitol 6 Movie Theatre

Walk to the *Capitol 6* movie theatre.
Ask the ticket seller what is playing right now.

_____

Ask the ticket seller what time the movies start.

_____

Ask the ticket seller how much tickets are for matinees.

_____

Ask the ticket seller how much tickets are for children under 12 years old.

_____

Ask the ticket seller if there is a special day of the week when you can buy cheaper tickets. Which day is it? _____

_____

The Post Office

Walk to the post office.
Ask how much it costs to buy a money order (a check that you can send in the mail) of about $50.00. (Canadian dollars)._____
Ask how much it costs to buy a money order of about $60.00 (American dollars)._____
Ask the clerk what is the fastest way to send a letter to Winnipeg. How long will it take? How much does it cost?_____
Ask the clerk how many days it takes for a letter to arrive in Seattle by regular mail._____
Ask the clerk how many days it takes for a letter to arrive in Shanghai by regular mail._____

The Queen Elizabeth Theatre

Walk to the Queen Elizabeth Theatre.
There is a restaurant at the theatre that serves a buffet. Ask the host how much the buffet costs and at what time does the buffet open and close.

_____

Go to the box office. Ask the ticket seller what is playing now.

_____

Ask the ticket seller how much tickets are for adults.

_____

Ask the ticket seller how much is the group rate and for how many people it applies to._____
Ask the ticket seller what time the doors open before a show._____

Tips To Get Mouths To Open

1. Give students a purpose in having the discussion. Provide useful language patterns, expressions, and vocabulary.

2. Check the physical environment of the classroom. Are the tables and chairs set-up to facilitate small group discussions? How is the temperature of the classroom? Is there air circulation inside?

3. Familiarize your students with the rules of conversation etiquette. Model appropriate and inappropriate behavior so students understand what is and isn't acceptable.

4. Model the kind of responses you expect from your students from the task discussion. If you expect detailed responses, provide an example detailed response. Students should see what kind of response you expect from them so they know how to participate in the discussion.

5. Tell students that you will be monitoring them for participation and if you see any dismal responses, you will consult with their group leaders.

6. Assemble students in small groups of 4–5. Small group discussions are less intimidating than large ones.

7. Appoint a group leader for each table. Having a group leader to chair the discussion will help the group focus on the task at hand and ensure everyone has a chance to voice their ideas in a respectable environment.

8. Establish a system that authorizes only 1 person to speak at a time. In some native tribes of North America, a "talking stick" is utilized in special table

discussions. Whoever is in position of this stick has the floor to speak while others must listen and wait for possession of the stick for their turn to speak. You can distribute one "talking stick" to each group for leaders to manage its distribution.

9. Distribute poker chips to each group if utilizing the poker-chip method as outlined in this chapter for getting shy students to speak.

10. Distribute one guided discussion sheet per table (only for the group leaders) so the other students are more focused on the discussion at hand rather than on reading what's written on the paper or what's coming up next.

11. For discussions with controversial topics, assign opinions or roles to take the heat off students.

12. Provide feedback on any common errors heard in your monitoring.

13. If you discover specific groupings of students who work well together, consider assembling them for further discussions.

Fluency Activities

The following activities require teachers to ensure students have the certain speaking skills needed to accomplish what's required. Teachers must also pre-plan their instructions so students can clearly understand what to do.

1. Survival Game

Students are assembled in small groups to brainstorm 10 essential items needed to survive being stranded on a deserted island or out in space. Afterwards, lists among the groups will be compared.

2. "$25,000 Pyramid Game"

Following the famous T.V. game show, students are assembled into teams. Teams are given a category. A member of each team gives clues for seven words that fall under that category for his teammates to guess. If the category was "wet" and the seven items were: milkshake, beer, coffee, grapefruit juice, hot chocolate, paint, rain, then a team member must provide clues to his teammates so they can guess all seven items. To make it more challenging, a teacher can ban certain words that a clue-giving member may use so as not to make the task too easy to accomplish. If banned words are heard, penalties can be imposed.

3.   Guessing Games

Students are assembled in pairs and are given a pile of cards (turned face-down) with vocabulary on them. One partner discreetly flips over one card to see what the word is and mimes it to the other partner for guessing. Afterwards the other partner repeats the procedure for the next card.

Another variation is to have cards with simple sentences written on them for miming. Guesses to the sentence can be approximate.

4.   Odd-thing Out

Similar to the "Odd-Man Out" game, students are given a list of items that all have a commonality except for one item. Students are to find which item on the list doesn't share a common trait that the others have.

Another variation is to give a list of items with no obvious "Odd-Thing Out" and students are asked to find one and justify their choice.

5.   Connections Games

Small groups are given several items (eg. one group can be given an ashtray, a football, a dictionary, and a hammer) and each group must brainstorm a story that incorporates all the items in it

Another variation of the above game is to have groups brainstorm what all the things have in common.

6.   Picture Differences

Assemble students in pairs facing back-to-back and distribute similar, but not identical pictures. Each picture has a certain number of subtle differences and students must discover the differences by talking and trying to find where the differences are.

7.   Story Sequencing

Students are given a line in a story to memorize. The object is to put the story in sequential order by having students talk about their lines and working out a reasonable order.

8.   Jig-Saw Listening

Similar to a Jig-Saw Reading activity, students are given specialized information to discuss in small groups. The groups are then divided into new groups with each member knowing different information so he can share his expert knowledge.

9.   Brainstorming Categories

Students are given a category to brainstorm ideas for it. For example, you can give them the category, "Ways to Get Money Fast" and groups would brainstorm different ways to get money fast through receiving inheritance, marrying a rich person, winning a lottery, doing hard work, etc.

10. Group Planning

Students can be assembled in small groups to plan debates, business proposals, surveys, political campaigning, parties, city development, etc.

Improvisation

Before beginning any improvisation, there are two rules that will help teachers conduct these activities. Teachers must introduce terms to help students participate in these role-plays. If a student doesn't play along with the story well and rejects any idea given to him (by saying for example, "There's no car over there, there are only tables and chairs"), the teacher can introduce a term such as "Reject" and tell a student "Don't reject!" if the student is observed denying an improvised idea. If a student gives a dismal response in a conversation and simply says "Yeah", "I know", "I guess so", etc., the teacher can introduce the adjective, "lazy" and tell students who are giving dismal responses that they're being "lazy" in their responses. Here are some improvisation ideas you can use in the classroom:

a)   One Scene Variations

Students are assembled in pairs or small groups to act out a particular scene provided by the teacher. The scene involves a common day-to-day situation.

Another variation is to have students watch a video and imitate a scene with transcripts or act out a scene that predicts the outcome of a video.

b)   Chain Stories

This is a great warm-up activity to practice fluency for advanced students. Lower-level students can do this activity to work on speaking accuracy. Students are assembled in a circle and they must create a story by adding one word each. A couple of students can be assigned in the group to act as error identification spotters. The teacher may participate in the circle. Speed is important so if a student can't think of a word, the story is passed onto the next student. The teacher may occasionally have to repeat the sentence in progress to progress the activity.

Another variation is to have students do a chain story in pairs so that it goes back and forth between just two students.

c)   First Lines

This is a classic improvisation stage performance. The teacher prepares "first lines" to be written out of different possible stories on slips of paper (Eg. "Justin's clothes are all gone!", "I've been robbed!", "I would like a refund please.", etc.). Students are to memorize their lines and are joined with a partner to begin an improvised story. The teacher may have to use herself as a partner to demonstrate the activity to the other students. Student # 1 says his line and the teacher plays along with the story by improvising the conversation with him for about a minute. After a minute, the teacher leaves "the stage" and points to Student # 2 who then enters "the stage" to say his line and engages in an improvised one minute conversation with Student # 1. Afterwards, Student # 1 leaves and prompts Student # 3 to enter the stage. It continues until all students have had a turn at speaking. This activity is good for upper intermediate and above levels.

d)   Theme-Based Scenes

Teachers can arrange students to act out a scene that focuses on a theme (Eg. cultural or historical points). If the theme of the week was appropriate table manners in North America, then students can act out what they've learned with regards to appropriate and inappropriate social behavior at the table during meals. Issues such as relationship conflicts, parenting, and other social contexts can be acted out as well.

e)   Story-Telling Face-Off

This activity works best at the advanced levels. A teacher provides a location, the main character, and a special circumstance for a story. All students in the classroom stand up. The teacher points to a student to begin a story based on the information provided. The student must continue speaking until the teacher points to another student to continue where the sentence is left off. The second student must continue speaking until a third student is pointed at to continue. This continues until a logical conclusion is reached or the teacher intercedes. A student who cannot continue a story is forced to sit down and whoever is standing is selected to continue. If the story continues too long, the teacher may force an ending but ideally whoever remains standing to tell the story becomes the winner.

Recommended Reading List

A. Listening & Speaking Reference Books

Anderson, Anne & Lynch, Tony. (1988). *Listening*. Oxford: Oxford University Press.

Richards, Jack C. & Rodgers, Theodore S. (2001). *Approaches and Methods in Language Teaching*, second edition. Cambridge: Cambridge University Press.

Stempleski, Susan & Tomalin, Barry. (1990). *Video In Action*. London: Prentice Hall

Ur, Penny. (1981). *Discussions That Work: Task-Centered Fluency Practice*. New York: Cambridge University Press.

B. Listening & Speaking Textbooks

Carver, Tina Kasloff & Fotinos, Sandra Douglas. (1998). *A Conversation Book 1*. New York: Prentice Hall Regents. (High Beginner)

Carver, Tina Kasloff & Fotinos, Sandra Douglas. (1998). *A Conversation Book 2*. New York: Prentice Hall Regents. (Intermediate)

Jones, Leo & Kimbrough, Victoria. (1987). *Great Ideas*. Cambridge: Cambridge University Press. (Intermediate)

Richards, Jack C., Bycina, David & Kisslinger, Ellen. (1995). *New Person to Person Book 1*. New York: Oxford University Press. (High Beginner)

Richards, Jack C., Bycina, David & Kisslinger, Ellen. (1996). *New Person to Person Book 2*. New York: Oxford University Press. (Intermediate)

Richards, Jack C. & Lesley, Tay. (2001). *New Interchange: Intro*. Cambridge: Cambridge University Press. (Beginner)

Richards, Jack C. with Hull, Jonathan & Proctor, Susan. (1997). *New Interchange 1* Cambridge: Cambridge University Press. (High Beginner)

Richards, Jack C. with Hull, Jonathan & Proctor, Susan. (1998). *New Interchange 2*. Cambridge: Cambridge University Press. (Low Intermediate)

McKay, Irene S. (1999). *Have Your Say!* Don Mills: Oxford University Press. (Intermediate)

C. Listening & Speaking Teaching Ideas

Cunningham, Helen & Kozakiewicz, Nina. (1992). *What Do People Really Say?* Vancouver: Vancouver Community College Press. (Guide & Video) (Advanced)

Jones, Hughie. (1998). *Talk It Up.* Vancouver: Vancouver Community College. (Advanced)

Nolasco, Rob & Arthur, Lois. (1987). *Conversation.* Oxford: Oxford University Press.

Tiittanen, Mike. (1998). *Brain Waves: Intermediate and Advanced Communication Activities.* Toronto: Oxford University Press. (Intermediate—Advanced)

Yorkey, Richard. (1985). *Talk-A-Tivities: Problem Solving and Puzzles for Pairs.* Reading: Addison-Wesley.

CHAPTER 18:

Teaching English for Academic Purposes—Cruising the Highway

The E.A.P Student

Here is an area of English that is at the forefront for students wishing to gain entry into English speaking post-secondary institutions: English for Academic Purposes (E.A.P.) or Academic English. Academic English prepares students for entry into higher educational institutions such as universities or colleges. It teaches them the necessary skills to succeed, such as study skills, analytical reading, learning how to research, writing academic reports and term papers, rules in referencing and plagiarism, speaking fluently, tackling common E.S.L. grammar trouble spots, and so forth in post-secondary institutions.

Who is your typical E.A.P. student? E.A.P. students will tend to have at least a 500 level score on the TOEFL exam and have a relatively high level of English proficiency. They may be able to read a Grade 8 level textbook with relatively little difficulty but they may face problems reading text books at higher levels. E.A.P. students also tend to make common E.S.L. grammar errors with articles, prepositions, gerunds, infinitives, and some verb tenses. Most E.A.P. students have attained a functional level of proficiency in practical uses outside the classroom but may need to sharpen their functional skills in reading, writing, listening and speaking in a more formal higher-level academic setting.

Success Skills

Most E.A.P. students, and E.S.L. students in general, may not have learned the good study skills that ease the path towards academic success. They may have learned study skills from their own native countries that are not suited to an English classroom. E.S.L. students exposed to the public school system of the West may have been taught study skills but didn't absorb them because of limitations in language proficiency. These success skills encompass eight different areas: time management, dictionary skills, memory techniques, strategies for note-taking, library skills, test-taking, and critical reading skills.

A. Time management

Successfully managing time by balancing school work, socializing time, studying outside of classes, and perhaps working or volunteering is a skill successful students have. Successful students know how to prioritize and tackle, rather than avoid, tasks that need to be done. On the other hand, unsuccessful students point to the biggest factor in their lack of success: *falling behind*. How do students avoid falling behind in their work? They have to realize that learning doesn't stop when the bell rings; they have to take personal responsibility for their learning by allotting a ratio of about one to two hours of study time for every hour of class time. Taking personal accountability for studying takes discipline and planning, which is what time management is all about.

A big weapon to help students manage their time is scheduling. Two great books for learning how to schedule are *Making Your Mark* by Lisa Fraser and *Keys to Success* by Carol Carter et al. Have students use schedules of various types (monthly, weekly, and daily) to give them a visual reference of how much

work needs to be done. Keeping
schedules will help students tread
water so they can prevent themselves from drowning in a sea of
homework and avoid the all-night
cramming sessions when it comes
down to the shark attacks (exam
time). When scheduling, students
should post on a wall all the impor-
tant semester dates on their monthly schedules to remind them of what's com-
ing. Weekly schedules can be filled in with the week's activities that include
study time, household chores, errands, and socializing. Students should be as
realistic as possible in their scheduling and in particular, arrange to have some
quiet time for themselves when nothing is deliberately being done. It's important to have some "unproductive time" to give the gerbil that's running the
wheel in the brain a chance to regenerate. A daily schedule is a list of reminders
of tasks that need to be done for the day. Students should prioritize these tasks
on levels of importance. Students can mark "A" for highly important tasks, "B"
for less important tasks and "C" for tasks that would be nice to get done but
can be left undone for a later time. If there are a lot of "C" tasks that aren't getting done, students have to learn to let go of the guilt and feel proud that the
essential "A"s have been completed.

Students should have a regularly scheduled time for quiet study. The ideal
place for study should be properly lit, have a comfortable temperature with
good air circulation, and be void of distractions. Regular study time is essential
in establishing the habit of reviewing lecture notes and making studying for a
test a quick review rather than a massive task that requires pulling in "all-
nighters". Students should avoid being near the strong temptation of a television when studying. Tell students to buy a set of blank video tapes and record
their favorite programs on a video machine for later watching. They can
reward themselves after they've completed their studying for the day by watching their beloved programs.

Students should also start projects as soon as they're assigned. Big projects
should be broken down into manageable chunks. Students should write down
their steps and do a little work on the project each day. Doing a little chunk
each day will allow students to put more quality into their work, whereas students who wait to finish projects on the last day tend to allow speed to over-
rule quality. It's important to communicate to students that they must
constantly be pro-active in their studying and that they have nobody to rely

on but themselves to ensure their academic progress. Many students, either E.S.L. or local, are unfamiliar with taking a self-leadership role and being proactive in their academic career. Students can also consolidate tasks by utilizing an answering machine to return calls at a later time, combine errands into one big trip, and do multiple activities where possible (such as folding the laundry while watching T.V., or reading a chapter in a textbook while waiting for the dryer to finish with the laundry). If students return all calls at a specified time and then find themselves conversing with a long-winded friend, they should learn the art of excusing themselves to end the long conversation by saying they need to get back to studying or need to do something.

The big enemy of time management is procrastination. Procrastination refers to the avoidance of doing an action by putting it off for a future time. There are many reasons (other than the common "laziness" reply) why people procrastinate. A good source that advises how to tackle procrastination can be read in the pamphlet, *Overcoming Procrastination* by the Board of Trustees of the University of Illinois. Procrastination may occur because of several reasons: people lack the planning ability or knowledge to do a job; the job isn't relevant in the student's world; the objective of the job isn't clear; the student feels apprehension at being judged by his performance; etc. Fortunately there are as many ways as reasons on how to combat this time robber. Students can be more consciously aware of when procrastination sets in and ask for help. Help can come from the instructor who can clarify details in what's required in a job, a counselor who can assist in anti-procrastination tips, or friends who may provide mental support. Much of procrastination's advances can be combated with the aforementioned time management techniques and knowing how to balance work from pleasure. Students should use reward as a motivating tool to accomplish tasks. They can do the most difficult job first on their agenda or they can sandwich it between two easy tasks to build momentum. Students can also use the power of the mind in creating a worst-case scenario if a task is not done and use the nightmare situation to push them to take action. People more often act on something to avoid pain than to feel pleasure.

B. Dictionary skills

Most E.S.L. students have not had instruction in the use of an English dictionary. Many rely on electronic bilingual dictionaries but teachers should encourage students to switch to using a good English dictionary, such as *Webster's Concise Dictionary* or *Funk & Wagnall's Standard Dictionary*. Some electronic dictionaries have been proven to have some inaccurate or confusing entries in the definition of words. Students should get some practice in how to read an

English dictionary in book form. Teachers can conduct activities that practice alphabetizing, deciphering abbreviations used in entries, syllable notation, interpreting pronunciation symbols, finding alternative word forms, etc. Teachers can reproduce a page from a dictionary onto a transparency and use it on an overhead projector to cover how to read dictionary entries.

C. Memory techniques

According to memory experts, there are certain techniques that students can use to make remembering things easier. One technique is making visual associations to places. For example, if a student needs to memorize a list of items, he can associate that list in a fictitious environment. such as in a house. If you needed to memorize a list of items to buy, you can imagine yourself walking into a house and seeing each item on the shopping list at various places around the house, regardless of its logical location. For example, imagine walking into a house and you see socks (item # 1 on the list) on the living room floor and a pair of jeans (item # 2) on the T.V. You can continue to enter each room of the house and see more items from the list at various locations. Pretty soon, you've placed all shopping items at their designated places in your imagination. Afterwards, you can go back and re-enter the house and try to recall where those items were located as you repeat your movements around the house. The environment doesn't have to be a house—it can be a scenic outdoor setting, a school, or any area real or imagined. People tend to remember things when they're associated with something that can be recalled more easily than by remembering the item by itself. You can even create surreal images from your shopping list, such as the pair of socks arguing with the pair of jeans. The more outrageous the image, the more memorable it'll stick in your mind.

Memorizing a speech can be done in the same manner by breaking down each part of a speech into visual associations of surreal images. If you had to prepare a speech to a group of executives about the financial state of your company, you would think of pre-planned surreal images that are associated with each sentence in your speech. After memorizing these surreal images, you would then be able to decipher the connection by thinking of them and successfully linking them with the real intended content of your speech. For example if part of your speech was to say, "The expansion of the marketing department is necessary to maintain growth", you could imagine an expanding balloon that's labeled "marketing" and see it floating away to meet a plant growing out of the ground with leaves that say "growth" on them. By imagining a scene, you can link up what you really intend to say to your audience.

D. Note-taking

Developing a good note-taking system is important because students tend to forget 80% of what was said in class after only 24 hours. The only way to counter this percentage is to develop an effective note-taking system that would help you review and retain information from lectures. Many students, E.S.L. and native English speakers alike may not have learned effective note-taking techniques. Being able to listen to a lecture in university or college and take relevant notes are key ingredients to academic success. A recommended method of note-taking was developed by Cornell University called the *Cornell System of Note-taking*. Some bookstores carry note-taking paper designed for this system called *Cornell paper* or *4R* paper (the "4 Rs: Record, Reduce, Recall, Review). In this chapter, we'll add an additional "R" for *reflect* after the *review* process to describe this note-taking technique. If you can't find Cornell paper, students can format their own paper under its method of design. It's a simple system to follow and essentially transforms your notes to being your review notes. Here's how it works:

1) Before class, prepare your notepaper by drawing a vertical line about 2-1/2 inches from the left edge of the paper. The wide area on the right will be where your notes will take place. The narrow area on the left is the recall column where summary notes from the adjacent side will be taken. The last page of your notes should have a horizontal line drawn about 2–3 inches from the bottom. This is the summary area where you can summarize the main points covered in the lecture writing 2–3 sentences. On each page, record the course name, date, and page number (example: *Page 2 of 4*) on the top right hand corner

See an example of Cornell note-taking paper below:

recall column	course, date, page number lecture notes
Summary (This section is for the last page of your notes.)	

2) Next, we come to the 5 steps: Record, Reduce, Recall, Review, and Reflect.

   a) Record:

     ➢ Record the main ideas of the lecture in the wide column of your paper using short telegraphic sentences.

     ➢ Be aware of the key transition words used to signal a lecture's organization.

     ➢ Leave space between ideas so additional information can be added.

     ➢ Leave a little more space between topics so additional information can be added.

     ➢ Develop a customized short-hand to enable you to write faster (eg. = example, imp = important, def = definition, with = w/, without = w/o, etc.)

     ➢ Notes can be organized under main ideas and related subtopics or details.

➢ Leave blank spaces if you can't keep up and get together after class with a class mate to consolidate your notes to fill in missing information.

➢ Write on one side of the page only

b) Reduce:

➢ Reduce notes into key words, formulas, and summary points in the recall column on the left side.

➢ You can anticipate possible themes or questions that may be asked on a test and write them in the recall column.

➢ The recall column will be your study notes, which will save you time from re-writing.

➢ Record a summary of the notes at the end in the summary box of your last page.

➢ Summarize your notes using 2–3 sentences.

c) Recall:

➢ To study, cover the right side of the paper comprising of the lecture notes and test yourself on the key words, formulas, and summary points in the left column.

➢ Recite the information out loud to maximize recall.

➢ Uncover your notes to check how accurate you were.

➢ This method of self-recitation is extremely effective in putting the information into long-term memory so that studying for an exam would be a matter of review rather than a monumental task.

d) Review:

➢ Review notes within 24 hours to maximize information retention.

➢ 80% of material not reviewed after 24 hours will tend to be forgotten.

e) Reflect:

➢ While looking at your notes, try to draw out opinions from them and reflect how the recorded information pertains to the course as a whole or to other courses.

➢ Ask yourself how you can apply this information in your life.

➢ Self-reflection prevents the information from being inert and soon forgotten.

3) Regularly reviewing your notes is key to retaining information. It's suggested that students spend some time every week to review their notes to enhance memory retention. The following illustration is an example of notes using the Cornell system. Note the use of short-hand in the notes. Students will have to develop a method of short-hand that will permit them to record lecture notes as quickly as possible.

<u>Teaching E.S.L.</u>

Why teach E.S.L.?	<u>Job Opportunities</u> overseas jobs → schools, gov't agencies, multinat'l co.s contracts, paid benefits (airfare, accomodat'n, health, vacat'n) big demand, highly mobile career local mkt → pvte schools, community centers, tutoring
How do I qualify?	<u>Qualificat'ns</u> undergrad degree preferred TESOL certificate (Teaching Engl to Spkers of Other Languages) experience → teaching, volunteer work, cultural

What's TESOL?	<u>TESOL Certificate</u>
	teaching grammar, reading, writing, listening & speaking, Engl for academic purposes
	teaching methodology/techniques
	job-ready certification
	p/t or f/t studies
	req'd practicum w/in-class prgm
	Global Excellence International, Ltd
	    ➢ in-class 1–2 month prgm
	    ➢ days, evenings, weekend class times
	    ➢ on-line prgm

<u>Summary</u>: You can be an E.S.L. teacher worldwide or locally with a TESOL certificate. Global Excellence International offers a TESOL program with convenient in-class or online programs.

Lecture Tips

☐ Students should read and skim their text before class to get a gist of what the lecture topic is going to be about.

☐ Skim texts by seeking content words in a passage (see Chapter 14 on content vs. function words).

☐ Previewing the text before a lecture will enable students to flag unfamiliar vocabulary that might be introduced by the professor.

☐ Students should arrive to class on time to find a seat at the front of the class. Sitting at the front enables students to hear what the professor is saying and provides fewer distractions from the lesson. In addition, statistics show that students sitting at the front of the class tend to get higher marks than students sitting at the back.

☐ The beginning of the lecture is important in getting information on what the lecture is going to be about and the main points that will be covered.

☐ The end part of the lecture is important as well. The professor will usually summarize the main points or try to quickly fill-in information that he didn't have time to elaborate, thus it's a good idea not to leave early or put away your notepad prematurely.

☐ Professors tend to give various clues to indicate important points such as using transition words, writing something on the board, using the overhead, showing videos or slides, repetition of explaining certain concepts, brief delays to examine lecture notes before presenting a point, summary statements, body gestures, high voice pitches, etc.

☐ Lectures are usually formatted with an introduction, body information, and a conclusion (much like an essay)

☐ Professors will provide key phrases to indicate main points such as, "*Today I will be discussing..., Let's look at the second..., On the other hand..., Finally,.... etc.*"

☐ In addition, students should be exposed to some language redundancies (babble) that may affect student understanding such as, "Okay, now, let's see where I put those notes,...oh here they are, it's been a busy day for me,...."

☐ Use a separate binder for each subject and divide the binders into sections: a section for lecture notes and a section for textbook notes

Teachers can slowly introduce note-taking by providing short and simple activities such as fill-in-the-blank exercises for a short presentation. Teachers can gradually progress to delivering short lectures to begin note-taking practice and gradually increase the lecture time with each session. Recorded lectures can be introduced to students after they feel comfortable with the short in-class lecture series. Be aware that lectures recorded on video are more favorable than the audio formats due to the presence of visual cues. Teachers should go over some of the visual clues instructors make, such as voice pitch changes, repeated gestures, body language, and so forth, when an important point is about to be presented or emphasized. If using audio lectures, teachers may have to stop the tape/CD at various points to check for student comprehension. Further exercises such as making summaries based on note-taking tasks can be assigned.

E.S.L. teachers can model various forms of note-taking by playing a recorded lecture, on video. The video can first be shown without sound so students can study the body language, and later it can be shown with sound. When the video is shown the second time around but with sound, students can be instructed to just listen and not take any notes. Afterwards, the teacher can play the video for a third time and simultaneously take notes on an overhead while students watch the video and the note-taking. By giving the students a manuscript of the lecture, they can discuss or ask questions about what was noted down or omitted. You can repeat this procedure with another video but have students take down notes on their own and then discreetly make a set for yourself on another transparency. Afterwards students can make comparisons with their notes to the set you wrote. Listening and note-taking a lecture can be a stressful experience for students so teachers can introduce relaxation methods that can be done before a lecture such as breathing and muscle relaxation exercises.

Textbook Note-Taking

Note-taking for textbooks follow a similar format to the lecture version. Textbook note-taking follows a S4R method: survey, read, write, recall and review. Students should spend about five minutes to survey the assigned reading and try to identify the general ideas that will be covered. Next students should read the passage and look for main ideas or subheadings that may be introduced by key phrases such as *"Another factor is....., Ultimately the goal of..., For example,...etc."* While students read, they should look for potential test questions. After reading their assignment, students can use the Cornell note paper to write down main ideas and details in the note column and the summarizing phrases, questions, and formulas in the recall column. A summary of the reading can be written on the bottom of the last page of the notes.

Afterwards, students can try to recall aloud the content of their notes by covering up their notes and taking cues from the recall column. Upon completion, students should regularly review their notes to retain the information from the reading.

E. Library Skills

If you're teaching students in a western country, take them to the local public library to apply for library cards and do a tour. Students need to know the library system to research information for assignments or for personal use. A pre-teaching session on library terms will be necessary before arranging a tour. Vocabulary related to the library should be taught such as *stacks, catalogue, periodical section, reserved books, audio-visual resources,* etc. prior to a visit. A discussion of censorship and freedom of information can be covered as well in a pre-teaching session. Librarians are usually happy to provide students with the necessary information on using the library. When students are familiar with library terms, it will be easier for them to absorb more information from a library tour.

F. Test-Taking Skills

Test anxiety is a major obstacle in academic success. Mental preparation will help students combat negative feelings that pop up when it comes time to facing the sharks. If students have undergone their time management techniques and have conducted regular reviews from their notes, test anxiety should be kept to a bare minimum. Inform students to prepare their materials (pen, pencil, eraser, notebook, student identification card, a watch, and any other essentials), eat well, and get plenty of sleep the night before a test. Have students practice positive visualization techniques that get them to imagine themselves writing the test and successfully doing well. Train students to create positive affirmations such as *"I've studied this material and I know it well. I'm fully prepared for what comes my way."* Positive mental images will create a positive attitude, which tends to produce positive results. Teachers can introduce relaxation strategies such as deep breathing and muscle relaxation exercises to help students reduce test anxiety.

Students should also realize that writing a test is only a fragment of their educational experience and that in the overall scheme of life, it doesn't reflect on their individual characters. Students should be reminded of this as all too often they pressurize themselves to the point where they believe utter devastation in life occurs if less than expected results come their way. Students should arrive about thirty minutes early so they have time to use the washroom, relax and mentally prepare themselves for the task to come. As soon as the exam begins, students should write down somewhere on the test any memory cues, formulas, facts, acronyms, or other notes that may be essential, in case they forget the information due to oncoming anxiety. Students should also utilize the full time allotted on tests and guess on any answers they don't know. Difficult questions should be skipped and done last to efficiently utilize time spent for questions that students know the answers to. Students should have a watch to keep track of the time allowed and pace themselves appropriately.

G. Critical Reading Skills

Reading and examining a passage to draw out relevant opinions and ideas is an essential skill in higher education. In addition to following the SQ3R method of reading as was described in Chapter 9, students should be introduced to critical reading skills. These skills involve aspects beyond inferential processing. A student with critical reading skills has the ability to interpret the message in a reading passage and *judge* its validity as a reliable or impartial source of information. How do students judge the merits of a passage? Teachers can practice looking at some articles by going through the following "Objective Reader's Checklist" of critical reading points.

OBJECTIVE READER'S CHECKLIST

A. Check for authorship and publication source.

- When was the article written? Is the time period relevant to the content of the writing?
- Does the publication have a good reputation? Is it from one of those "underground" publication companies?
- Does the writer have the qualified background to do the written work?

B. Check the article for objectivity.

- Does the article cover both sides of an argument? (pros and cons)
- Was any information left out?
- Were both sides of an argument judged with the same standards?
- Based on the information given in the article, do you have the same conclusion as the author?

C. Identify faulty arguments

- Are the conclusions based on weak support?

- Are inferences based on opinion rather than fact?
- Are unproven hypotheses assumed to be true?
- Are alternatives deliberately limited?
- Is there desperate questioning of the perceived truth?
- Is there an illogical conclusion that says one effect is pointed solely to one cause?

D. Look for opinion words.

- Look for words expressing opinion—*I feel, I think, In my opinion, I believe,…*
- Is support based on direct experience, observation, or third party accounts?

E. Look for words of emotion.

- Did the author use emotional words and phrases in his arguments?
- Do you recognize words that deliberately give false conclusions?
- Is the information written in a personal format?
- Are any stereotypes mentioned?
- Does the author deliberately use comparisons that have unmentioned conclusions?
- Does the author try to appeal to a vulnerable group that could be emotionally charged, such as striking workers?
- Is the information supportive of unrecognized authority figures?

To gain more practice in critical reading skills, teachers can distribute a passage to students for assessments based on the above checklist. Passages can be from existing material or self-produced by the teacher. Students can also be assigned to go to a library and pick out examples of passages or books that express propaganda, faulty reasoning, emotional appeals, etc and write an appraisal report. It's important for students to be able to judge a reading passage for its merit before assigning any value to its use in academic research.

Research Papers

See Chapter 10 on the world of essay writing on how to create well-written paragraphs and essays. Writing research papers is a branch of essay writing that involves extensive research on the student's part to answer a topic question. Research papers differ from essays in the sense that research papers are more scholarly and require the student to selectively gather facts and opinions from different sources to form a thesis to answer the topic question. In addition, research papers must follow certain formal writing guidelines for submission. Research writing should incorporate the following points:

1) Writer's Stance

   - The research paper is the work of the writer, thus the writer's position is generally expressed in the thesis statement.

2) Formality

   - Students shouldn't use the first or second person in traditional formal writing.

   - Avoid asking questions to the reader unless it's part of the introduction to indicate that the paper will be providing an answer to it or it's part of the conclusion as a question of reflection for contemplation purposes.

3) Reasoning

   - Students should ensure that their supportive sentences have a logical relationship to the ideas presented.

4) Style of Documentation

   - Students should check to see which style of documentation the professor expects.

   - Style of documentation can be A.P.A. (American Psychological Association), M.L.A. (Modern Language Association), Chicago Style, etc.

5) Document Design

   - Papers should be typed double-spaced on one side only and follow the format particular to the style of documentation (A.P.A., M.L.A., Chicago Style, etc.).

   - Fonts should be standard for all papers and not entirely typed in bold, italicized, or capital letters.

   - Papers should be fastened together with a paper-grip folder and not submitted as a pile of loose papers.

   - The student's name should be clearly visible on the front of the folder.

Unlike the outline of an essay, research papers have a different outline format. Compare the outlines below:

1) <u>Paragraph Outline:</u>

Topic Sentence (what this paragraph is going to discuss)

    A) Supporting Sentence

        i) Supporting Detail*

        ii) Supporting Detail*

    B) Supporting Sentence

        i) Supporting Detail*

        ii) Supporting Detail*

        iii) Supporting Detail*

    C) Supporting Sentence

        i) Supporting Detail*

        ii) Supporting Detail*

Concluding Sentence

* Supporting details may vary in number. Each capitalized letter introduces a different point that supports the topic sentence.

2) <u>Essay Outline:</u>

    I) Introductory Paragraph
      Thesis: _____(the topic + what you want to say about the topic)_____

    II) Body Paragraph One
        *

    III) Body Paragraph Two
        *

    IV) Body Paragraph Three
        *

    V) Concluding Paragraph**

    * See paragraph outline.

3) <u>Research Paper Outline</u>

    I) Introductory Paragraph

      A) "Hook"

      B) General information

      C) Thesis: __(the topic + what you want to say about the topic)__

II) Body Paragraphs

   Number of paragraphs will vary.*

   Organization may not be as structured as an essay.

   Answers and supports the thesis.

III) Concluding Paragraph

   A) Echoes the thesis

   B) Personal comment/evaluation/advice/quotation/anecdote/summary

   C) Final thought (irony/humor/statement of reflection, etc.)

   * See paragraph outline.

Due to the varying parameters of what a research paper calls for, the body paragraphs offer flexibility in terms of organization whereas the essay outline follows a more structured format for its body. Research papers may call for analyses in the pros and cons of a topic, the cause(s) and effect(s), and comparing and contrasting—all of which require flexibility in organization of body paragraphs. Below are some example outlines for certain types of research papers:

A. <u>Pro-Con Research Paper Outline</u>

Pro-Con Model 1	Pro-Con Model 2
INTRODUCTION	INTRODUCTION
PRO-position A. B. C.	CATEGORY 1 A. Pro B. Con
CON-position A. B. C.	CATEGORY 2 A. Pro B. Con
CONCLUSION	CATEGORY 3 A. Pro B. Con
	CONCLUSION

B. Cause and Effect Research Paper Outline

Cause & Effect Model 1	Cause & Effect Model 2
INTRODUCTION	INTRODUCTION
CAUSE # 1	CAUSE # 1
CAUSE # 2	EFFECT # 1
TRANSITION PARAGRAPH	CAUSE # 2
EFFECT # 1	EFFECT # 2
EFFECT # 2	CAUSE # 3
EFFECT # 3	EFFECT # 3
CONCLUSION	CONCLUSION

C. Comparison (finding similarities) and Contrast (finding differences) Research Paper Outline

Model 1	Model 2
INTRODUCTION	INTRODUCTION
SIMILARITIES	POINT # 1 A. Feature 1 B. Feature 2 C. Feature 3
DIFFERENCES	
CONCLUSION	
	POINT # 2 A. Feature 1 B. Feature 2 C. Feature 3
	POINT # 3 A. Feature 1 B. Feature 2 C. Feature 3
	CONCLUSION

Index Cards

When conducting research, students should be introduced to the world of 3"x5" or 5"x7" note cards. These cards help catalogue information sources to be later cited in the paper.

A. Bibliography Cards

On bibliography cards, students should write the following information:

➤   author's last name first and the first name; any editors or translators of the book

➤   title and subtitle of the book (and applicable edition number), article, or periodical (with volume and issue numbers)

➤   publishing information (city, publishing company and year of publication)

➤   library name and call number of the book for future reference on the student's part if needed

Bibliography card for a book.

> Sedgwick Library PD574.R87 L32 2003
>
> Jones, Mary. Cultural Diversity: Life in the Modern
> New York: Alpha Delta Press, 2003.

Bibliography card for a periodical.

> Main Library
>
> Smith, John. "Great Inventions Our Way."
> Technology Today 30 November 2003: 59-62.
>   (page numbers)
> (volume & number: none)

B. Note Cards

Carolyn M. Spencer and Beverly Arbon provide a good model for how to set up note cards for a research paper in their book, *Foundations of Writing.* They indicate that the following information should be recorded on note cards:

➤   the author's last name, year of publication, and page number in the top left corner

➤   a word to categorize the information in the top right corner

➤   the recorded information in the center of the card

Note card for a book.

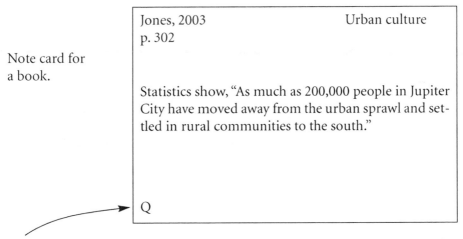

Jones, 2003   Urban culture
p. 302

Statistics show, "As much as 200,000 people in Jupiter City have moved away from the urban sprawl and settled in rural communities to the south."

Q

A signal at the bottom left corner should be made to indicate how the information was referenced (Q = quote, P = paraphrase, S = summary). Ensure that quotations have quotation marks surrounding the exact reference.

Plagiarism

Students doing research need to know that appropriate forms of acknowledging and citing the ideas of others are required in writing essays or research papers. It's imperative for teachers to communicate the importance of academic honesty to students. Students who come from countries where plagiarism is not considered a major crime will not be heard when they proclaim to administrators, *"I didn't know pirating was illegal!"* The word

"plagiarism" refers to the stealing of other people's ideas or words and using them as your own. In fact, the Latin root meaning of plagiarism is *"to kidnap"*. Universities and colleges have strict rules on plagiarism that can lead to possible failure in a course or expulsion from the school. Students, who cheat on tests, get other people to do their homework, or purchase readymade papers from the many different companies that sell them, can also face possible expulsion or failure in a course. To protect themselves from plagiarizing, students must learn how to properly cite information from sources (following the guidelines of the particular style of documentation) and use a system (such as using note cards) that helps them credit information used in their research.

The Art of Paraphrasing and Summarizing

When using information from printed sources, students must know how to paraphrase using synonyms and adopt their own sentence structure for expressing ideas. Simply using synonyms to paraphrase isn't good enough—students must change the sentence structure in their paraphrasing to avoid plagiarism. Teachers should provide plenty of practice in paraphrasing, summarizing, and making direct and indirect quotes in their writing classes.

Paraphrasing Examined

Teachers should model an example paraphrasing activity for students before they begin to try it themselves. A transparency of a passage can be put up on an overhead projector and a paraphrasing activity can be done simultaneously on the board for students to compare. After a couple of demonstrations, students can try some paraphrasing activities on their own. Here are some sequential steps for paraphrasing:

1. Read and fully understand a passage.
2. Look up unfamiliar words (note the synonyms).
3. Take notes or make a brief outline (don't write full sentences).
4. Begin re-writing the main ideas from memory (no peeking at the original passage).
5. Check for accuracy from the original passage and add any important information that was omitted in the re-writing.
6. Name the source. (Eg. Jones, 2003)

Summarizing Examined

The steps for summarizing are similar to those following paraphrasing. The only difference would be Step 3:

>   3.   *Using only a few words, write down the main ideas.*

A summary is shorter in length, omits the details and expresses only the main ideas or points. Teachers should model an example summarizing activity for students on the board using a transparency of a passage on the overhead projector. After a couple of demonstrations, students can try some summarizing on their own with newspapers, magazine articles or short stories.

The Art of Unity and Coherence

Academic writing demands two essential characteristics: coherence and unity. A piece of writing with good unity means that every sentence mainly discusses and is very closely related to the topic at hand whereas good coherence describes a piece of writing with sentences that flow smoothly with each other with good transitions and logical ordering.

Unity Examined

How do you achieve good unity in writing? Unity is achieved when all of the sentences work together to communicate the central idea. Unity should be achieved at the essay level and the paragraph level. Achieving unity in a paragraph requires all supporting sentences to give "power" to the topic sentence while unity in an essay requires all paragraphs to give "power" to the thesis of the paper. Writers should separate main ideas of differences from main ideas of similarity or group ideas of commonality together. For example, if the topic was to discuss the causes of cancer, you don't want to discuss the financial costs of fighting cancer because it would be unrelated to the central theme. On the other hand, if you were discussing smoking and breathing in second-hand smoke as cancer-causing factors, you can group them together because they are closely related to each other. Irrelevant sentences must be avoided.

Coherence Examined

Good coherence in writing means that sentences flow smoothly with each other and are presented in a logical order. Writing with coherence can be easily achieved by following the tips below:

a) Avoid short choppy sentences.

b) Alternate between using key nouns and pronouns in a paragraph.

c) Use transition signals to give smooth transition between ideas and support.

d) Arrange sentences in logical order.

Teaching Literature

How do you select literature that would be appropriate for your students? Barbara Gray-Richards lists in her book *Teaching English for Academic Purposes* some important factors teachers should consider in their selection of literature. There may be other factors involved that add to the list below but keep always keep in mind the perspective of the students when adding literature units in your academic curriculum.

A) Language
   - ❏ Teachers should avoid literature with archaic language or style.
   - ❏ Literature with difficult language structure would require too much class time in explaining them and too little class time in generating ideas for discussion.
   - ❏ Students appreciate literature more when the language is easily accessible to them.

B) Study Time
   - ❏ Teachers have to carefully weigh the amount of time in the course with the time it would take to study chosen pieces of literature.
   - ❏ Gray-Richards points out that students will tolerate a short piece of work that they don't like more than one that is longer in length.

C) Teacher's Personal Taste
   - ❏ Teachers should select material that they can be enthusiastic about and eventually communicate those feelings to students

D) Cultural Content
   - ❏ Teachers should select subject matter that helps students increase their cultural knowledge of their host country. The more the students learn about the host country, the more adaptable they can become with the effects of culture shock.

E) Plot and characters

    ❑ Students tend to enjoy and respond more to stories with a well-developed plot and strong characters; thus creating a deeper appreciation.

F) Literary Value

    ❑ Teachers should only choose works that have great merit when there is only a limited time to teach them.

Students should be exposed to the different classifications of English literature such as the novel, the short story, fiction, non-fiction, prose, and poetry. To teach fiction, students need to be pre-taught terminology related to it. Below are the elements of fiction that students should be introduced to:

1) Setting

- Refers to the time and place of the story.
- Teachers can discuss with students the relevance of the setting to the plot of the story.
- Activities that explore the story's setting can be devised to give further understanding of how it connects with the plot.

2) Plot

- Refers to the situations or chain of events in a story.
- Can be categorized as conflicts (man vs. man, man vs. society, man vs. himself, etc.).
- Resolutions of the plot generally expose the theme of the story.

3) Character

- Students should distinguish major and minor characters.
- Protagonist vs. Antagonist

4) Point of View

- First person: The author assumes the role of one of the characters in the story and uses the pronoun, "I".
- Limited Omniscient Point of View: A narrative that allows the author to use the third pronoun of "he" or "she" to tell the story through the eyes of one of the characters.
- Omniscient Point of View: The author tells the story through the eyes of several characters and makes comments on their behaviors and their implications to the story.

- Objective Point of View: The thoughts and emotions of characters aren't revealed; thus the story is devoid of emotion.

5) Irony
- Refers to two contrasting elements that display contradiction.
- Irony can be verbal or situational.

6) Tone and Mood
- Sentence structure, figures of speech, and diction all play a part in studying the writing style and attitude of the author towards the reader or the characters.

7) Theme
- The main idea of the story.
- Can be deduced by studying the central conflict of the story and making a generalization.

8) Symbols and Motifs
- Symbols reinforce meaning in a story.
- Motifs are recurring symbols, phrases, or images.
- The concept of inferring a deeper meaning to a symbol should be practiced with students.
- Since symbols can be highly cultural, students may have problems interpreting their meanings.
- Symbols are generally recognizable due to emphasis by the author.
- Example symbolism: white = purity, black or darkness = death, dove = peace, island = isolation, etc.

Teachers should introduce these literary terms with a simple short story with clear-cut and easy-to-understand elements of fiction. By modeling these literary terms with a simple short story, students will have a base to further build their understanding of literature with future more complex works.

Before presenting a piece of literature, teachers should pre-teach any cultural aspects associated with it. For example, if students were to study the short Canadian story, *The Sweater* by Roch Carrier, students would need to understand the cultural and historical details of life in Quebec, Canada in the 1940s to 1950s and Canada's love of hockey to appreciate the story's plot.

Teaching Poetry

Since learning poetry is on the bottom of many students' lists of favorite literature pieces to study, teachers have to take extra care in the amount of time spent and the selection of poetry in the classroom. Teachers should choose poems that have readily accessible themes, strong rhythms, and understandable language. Studying poetry encompasses a range of terminology covering various devices of sound. These terms can be overwhelming for learners. As a result, it's best to limit poetry analysis to a maximum of three terms per poem from the following list:

Devices of Sound

1) Alliteration
2) Assonance
3) Onomatopoeia
4) Rhyme
5) Rhythm
6) Onomatopoeia
7) Oxymoron
8) Paradox
9) Personification
10) Simile
11) Symbol

Figures of Speech

1) Allusion
2) Euphemism
3) Hyperbole
4) Imagery
5) Metaphor

Poems can be presented as dramatic readings that require them to be read aloud by the teacher, chorally by the class or by students in small groups. Since most poems are written to stir an emotional response, teachers can try to elicit any feelings students may have from hearing a dramatic reading and explore the deep meaning behind poems.

References

Gray-Richards, Barbara J. (1993). *Teaching English for Academic Purposes.* Vancouver: Vancouver Community College.

Spencer, Carolyn & Arbon, Beverly. (1996) *Foundations of Writing.* Lincolnwood: National Textbook Company.

Recommended Reading List

A. English for Academic Purposes Reference Books

Blue, George M. (Ed.), Milton, James (Ed.) & Saville, Jane (Ed.). (2000). *Assessing English for Academic Purposes.* New York: Peter Lang Publishing.

Board of Trustees of the University of Illinois. "Overcoming Procrastination" Pamphlet. (1984).

Carter, Carol, Bishop, Joyce, Kravits, Sarah Lyman & Bucher, Richard D. (2002). *Keys to Success.*, 4th edition. New Jersey: Prentice Hall.

Fraser, Lisa. (1996). *Making Your Mark*, 5th edition. Port Perry: LDI Publishing.

Glendinning, Eric H. & Holmström, Beverly. (1992). *Study Reading: A Course in Reading Skills for Academic Purposes.* Cambridge: Cambridge University Press.

Gray-Richards, Barbara J. (1993). *Teaching English for Academic Purposes.* Vancouver: Vancouver Community College.

Hacker, Diana. (2001). *A Canadian Writer's Reference.* Ontario: Nelson Thomson Learning.

Jordon, Robert R. (1997). *English for Academic Purposes: A Guide and Resource Book for Teachers.* Cambridge: Cambridge University Press.

McKellar, H.D. (1972). *Teaching the Short Story.* Agincourt: The Book Society of Canada.

Oshima, Alice & Hogue, Ann. (1999). *Writing Academic English*, 3rd edition. New York: Pearson Education.

Spack, Ruth. (1985). "Literature, Reading, Writing, and E.S.L.: Bridging the Gap." *TESOL Quarterly.* 19 (4): 703-725.

Spencer, Carolyn & Arbon, Beverly. (1996) *Foundations of Writing.* Lincolnwood: National Textbook Company.

CHAPTER 19:

Testing and Test Designs—The Car Pool Lane

The first test that almost all E.S.L. students encounter, other than asking "Where is the bathroom?", is an English assessment test to determine the appropriate study program they should enroll in. Other than placement tests, what kind of tests can teachers develop in order to burden the lives of their students? Okay, that was a joke. First, we need to determine what the goal of the teacher is in administering a test. If the test is in the middle of a course, you'll be writing a progress test. If the test is at the end of the term, you'll be writing an achievement test. There are 4 points to consider when test designing: the content, the validity of the test; the reliability in testing the student's knowledge of the taught material; and the practicality of administering the test in terms of how it is to be marked by the teacher.

Content Validity

Throughout your teaching career, there may be times when your grammar students complain that they should be upgraded to the next grammar level because the course content is too easy. Rather than sneer at the students and accuse them of being over-confident for their own good, consider alternative test formats to challenge their knowledge. Indeed, some grammar textbooks with ready-made tests such as fill-in-the-blank exercises can be considered easy for some students and not very challenging. In order to add a twist of variety, you can change a written grammar test to become an oral grammar test. Oral grammar tests lean towards a speaking and listening test except with more emphasis on accuracy.

For a midterm exam, I used cued dialogues that students had to follow by making correct questions and answers based on the cues. For example, a cued dialogue for a high beginner class may follow the format of a 2-person dialogue (Student A and Student B) as illustrated in Figure 19.1 and Figure 19.2. In order to expedite the evaluation process, you can also create 3-person cued dialogues as well. When marking a test involving 2 students, you'll need 3 copies of the dialogue (1 for yourself and 1 each for the 2 participants). Pre-plan how many marks you will give on each conversation point. On the teacher's copy, place a clear transparency over the cued dialogue and use an overhead pen to make notations on points that were said incorrectly by the participants. At the end of the dialogue, tally up the errors and calculate the total scores for each student. Testing and marking is done quickly and efficiently as soon as the dialogue is over. Afterwards you can just erase the notations from the transparency with a wet and dry rag, have time to sip your coffee, and repeat the process for the next pair of students.—P.D.

Figure 19.1: Example oral grammar test for high beginners (Sample 1)

MODEL 1: High Beginners' Oral Grammar Test

STUDENT A

STUDENT B

1) Hi. (How are you?)*

2) [answer] + (How are you?)*

3) [answer] + simple present - habit (yes/no) question

4) [answer] + simple present (information) question

5) [answer] + simple present - non-action

6) [answer] + present progressive - future (yes/no) question

7) [answer] + present progressive future (information) question

8) [answer] + present progressive (information) question

9) [answer] + simple past (yes/no) question

10) [answer] + simple past (information) question

11) [answer] + simple past (information) question

12) [answer] + simple past (yes/no) question

13) [answer] + "I'm thirsty _____"

14) Suggestion

15) [answer] + Direct and Indirect Object Sentence

16) Repeat sentence with Direct and Indirect Object Pronouns

* *Use another sentence with the same meaning as "How are you?"*

Figure 19.2: Example oral grammar test for high beginners (Sample 2)

MODEL 2: High Beginners' Oral Grammar Test

STUDENT A

STUDENT B

1) Hi. (How are you?)*

2) [answer] + (How are you?)*

3) [answer] + simple present (information) question

4) [answer] + simple present (yes/no) question

5) [answer] + simple present - habit (yes/no) question

6) [answer] + present progressive - in progress now (yes/no) question

7) [answer] + _What + NOUN_ question

8) [answer] + _Whose_ question

9) [answer] + simple past (yes/no) question

10) [answer] + simple past (information) question

11) [answer] + simple past (information) question

12) [answer] + simple past (yes/no) question

13) [answer] + "I feel _____ "

14) Suggestion

15) [answer] + Direct and Indirect Object Sentence

16) Repeat sentence with Direct and Indirect Object Pronouns

* _Use another sentence with the same meaning as "How are you?"_

Test Reliability

How can teachers ensure that their tests are indicative of student performance? Sometimes a student may earn a poor mark on a test because he/she didn't understand the written instructions. You must ensure that students are familiar with the wording of common instructions given in textbooks and tests. Do students know what parentheses are? Do they know what "Fill in the gaps" or "Circle the correct word" mean? Do they know what "Edit the following passage" entails? Any test being made should have the same consistent instructions that students have been familiar with throughout the course. You also have to be careful with the wording of the instructions. The longer the instructions are written, the more confusing it may be for students to understand, so make sure that instructions are short and concise.

Test Practicality

The most time-consuming test to mark for teachers is the writing test. You will find yourself spending a lot of time marking compositions, especially when you have a large class. In-class assignments can take advantage of the peer-editing process, but when you have to mark compositions that involve several paragraphs for each, expect to quickly say goodbye to your weekend with marking if you have a class of 20 students. In the past, I (Pinky) have spent 4 hours marking essays of 800 words each written by a mere 8 students.

There is a variety of test formats you can consider. Below is an overview of some common test questions; however don't limit yourself to the list below. Testing can hold a lot of creativity.

Common Test Questions

A.   Matching Exercises

Match the words in column A with the definitions in column B. You have 2 minutes to complete this task.

A	B
aid (verb)	to be bashful
shy	to have an effect
quit	to help
influence	chief element
principle	to stop a process

Put the two parts of a sentence together by matching column A with column B. You have 1 minute to complete this task.

1. John flew	a. a delicious chocolate cake.
2. Cheryl made	b. all night and kept me awake.
3. The dog barked	c. back home to visit his mother.
4. The repairman fixed	d. 2 feet in a month.
5. School finished	e. early because many teachers were sick.
6. The flower grew	f. my car yesterday.

B.   Guided Word Choice

Insert the correct word from the list below to complete the passage.

Shirley _____ home late last night and _____ Frank _____ the couch. She asked him, "_____ you wash the dishes in the sink?". He replied, "_____, and I _____ the house too."

vacuumed   no   arrived   on   did   saw

C.   Fill-In-The-Blanks

Complete the sentences below by inserting an appropriate word.

I'd _____ teach E.S.L. than Math.
Answer: rather

*Instructions need to be clear as more than one answer may be possible.

I think _____ English is _____ than _____ Math.
Possible answer: teaching, better, teaching

D.   Word form

Provide the correct form for the word in parentheses.

He spent years studying to be a _____
                                (geography)

E.   Multiple Choice

Choose the word or phrase which best completes each sentence.

I _____ love to travel and teach E.S.L. abroad.
a) am   b) can   c) would   d) will

F.   True-False

Circle "T" for true or "F" for false for the following statements based on the story you have read.

Norman went to Paris before he studied at the University of Alberta.   T   F

G.   Sentence Alteration

Add the given words in parentheses to each sentence.

She loves children, but she craves for solitude. (Although….)
Answer: Although she loves children, she craves for solitude.

Change the following sentences so that they describe the <u>past</u>.

He is learning to teach English while he is living in Vancouver.
Possible answer: He learned to teach English while he lived in Vancouver.

Rearrange the words to make a complete sentence:

TESOL / at / pace / You / your / can / study / Certificate / a / pace / for
Answer: You can study for a TESOL Certificate at your own pace.

Create a sentence by using the given words and adding words of your own.

ran / dog / Although / the
Possible answer: Although the dog ran away, Sally kept her spirits up.

H.   Editing Exercises

Cross out the incorrect word:

She is goes shopping in the mornings.

Re-write the sentence to make it grammatically correct.

Bob and Martha are eat dinner in front of the T.V. every night.

Correct this composition. There are twenty mistakes.

[Teachers would create a short story with 20 grammar mistakes]

I.   Pictures Labeling

Write the correct word under each picture.

Teaching Aids: drawings of objects on paper

J.   Word Categorization

Arrange the following words under the correct category: *fox, snow, rain, statistics,* donkey, bull, history, fog, biology

Subjects	Animals	Weather
history	donkey	snow
biology	bull	fog
statistics	fox	rain

Marking Criteria

Since marking students' work can demand a considerable amount of energy, you have to decide what criteria you're going to establish and follow before you begin the task. Do you give half marks or only full marks? If a small word is omitted in a student's answer, do you mark the entire answer wrong, deduct a half mark, or mark it correct and give a warning not to do it again? The most-time consuming marking task E.S.L. teachers will encounter is correcting writing-homework/tests. When marking student writing, you can refer to Chapter 10 for a list of marking symbols. To cut down the time consumption of marking writing tests, teachers can deduct marks for only certain errors made that students have previously been taught and made aware of such as run-on sentences or sentence fragments. Teachers can also focus their mark distribution primarily on content and organization rather than grammar structure in student writing. The more specific the criteria, the more efficient your marking becomes.

> Always remember to give some kind of positive feedback when correcting tests or assignments. Students need continual encouragement and an excess of negative feedback will only encumber their learning process.

There are 2 methods of distributing marks on tests: positive marking and negative marking. Positive marking gives marks to correct answers only. Negative marking gives marks to correct answers but deducts marks for incorrect ones (omitted answers are not penalized). The quicker and better method is positive marking, as the negative one usually requires more calculation effort on your part. Since E.S.L. teachers don't specialize in math and time is precious to them, it'll be more convenient to choose the positive marking technique. In addition, positive marking encourages E.S.L. students to take more risk in learning the language and experimenting with their knowledge since they know they won't be penalized for errors. Below are a student's answers to an exercise. Note the differences in positive marking versus negative marking.

1. I <u>went</u> to school yesterday. (correct)
2. John <u>fly</u> kites everyday. (incorrect)
3. The equipment <u>are</u> in the room. (incorrect)
4. We <u>were studying</u> last night when the phone <u>rang</u>. (correct)
5. Whose pen <u>is it</u>? (correct)

6. They _____ to the park. (omission)

7. Where <u>go</u> he? (incorrect)

8. Do you often <u>come</u> here? (correct)

9. When does the train <u>arrive</u>? (correct)

10. <u>Can</u> you swim? (correct)

Positive marking: This exercise would have a mark of 6/10
Negative marking: This exercise would have a mark of 3/10

Oral Evaluations

Oral testing for conversation classes require careful time keeping. All too often, presentations become too long and before you know it, the class goes into overtime because there are still some students who have yet to have their turn on stage and you were too generous in giving time to the earlier presentations. Make sure time limits are strictly adhered to so testing can be completed in one day. For general oral presentations, evaluations should cover all aspects of the speaking process in terms of organization, content and delivery. Here is an example evaluation grid that may be used for all types of oral presentations in conversation classes.

Oral Presentation Evaluation

Name:

Topic: Presentation Time:

1—poor   2—needs improvement   3—fair   4—good   5—excellent

Content	1	2	3	4	5
Introduction					
Is there a "hook" to pique interest?					
Is there appropriate background information?					
Is there a thesis presented?					
Body of Speech					
Is the information in logical order?					
Is the material informative?					
Is the material substantive?					
Conclusion					
Is there a summary?					
Is there a prediction, a recommendation, a solution?					
Delivery					
Is it a suitable topic?					
Is the voice loud and clear?					
Is the speech delivered at a good pace?					
How is the eye contact?					
Is the posture/body language appropriate?					
Does the speaker project enthusiasm?					
How is the speaker's: pronunciation?					
fluency?					
grammar?					
Are there any props and visuals?					
Is the speech within the allowable time limit?					

TOTAL

95

Comments:

All in all, the primary considerations when teachers design tests should be in the relevant content, the validity of the test design in its content, the reliability in testing the student's receptive skills, and the practicality of administering the tests in terms of the amount of time required to mark them all. Since the teacher has control over testing of content material, he also has the freedom to be creative in his testing techniques. Provide students sufficient time to prepare for an upcoming test and warn them on what topics are going to be covered. The more guided information you provide students on what to expect on a test, the more students will appreciate your fairness and be able to study more efficiently. Language learning encompasses a vast area and students need to know what they should be doing on their part when it comes time for evaluations.

Recommended Reading List

Testing Resources

Folse, Keith S. et al. (2000). *100 Clear Grammar Tests: Reproducible Grammar Tests for Beginning to Intermediate E.S.L./E.F.L. Classes.* Ann Arbor: University of Michigan Press.

Jacobs, Holly. (1981). *Testing E.S.L. Composition: A Practical Approach.* Rowley: Newbury House Pub.

Lieu, Mark Wade. (2001). *Test Bank for Understanding and Using English Grammar*, 3rd edition. New York: Pearson Education.

CHAPTER 20:

Multimedia and Teaching Resources— Accelerating Speed

Many years ago, when I (R.R.) was a high school student in Europe, the only medium used in teaching was a blackboard and dusty white chalk. As a kid, it was an honour to be asked to clean the brushes. We have come a long way! Media is the plural form of medium. How do we define media in language teaching? Media in language teaching is very inclusive; we usually think of the technological innovations, the various aids in audiovisuals and mechanical gadgets. Let's not over-look the teacher-made non-mechanical aids and props that we use in daily life. Have you ever watched kids unwrap their presents at Christmas? They certainly liked the mechanical toys; however, it was the boxes in which these toys were packaged in that initially stimulated the children and lead to hours of fantasy play. Sometimes the least expensive items command more attention than the ones bought at a premium price.

The range of classroom media is indeed very large and ever expanding as technology presents us with new advances, such as computer-assisted instruction, interactive video and satellite transmission. Language teachers incorporate this technology into their repertoire of aids. It may not always be possible to use the latest gadgets that are on the market and we sometimes improvise with cereal boxes and hand puppets. Whiteboards have replaced blackboards and you may see chalk as archaic as the 8-track cassette. There are numerous media utilized in the classroom but the basic modern tool is still the whiteboard and whiteboard markers. If one day you or someone else accidentally marked your whiteboard with a permanent felt marker, don't despair. Simply take one of your whiteboard markers and mark over the offending permanent mark. Afterwards, you should be able to erase the permanent mark off the board.

Photocopy Machines

You will likely find yourself engaged in battles with the photocopy machine at various times throughout your teaching career. Paper jams are all too common in these battles and accumulated experience will be your best teacher in unjamming your paper. Since machines range in make and models, paper jams can happen for a variety of reasons; thus there's no hard and fast formula here. Try to find a mentor who can help you with operating the photocopy machine and ask him/her the basics in troubleshooting paper jams for the particular machine you will be using. Try to make double-sided copies to save on paper; students will appreciate the lower paper volume in their notebooks. If you have a machine that tends to jam when copying double-sides, you can "win" this particular battle by having the machine do one-sided copies on both sides of your paper. How? You take your completed one-sided copies, flip them over to expose the blank side, and put them back in the paper compartment. You may have to experiment with the flipping part to ensure you have the correct orientation when you load up the paper compartment. Put the second page on the glass surface of the machine and continue to make another "one-sided" copy. Now you have double-sided copies made with the one-sided copy mode.

If you are making photocopies of exercises for your class but you wish to retain an original copy for yourself, you can take a big yellow highlighter pen and mark originals with a big "M" on it to indicate that it's the master copy. Ink from a yellow highlighter pen will not show up in photocopies. If you are making notes for reference, you can color-code them for your students by photocopying reference notes with one paper color and exercise sheets on another paper color. You can experiment with different paper colors (if your school has an assortment of them) to see which works best for your curriculum. Color-coding your handouts is also helpful for students to organize their binders.

Teaching Aids

Teaching aids can be categorized as technical or non-technical. Let's look at a list of some possible material you may find yourself using in your lessons:

<u>Non-technical</u>

Black boards

Whiteboards

Magnetic boards

Bulletin boards

Card games

Index cards

Menus

Charts

Maps

Board games

Newspapers/magazines

Puppets, dolls

Miscellaneous role-play props

Art work

Photos

Cartoons

Pamphlets and flyers

Flashcards

Maps

Game boards

Posters

Scrolls

Mounted pictures

Grocery containers

Clothing items

<u>Technical</u>

Record player

Tape cassette player/recorder

CD player/recorder

Video cassette player/recorder

DVD player

Radio

Television

Computer printer

Tachistiscope **

Filmstrip

Film projector

Slide projector

Overhead projector

Opaque projector

Computer

Computer software

Language masters

Photocopy machine

** A tachistiscope is a projector that shows words on a screen for short periods of time; thus forcing students to read the words as quickly as possible. The timing is pre-set by the teacher. This machine assists students in improving their reading speed.

You may not use all of the equipment listed above or the school you're working at may not even supply them at all. The most common machines you'll likely encounter at language schools will be the overhead projector, the CD/tape cassette player and recorder, the television, the DVD player, the VCR player, and computers.

Overhead Projector

When using the overhead projector, ensure that you have plenty of cord length and have laid out the cord in such a way that you don't end up tripping over it when you're reaching for the next overhead transparency at a table. There are several key points to keep in mind when designing overhead transparencies. If you have access to a photocopy machine and you wish to make a transparency from a typed-up page, it's best to lay out the copying in a horizontal format (landscape orientation) for maximum viewing. The horizontal format makes writing easier to read since the vertical format prohibits the viewing of the bottom fourth of the sheet without moving the sheet, due to the overhead's square-shaped glass stage. (See Figure 20.1). You should also make sure that you buy the right type of transparencies. There are two kinds of transparencies: those that can withstand high temperatures and thus are suited for photocopy machines and those that are strictly for writing with transparency pens. Make sure you don't put in a transparency made for just writing into a copy machine, unless you want melted plastic inside your copier.

Figure 20.1

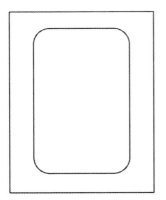

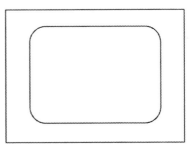

Horizontal transparency with a good view

Vertical transparency with limited view.

If you are presenting a transparency page, expose the information a little at a time by blocking out part of it with a piece of paper. By only exposing the information that's being discussed at hand, you will retain the student's attention more to what's being discussed rather than be ignored because students are busy reading or copying what they see on the overhead.

Dynamic overhead transparencies can have diagrams, charts, graphs, clip art, and other visuals that can assist in your teaching. If you're not using the transparency for class notes but for introducing ideas or concepts, make each sheet express one idea or it will look cluttered if you have too many ideas to explain at once. Transparencies can have key words, phrases or visual clues to introduce headings and subheadings. Font and images should be large enough for the person in the back of the class to see.

The most common complaint with overhead transparencies is lack of clarity. Viewers may complain that the transparency is blocked out by the instructor who's not paying attention to see whether the transparency is viewable; information is printed with letters that are too small and cluttered; the image on the transparency isn't centered, the writing is too light to see clearly; the projector is out of focus; or the transparency is put away too quickly for viewers to read. If you're using the overhead for the first time, allow yourself some time to familiarize yourself with its functions and applications. As you become more comfortable with the overhead, you'll soon master this valuable teaching tool.

Figure 20.2

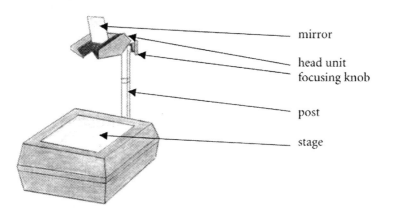

mirror

head unit
focusing knob

post

stage

The mirror of an overhead projector allows the image to be moved up or down on a screen. The focus knob sharpens the image. The stage is the glass area where transparencies are placed. On either side of the stage area there should be stage release buttons, that when pressed simultaneously, allows the stage to be opened so you can access the interior for maintenance (such as changing the light bulb). The overhead projector quickly gets hot when you start running it so ensure the interior fan is working properly and the air vents are unobstructed.

"Captain Video"

Videos in a classroom are great tools for teaching oral skills at all levels, particularly the lower ones. Videos are powerful in presenting contextual language for lower levels and great for advanced students in note-taking practice when preparing for university lectures. When choosing a video segment, keep in mind that the material should have a wide appeal for everyone watching; its length is between 30 seconds and five minutes (rarely more than ten minutes); the language is accessible to viewers; and unfamiliar vocabulary and background information have been introduced.

For great ideas on showing videos in the classroom, read *Video in Action* by Susan Stempleski and Barry Tomalin. Videos are great tools for the classroom and many students love the opportunity to practice their listening skills with them. Here are some basic techniques for showing videos in a classroom:

1) Pausing
   - ➢ Teachers can pause the video at strategic places of a scene and have students guess what is going to be said next and then play back the scene to compare.
   - ➢ Teachers can use this function to ask concept questions to check for the student understanding.
   - ➢ Teachers can pause the video at points showing particular facial expressions from the characters and have students guess what the characters are feeling or thinking.

2) Mixed-Up Scenes
   - ➢ If you have a DVD player, teachers can show scenes out of sequence for students to arrange in the correct chronological order.

3) Audio on/picture on
   - ➢ Teachers can give students a set of comprehensive questions before a clip and they are to try to answer them after the viewing.
   - ➢ Teachers can present some vocabulary items that are seen in the clip and students are to answer questions on its appearance, location, condition, and so forth afterwards.

> Teachers can present a particular scene from a video and students are assembled in small groups to predict and act out a conclusion from it. After presentations, teachers can show the students the conclusion of what really happened in the video for comparison.

4) Audio off/picture on

> Teachers can use the pause button on the video machine to stop the clip at strategic scenes to obtain student feedback on what's going to happen next or what was said.

> Students can also be asked to predict or guess the words that were spoken by the characters by referring to visual clues in the video; afterwards the teacher can rewind the segment and view it with the sound on to compare with the student responses.

> Teachers should choose short scenes that have obvious visual clues to what is being said in the clip and assign students to develop story lines or screen plays for comparison afterwards.

Video Sources

Most major publishing houses sell videos designed for E.S.L. teaching. Permission from local distributors or television networks must be granted for use of commercially-produced videos in the class but you may find some video sources such as government sponsored film boards, government agencies or community media outlets that generally waive copyright if their videos are used in the classroom (generally for public institutions). Video clips can be recorded from T.V. commercials, T.V. shows, weather reports, general interest stories from a newscast, game shows, talk shows, etc.

The National Film Board of Canada has a catalogue of videos that are cleared for classroom use. Check out their website: www.nfb.ca/e/ to request a catalogue.

Some of the movies I've incorporated into E.S.L. lessons are: *Indiana Jones and the Temple of Doom* (introductory segment only), *Jumanji*, *Mrs. Doubtfire*, *The Wrong Trousers* (animation), and *A Close Shave* (animation).—P.D.

Language Masters

Language masters are recording machines that come with long cards that have a magnetic strip on one side. These machines slowly swipe a card's magnetic strip which holds whatever is recorded or played on the card. A variety of small group activities can be conducted with language masters. For example, a vocabulary activity can be conducted whereby a teacher provides small groups with blank language master cards with a picture attached to each one. Groups would have to come up with the name of each item and record a sentence with it on the language master card. Recorded cards can be exchanged with other groups to check for accuracy. Pronunciation listening activities can be conducted with pre-recorded target sounds on the cards. Students would listen to the cards and circle the sounds they hear from a multiple-choice worksheet provided by the teacher. Grammar activities such as sentence de-scrambling can be done as well. Teachers can record scrambled sentences on cards for students to playback and record the unscrambled versions of them.

CDs and Tapes

Many E.S.L. books come with accompanying CDs or cassette tapes. Since the audio format lack visual cues needed in assisting listening, tasks based on them can be challenging. If you have a choice between choosing a CD or a tape cassette to accompany a textbook package, choose the CD format. It's easier to line up specified playback points on a CD and repeat playbacks are easier to manage than with a tape.

There are a variety of uses for CDs and tapes other than those presented in textbook/audio learning programs. Listening exercises involving music can be conducted with your students. Choose a popular English song students would probably be familiar with and create a worksheet with its lyrics on them. On the worksheet, omit some of the words so that students would have to listen to the song and decipher what the missing words are in the lyrics. Teachers can pre-teach useful vocabulary related to song writing such as *chorus, ballad, solo, duet, etc.* Students tend to enjoy this type of activity as it offers them a unique listening challenge. Ensure the songs have easily accessible language so students can clearly hear what's being sung. If you have a class of enthusiastic music-loving students, you can assign them in small groups to do a song-writing task. Teachers can facilitate this song-writing task by selecting and playing karaoke music that would accompany their songs and also by modeling a simple song to them so they have an idea of how to design and sing their own songs. This lyric writing task is challenging in getting the students to devise the correct rhythm and stress in their songs. Class performances can be done at the end of the week.

Recorded radio plays can also add variety to listening lessons (check copyright restrictions on them). Advanced classes would enjoy the challenge of listening to radio plays and then having their session interrupted with discussion exercises on what's going to happen in the plot. Later, small groups can get together to produce and record their own radio plays in class.

Recommended Reading

Stempleski, Susan & Tomalin, Barry. (1990). *Video In Action*. Hertfordshire: Prentice Hall Europe.

CHAPTER 21:

Fun E.S.L.—Heading for the Sunset

You've finally reached the final stretch of this life-altering book. Now that you have a good grasp on how to teach E.S.L., you can use your creative mind to create and incorporate the fun side of teaching. Adding fun to any academic program is the key in retaining student interest and motivation. How do you add fun to E.S.L. learning? Doing all kinds of supplemental activities outside of assigned textbooks is essential in the learning process. Students who study and do activities strictly from their textbooks will become bored as anyone would from being forced to do the mundane. Imagine yourself as a student coming to class and knowing daily lessons are going to lack stimulation because your teacher never strays from doing things beyond the textbook? Award-winning American public school teacher, Ron Clark, integrates his lessons by creating songs for students to sing in class and use as reference when studying. This great teacher from North Carolina developed unique ways to help motivate and guide students who had little interest in learning. Check out his great book, *The Essential 55* for tips on classroom management. By making your lesson plans fun for students, you will make the classroom environment more conducive to effective language learning.

Songs

If you think you have a bad singing voice, you'll have to overcome your fear of crooning to introduce music as a wonderful second-language teaching tool. Don't shy away from the useful tool of songs. Singing is a great way to learn the intonation and rhythm of English speech. The "music" of English speech follows certain patterns and can be quite useful in its study. Furthermore, the content of songs can also help students remember whatever they need to remember at the time when the lyrics are written. You can write a short song that describes how to use articles or other grammar points. Songs can be made into E.S.L. ballads or jazz chants. Jazz chants are simple melodies with a varying number of syllables that may be intonated with singing notes. The lyrics are usually simple sentences or phrases with or without rhymes and sung as a chant. You'll note that these chants usually have nothing to do with "jazz", however they're commonly referred to as jazz chants. Jazz chants are often sung with a rhythmic clapping of the hands as if you were doing a peaceful political demonstration. Although you may not feel comfortable singing or chanting in front of a class of students, your students may have personal inclinations towards music that you may not be aware of. You can make classroom singing a fun event by holding a "talent search" contest with the class or among classes of the same English levels. Participants can be assigned in teams to create lyrics that describe certain grammar rules and ultimately sing in a classroom music show. The opportunity to present learning through music can be an enjoyable, rewarding and memorable experience for everyone involved.

Board Games

You have probably enjoyed times in your childhood when you were able to happily defeat family members playing board games such as *Monopoly*®, *Pay Day*®, or *Life*®. After such victories, you were able to relish and brag about them for days to your defeated opponents. Students love challenges. When you assemble a small group of students together to compete with each other in a teacher-created E.S.L. board game, look out! Board games are great devices to challenge the egos of students in demonstrating their language-learning prowess. Board games are fun to create and a joy to see students delight in its play. You can buy game parts such as dice, player tokens, playing chips, fake money, poster paper (for the board) and other miscellaneous pieces at the toy department of major chain stores, "dollar" stores, specialty game and toy stores or stationery stores. Game designs are only limited by the power of your imagination. To begin the design of a board game, first you should decide what the learning objective of a board game is going to be. It could be a board game that tests the students' knowledge of verb tenses, past participles, sentence-making, question-making, cultural facts, specific language functions, etc. The more specific the objective is, the easier the play instructions are going to be. Next, you should decide what the rewards will be for participants with positive results—will it be the gain of fake money, poker chips, certain property on the board, points, or some other kind undetermined benefit? Afterwards you'll have to decide what exercises participants would need to accomplish in order to satisfy the learning objective and achieve their coinciding rewards. When designing a board, keep it simple to understand by keeping the playing rules simple. You should also determine how many boards are required in your class if you want to limit the numbers of participants for each board. After creating game boards, you may wish to laminate them in a stationery store or a copy center in order to protect them from wear and tear. Game boards are wonderful tools to end a lesson on a positive and fun note.

Bingo-mania

When you were little, you may have had the exciting opportunity to play the game of "Bingo" in school, at a festival, in a game hall, or other social function. However, if you are one of the few people on this planet who have never heard of the game of "Bingo", a brief description will be provided. The main goal of "Bingo" is to listen to a person call out numbers under 5 categories, which are the letters that comprise the word "Bingo": B—I—N—G—O. Numbers and their categories are determined by a drawing of marked balls in a drawing-cage. A caller may announce "B-15", or "G-25", and so on. Participants will have cards with various numbers printed on them under the categories of B-I-N-G-O and they are to check and mark their cards if they have the announced letter and numbers. Bingo cards will generally have a "free" square in the middle of the card that doesn't require any number. When participants have successfully marked off the required quantity of numbers on one card, they are to quickly say "Bingo!" to notify organizers who will then verify their results before awarding prizes. The quantity of marked numbers required on a winning Bingo card can vary. Organizers may require winners to have an entire Bingo card to be marked off; or a card with any vertical or horizontal line marked; or just the four corner numbers marked; or a card with an "L-shape" or other particular pattern marked-off.

E.S.L. teachers can transform this popular game into "E.S.L. Bingo". Teachers can transform typical Bingo cards into language learning cards by replacing numbers with grammar points. For example, a past tense Bingo game can require Bingo cards with various verbs in the past tense. Instead of drawing Bingo numbers, a teacher can draw the present tense version of the verbs on the bingo cards. When students hear the announced present tense verb, they must think of its equivalent past tense form, then check their Bingo-cards for its presence and mark it off. When the required number of Bingo squares is marked, the student yells "Bingo!" and is awarded a prize. At the end of "E.S.L. Bingo" games, it's best to reward all students small consolation prizes for participating. See Figure 21.1 for a sample past tense bingo card:

Figure 21.1

told	ran	flew	ate	went
came	did	sold	bought	blew
sought	won	FREE	grew	drank
swam	fought	wrote	made	got
brought	lit	sat	dug	drove

Telephone Conversations

Toy telephones could be used to add a sense of realism to telephone activities. For telephone conversations, ensure students are taught the necessary gambits in initiating a phone call before you assemble students together in telephone role-play—gambits such as "Could you repeat that please?", "Can I put you on hold?", "I'm sorry, John isn't here, would you like to leave a message?", etc. The dynamics of a telephone call should be divided into 3 parts: the introduction, the purpose, and the closing. Gambits for each of the 3 parts should be introduced to the students. As you teach different language functions, the big changes in gambits you would make in non-personal phone conversations is the purpose, while minor changes would occur with the introduction and the closing.

Language management techniques such as asking a person to repeat information, or spelling words on the phone should be taught to students as well. It's a good idea to introduce a special phonetic alphabet (unlike the pronunciation phonetic alphabet) for spelling words on the phone. Since the pronunciation of some letters such as "P" and "B" or "T" and "D" sound similar when spoken on the phone, a phonetic referencing system had to be developed. Back in the 1950s the North Atlantic Treaty Organization (NATO) developed a phonetic alphabet that was to be easily intelligible and pronounceable to all allies. When a word had to be spelled over the airwaves, phonetic alphabet users replaced letters with words that contained the required letters needed in the spelling. For example, instead of saying, "Apple is spelled A-P-P-L-E" you would say, "Apple is spelled 'A' as in alpha, 'P' as in papa, 'P' as in papa, 'L' as in Lima, and 'E' as in echo." With Canadian postal codes, you could say, "My postal code is Victor—3—Charlie, 2—Yankee—5" or in other words, your postal code is V3C 2Y5. Although there are other versions of such an alphabet, the NATO phonetic alphabet is widely used throughout North America and Europe in telecommunications and business.

Teachers can create word-spelling games in which students have to spell certain words just by using the NATO phonetic alphabet. Team games can be organized by dividing the students into teams to see which team knows their alphabet the best. Spelling pop quizzes can be organized involving the phonetic alphabet. Any telephone dialogue that requires the passing of information should be done with a phonetic alphabet such as NATO's.

NATO Phonetic Alphabet

A—Alpha	G—Golf	M—Mike	S—Sierra
B—Bravo	H—Hotel	N—November	T—Tango
C—Charlie	I—India	O—Oscar	U—Uniform
D—Delta	J—Juliet	P—Papa	V—Victor
E—Echo	K—Kilo	Q—Quebec	W—Whiskey
F—Foxtrot	L—Lima	R—Romeo	X—X-ray
			Y—Yankee
			Z—Zulu

Role-Plays/Skits

Integrating role-playing in your lessons will enliven any classroom atmosphere. Without role-plays, students would not have a chance to put their knowledge to practical oral use. Role-plays can range from doing simple telephone conversations; dialogues focusing on functional English; and acting out a small drama. The more props that you have for role-plays or skits, the more "real" it becomes and students tend to be more involved in playing their roles.

Making skits are wonderful improvisations in student-centered activities. Provided the students have been presented appropriate gambits related to the topics of the skits, teachers can assign small groups with a skit-card. A skit-card would contain brief information on the situation that they would have to role-play and the necessary characters involved. At the conclusion of their skits, students would have to provide a solution to any predicament involved in their situation. Here is an example skit-card for an advanced conversation class:

Situation:
You and your business partner want to start a business but you need a loan from a bank. You have made an appointment to a loans officer at a bank to discuss the possibility of borrowing some money.
The loans officer has to be careful not to lend money to careless business people. The officer has to ask many questions to the applicants to scrutinize their business before deciding to lend out any money. The officer has an assistant to help him/her. The conversation must end with the loans officer and the assistant making a decision whether or not to lend the business partners any money.

Characters:
2 business partners
1 loans officer at a bank
1 loans officer assistant at a bank

The skit-card assumes that students are familiar with the gambits of making requests, answering *wh*-questions, *yes/no* questions, modals and some aspects of business etiquette. Ensure skit-card language is accessible to students.

Programs with E.S.L. Story Books

Some publishing companies print stories in formats that E.S.L. students can read. A great selection of E.S.L.-formatted stories is from Penguin Readers.

Penguin Readers are graded reading books written for E.S.L. students. They offer a variety of stories from the classic to the contemporary. If you're a big fan of the classics such as Charles Dickens' *Oliver Twist*, you can order a class set of Penguin Readers of *Oliver Twist* and introduce an extensive study program by designing reading, writing, listening and speaking activities surrounding the story.

For reading class, pre-reading information should be introduced to the students before beginning any book. Teachers can survey the students if they know anything about the cultural or historical side of the book's setting. A teacher can question students about their knowledge and introduce some material in the form of historical books, pictures, internet material, maps, and so forth to pique interest. When students are familiar with the cultural and historical background, they will have a base from which they can refer to before reading the first chapter. In reading classes, students should do regular comprehension and vocabulary exercises from each chapter. Teachers should vary the exercises since there may be a lot of chapters to cover and students will be bored with answering the same type of comprehensive and vocabulary questions with every chapter.

A writing class can involve making summaries from each chapter of the book, making a critique from each chapter or a making a book report at the end. For *Oliver Twist*, a listening and speaking activity can have students view a video of *Oliver Twist* in segments (such as in ½ hour blocks) and do activities that compare the video and the book version of the story, or discuss particular features of the characters such as body language, facial expressions, phonological expressions, etc.

The conclusion of a unit such as *Oliver Twist* could involve doing a play with the students. The teacher could make an E.S.L. level script of the story with learned-sentence patterns, expressions and vocabulary and assign students to play certain roles. After several rehearsals, a final act could be performed in a show with a select audience. Students should know who the audience would be, since nervousness will be a major impediment in their performances. The effort of numerous rehearsals may be squandered if students don't know from the beginning who would be watching them perform. If other students would be the audience, it's probably best to limit the number of audience members by limiting it to other classes that are of the same or similar E.S.L. level as the performers.

Games with Cards

Another great small-group activity that students have fun with is playing card games. The following is a list of some card game activities:

1) <u>Sentence Scramble</u>

Scrambled sentences can be put together in the correct order by assembling together single-worded cards. Excess words should be created so students can spot any unnecessary words. Another version is teachers can create sentence strips that describe a short story and students would have to arrange the sentence strips in correct sequential order.

2) <u>E.S.L. Fish</u>

Picture cards can be played in the same fashion as the traditional "Fish" game with an E.S.L. twist. The goal of "Fish" is to accumulate as many matched pairs of cards as possible. Ensure students know the specific language needed to play the game. In groups of three to five students, each group has a small deck of cards (for example with pictures). Each player is dealt five cards facedown. The remaining cards are placed at the center of the table. Each player takes his cards and privately looks for matching pairs. Matching pairs are then placed on the table for all to see but the remaining cards are not to be exposed to other students. The person on the right of the dealer begins the game by asking a target-language question from the cards in his hand. For example, if the target language is asking for favors and the student needs a match for a card that has a picture of a baby, the student can specifically ask another student, "Jim, can you baby-sit for me tonight?" If Jim has a card with a picture of a baby, Jim would have to give a positive answer, "Yes, I can" and relinquish his card to the asking student. The asking student then has a matching pair to put down in his favor. All positive answers entitle the requester to make another request to the same student or to another student in the group until the requester receives a negative response. If Jim didn't have the card in question, he would have had to give a negative answer with an explanation, such as "No, I'm sorry. I have to do a lot of homework tonight." and the requester would have to pick up a card from the center of the table. The next turn would be the student on the right of the first requester. The procedure continues until a student doesn't have any cards left in his/her hands.

3) <u>Pronunciation Categories</u>

When testing students' knowledge of the phonetic alphabet such as vowel sounds, diphthongs, consonants and consonant clusters, and so forth, teachers can make cards with different words containing particular phonological features. Students would then have to read the words, pronounce them, and sort them under the appropriate phoneme.

4) Adjective Opposites
Teachers can test a student's knowledge of opposites involving adjectives. Cards with adjectives can be created for students to match them with their corresponding opposite.

5) Phrasal Verb Match
Teachers can test a student's knowledge of phrasal verbs by making cards with a phrasal verb on each. Corresponding cards with synonymous verbs to the phrasal verbs can be made for students to match together.

6) Vocabulary Grouping
Teachers can test a student's knowledge on logical vocabulary grouping. The categorical groupings are not given so students would need to determine what they are. Words that correspond to certain groupings can be made on cards and students would need to determine what certain words have in common and figure out what the name of the category is. For example, you can create cards with the words, *water, cup, towel, toothbrush, toilet* and the category students would have to come up with to assemble them under would be "Things found in a bathroom." This game can be reversed by distributing a card with the category written on it already, "Things found in a bathroom" and having a student provide clues that would prompt the other group members to guess what the category is.

A good card game reference book is *Index Card Games for E.S.L.* by Pro Lingua Associates and *The Card Book: Interactive Games and Activities for Language Learners* by Abigail Tom and Heather McKay. It's best that the teacher models card games and their corresponding rules than delve into long explanations that may confuse students. Some students may be sensitive and resent the word "game" with these activities due to preconceived negative connotations with language learning. Instead, you may want to classify these activities as card-activities rather than card-games.

There are a variety of E.S.L. activity books on the market today to help you add fun to your lessons. Here are just some of the great fun resource books available for teachers: *Talk-A-Tivities : Problem Solving and Puzzles for Pairs* by Richard Yorkey; *Brain Waves: Intermediate and Advanced Communication Activities* by Mike Tiittanen; *Fun With Grammar* by Suzanne W. Woodward; *Grammar Games and Activities* by Peter Watcyn-Jones; and *Zero Prep* by Laurel Pollard and Natalie Hess.

Recommended Reading List

Fun E.S.L. Resources

Pollard, Laurel & Hess, Natalie. (1997). *Zero Prep*. San Francisco: Alta Book Center Publishers.

Pro Lingua Associates. (1992). *Index Card Games for E.S.L.*, 2nd edition. Brattleboro: Pro Lingua Associates.

Tiittanen, Mike. (1998). *Brain Waves: Intermediate and Advanced Communication Activities*. Toronto: Oxford University Press.

Tom, Abigail & McKay, Heather. (1991). *The Card Book*. New Jersey: Prentice Hall Regents

Watcyn-Jones, Peter. (1995). *Grammar Games and Activities for Teachers*. London: Penguin Books.

Woodward, Suzanne W. (1997). *Fun With Grammar: Communicative Activities for the Azar Grammar Series*. New Jersey: Prentice Hall Regents

Yorkey, Richard. (1985). *Talk-A-Tivities: Problem Solving and Puzzles for Pairs*. Reading: Addison-Wesley.

Last Words

As you begin your E.S.L. teaching career, you will realize the profound impact you can have on international students who depend on you for language guidance. This impact gives you a self-satisfied feeling that you've made a difference to somebody in this world—a difference that will last a lifetime for that person as his or her mentor or life-long friend. There are few jobs in life that is as mobile and personally rewarding as teaching E.S.L. Your language skills are a gift and with the assistance of this book, you can pass on your gift to others to help them become more independent citizens in the English-speaking community.

> *The value of my teachings were clearly understood for me back in 1996 when I was assigned by a community outreach program to tutor a middle-aged woman who was a new immigrant from India. She had recently become a widow and was raising an eleven-year old daughter on her own. The weekly lessons were held in her home and I was teaching her survival English skills such as talking on the phone, making medical appointments, going shopping, etc. One day I had decided to teach my student how to dial 911 for emergency calls. I arranged an extensive lesson on making emergency calls that lasted 2 sessions. At the end of the second session, I informed my student I was canceling next week's session because of vacation plans I had made.*
>
> *At the end of two weeks I went back to see her for our next tutoring session. When I walked in her house she greeted me with excitement. She proceeded to tell me an incredible story. She informed me that one night while I was on my vacation, she was struck with intense stomach pains that made it difficult for her to move. She thought the pain would be short-lived but it persisted and intensified for several hours. She got her young daughter, who also had limited English, to call 911. The daughter didn't know what to say to the 911 operator so she passed the phone to my student. Following the lesson I had given, my*

> *student was able to communicate with the operator and say what she needed, her name, address, and her condition. An ambulance was dispatched and my student was taken to the hospital where she was treated. I was in utter amazement to hear her story. I had a profound sense of gratitude in my teaching skills when I realized the impact I had made for this woman's life. After hearing her story, a tremendous sense of life purpose came upon me. I began to see teaching E.S.L. not as a 9:00–5:00 job opportunity, but more as a social service to the world community. We sometimes don't realize the impact we make on others when we go about our day-to-day business but in E.S.L. teaching, the impact can be unimaginably great as I've learned from my student.*
> *—P.D.*

Although you and I have overcome a few hurdles throughout this book in learning how to teach different aspects of the English language, the ultimate ingredient in your success will be your attitude. You can be the most knowledgeable grammar teacher on this planet, the author of several textbooks, holder of a few degrees, and have 5 years experience under your belt, but those qualifications won't be enough if you don't have the right attitude to take with you to the classroom.

As you start out your career, you will begin to learn more about yourself and develop a system of classroom preparation and lesson planning that works best personally for you. You will become a master planner, a master speaker, a master entertainer, and eventually a master at un-jamming the photocopy machine. The rich rewards of taking your teaching skills overseas cannot be overstated. You will learn more about yourself and about how the human mind works in language acquisition as you embrace and explore other cultures.

We wish you all the best in your new career. May the journey ahead be the start of new adventures towards your own highway to the sunset.

Warmest regards,

Pinky Y. Dang
B.A., TESOL

and

Rik Ruiter
Psy.D, CELTA

Course Planning

Course Syllabus, Teaching Records, Lesson Plans

Course Planning

Format 1

Level: Time: Date:

Class Profile:

Aims:

Assumptions:

Anticipated Problems: Solutions:

Aids:

Miscellaneous:

Time	Stage	Aim	Procedure	Interaction	Aids

Lesson Evaluation:

Sample Format 1

Level: Beginner   **Time:** 60 minutes   **Date:** Feb 25

Class Profile: Academic students staying in Canada for 4 months to study conversational English.

Aims: To elicit reading comprehension and speaking abilities for story telling
     To practice the simple present and the simple past verb tenses.

Personal Aims (of the teacher): To avoid excessive instructions.

Assumptions: Students understand the instructions. They do not understand the vocabulary related to sports—for example, the difference between mountain climbing and rock climbing.

Anticipated Problems: Differentiating the activities of mountain and rock climbing.

Solutions: Elicit the difference from students via story telling, modeling, or questioning.

Aids: Textbook—John Soars & Liz Soars <u>Headway: Intermediate</u> (1986), New York: Oxford University Press, p. 86-87, blackboard, chalk, chalk eraser, picture of rock singer Avril Levine and a rock climber.

Time	Stage	Aim	Procedure	Interaction	Aids
0.00	Lead-in		Elicit different sports	S → T	
0.02	Task	Ss activate vocabulary	Spider graph indoor/outdoor sports	S → S	
0.05	Feedback		Ss fill in spider graph	S → S	Board
0.08	Check	To see if ss understood vocab	Check spelling, pronunciation and stress	S → T	Board
**					
0.11	Lead-in		Classify dangerous sports vs. safe sports	S → T	Board
0.15	Task	To create interest in dangerous sports to lead into rock climbing.	Ss list dangerous/safe sports	S → T	Board
0.19	Feedback		Write dangerous sports on board	S → T	Board
0.21	Introduce		Present rock star and rock face	T → S	Book
0.22	Task	Activate vocab.	Ss define rock star and rock face	S → S	Book

Time	Stage	Aim	Procedure	Interaction	Aids
0.25	Feedback		Ask concept questions on rock star and rock face	S → S	Book
0.28	Introduction		Rock star-Avril Levine	T → S	Picture
0.29	Task	Practice speaking ability	Ss create story from pictures	S → S	Book
0.34	Task	Ss read for gist	Ss skim the text on rock climbing	S	Book
0.39	Task	Ss read for details	Ss match headings with paragraphs by scanning	S → S	Book
0.42	Feedback		Ss comment on text	S → T	
0.43	Task	Ss read for understanding	Ss read text carefully and answers questions/T monitors	S → S	Book
0.48	Feedback		Initiate when errors are detected in monitoring.	T → S	
***					
0.49	Lead-in		Review simple present and simple past structures	T → S	
0.50	Task	To check grammar knowledge	Find sentences with verb tenses	S	Book
0.53	Feedback		Ss compare answers	S → S	

Lesson Evaluation:

The lesson went well and the students gave a lot of good feedback. Students had trouble seeing the pictures—find bigger sized pictures for next time.

References

Soars, John & Soars, Liz. (1986) *Headway: Intermediate.* New York: Oxford University Press.

Format 2

Topic: Time:
Level:
Aims:

Assumed Knowledge:

Anticipated Problems:

Solutions:

Aids:

Warm-Up/Review   Time:
Aims:
Focus:
Aids:
Procedure:

Language Acquisition/Learning Stage   Time:
Aims:
Focus:
Aids:
Procedure:

Controlled Practice Stage   Time:
Aims:
Focus:
Aids:
Procedure:

Less Controlled Practice Stage   Time:
Aims:
Focus:
Aids:
Procedure:

Closing   Time:
Aims:
Focus:
Aids:

Procedure:

Lesson Evaluation:

Sample Format 2

Topic: To introduce count/non-count nouns   Time: 1 hour
Level: High beginner academic English students
Aims: To identify count/non-count nouns and associated expressions of quantity.
Assumed Knowledge: Ss are familiar with numbers, articles, yes/no questions and Wh-questions, "There is/are"
Anticipated Problems: Determining which nouns are non-countable.
Solutions: Ask concept questions that fit the criteria of nouns that are countable (Eg. Is there an "s" at the end of 2 count nouns [except for irregular count nouns, such as people]? Yes (2 chairs) Is there an "s" at the end of 2 non-count nouns? Common error: "2 homeworks"
Aids: pictures of count and non-count nouns, worksheets, a few apples, books, pens, chairs, a bottle of water, a cup of rice, whiteboard, markers, whiteboard eraser, picture of a beach, text book

---

Warm-Up/Review   Time: 10 minutes
Aims: To review numbers and articles and the expressions "some", "any"
Focus: T → S
Aids: pictures of count nouns
Procedure:
1. Orally quiz ss on how many things are in some pictures of count nouns; ss respond by using the sentence "There is/are"
2. Ask comprehensive questions (yes/no and Wh-questions) with the pictures to elicit answers from the ss using "some" or "any"
3. Assembled ss in pairs and have them ask each other 5 yes/no questions that require numbers or expressions of quantity in their answers. Ss switch roles afterwards.
4. Have ss expand on the questions by asking 3 Wh-questions with numbers and 3 Wh-questions with expressions of quantity on any topic in general.

<u>Language Acquisition/Learning Stage</u>   <u>Time:</u> 15 minutes

<u>Aims:</u> To identify count/non-count nouns

<u>Focus:</u> T → S

<u>Aids:</u> a few apples, books, pens, chairs, a bottle of water, a cup of rice, whiteboard, markers, whiteboard eraser, picture of a beach

<u>Procedure:</u>

1. Show books and apples and ask "How many.......do I have?"
2. Write the questions and the elicited answers on the board
3. Elicit a student to ask the same kind of question with the pens and another student with the chairs. Elicit answers.
4. Show picture of a beach. Elicit the word sand. Ask "How many sand is there on the beach?" Motion the hands to indicate big quantity or little quantity without giving any verbal clues. Write the question on the board as #2.
5. Show the cup with rice. Elicit the words "cup" and "rice". Ask "How many cups do I have?" Elicit answer. Repeat with the rice: "How many rice do I have?" Motion the hands to indicate big quantity or little quantity without giving any verbal clues. Write the question on the board as #3.
6. Introduce the answers to questions #1-3 with "a little", or "a lot".
7. Show the bottle of water. Elicit the words "bottle" and "water". Ask "How many bottles do I have?" Elicit answer. Repeat with water: "How many water do I have?" Motion the hands to indicate big quantity or little quantity without giving any verbal clues. Write the question on the board as #1.
8. Differentiate the above terms by motioning the hands to indicate a big or small quantity
9. Repeat questions #1-3 by crossing out "many" and writing "much" above the error. Ask ss questions for #1-3 to elicit the answers "a little/a lot"
10. Ask ss questions with other non-count nouns to elicit the answers "a little/a lot"
11. Ask ss to ask other ss example questions using "How much" and eliciting the target answers.
12. Write the target answers on the board.
13. Repeat the above procedure with some count nouns but introduce the answers "a few", "several", "many", "a lot"

Controlled Practice Stage   Time: 12 minutes
Aims: To practice forming questions and answers with non-count nouns
Focus: T → S
Aids: worksheets, textbook
Procedure:
1. Distribute worksheets with lists of nouns to be categorized by the ss
    under count or non-count nouns
2. Have ss do any related exercises from the textbook
3. Class review of the answers afterwards

Less Controlled Practice Stage   Time: 18 minutes
Aims: To practice using questions and answers for non-count nouns
Focus: S → S
Aids: previous activity's worksheet
Procedure:
Pt. 1
1. Teacher models the next activity. T refers to the worksheet from the
    previous activity, looks at a word, turns over the sheet so T can't see
    it again, then makes a yes/no or Wh-question with a student. The stu-
    dent answers. T repeats and emphasizes to the student that the
    asker must look at the word on the sheet, turn over the sheet so he
    can't refer to it again and make the question.
2. The partner student switches roles with the T and repeats.
3. Ss are assembled in pairs and are to conduct the above exercise. T
    monitors to ensure ss aren't looking at the sheet excessively or show-
    ing it to their partners.
Pt. 2
1. T arranges a student to ask how a person makes a sandwich. T
    answers using numbers and expressions of quantity with the ingredi-
    ents and the directions. T asks a student how a person makes a pizza.
    Student responds by answering with numbers and expressions of
    quantity with the ingredients.
2. Ss are assembled in different pairs and are to ask each other how to
    make certain foods

<u>Closing</u>   <u>Time:</u> 5 minutes
<u>Aims:</u> To summarize the different questions and answers used for count/non-count nouns
<u>Focus:</u> S → S
<u>Aids:</u> none
<u>Procedure:</u>
1. Summarize with an evaluation grid on the board how to identify count/non-count nouns, and differentiate the questions and answers.
2. Ask ss questions using count/non-count nouns and ask others concept questions on the reported answers to verify understanding

<u>Lesson Evaluation:</u>

> good feedback and understanding on the lesson
> more time was needed for the less controlled activity as it seemed rushed
> some grammar difficulties on when not to add "s" for irregular plural count nouns (Eg. people, men, children, fish, etc.)

Format 3

Topic:				Time:
Level:				
Aims:				
Assumed Knowledge:				
Anticipated Problems:				
Solutions:				
Aids:				

Time	Stage	Aim	Procedure	Interaction

Lesson Evaluation:

Sample Format 3

Topic: Sign recognition   Time: 1 hour
Level: Intermediate level immigrant students from different nationalities
Aims: To provide listening & speaking practice in sign recognition
Assumed Knowledge: Ss learned vocabulary related to household products
from the previous lesson
Anticipated Problems: Ss may not recognize some warning or hazard signs
common in daily life
Solutions: Concept questions on health and consequences of different hazards;
use body language and facial expressions to suggest dangers
Aids: Pre-recorded audio tapes or language master cards, tape cassette players
or language master players, pictures of road signs, prohibition signs, common
danger signs from household goods, danger signs in everyday life, sample fake
warning sign, poster paper, markers

Time	Stage	Aim	Procedure	Interaction
0.00	Warm Up	To prepare ss for household product symbols	Present picture cards to review vocabulary	T → S
0.05	Lead-in	To introduce symbols and their meaning	T presents pictures of symbols commonly found on household products.	T → S
0.15	Intro.	To present new vocabulary	T expresses modals of prohibition necessity, and obligation; T drills pronunciation and writes structural form on the board. T asks concept questions to differentiate the scale of obligation.	T → S
0.25	Check	To present other safety signs	T presents pictures of road signs, no smoking sign, poison and electrocution warnings, etc. and elicits example sentences with target modals from each sign.	T → S
0.35	Task	To provide controlled practice	Students listen to pre-recorded cards or audio tapes and match the audio expressions with the appropriate signs; ss work in pairs	S

| 0.45 | Task | To provide less controlled practice | T presents a fake warning sign and encourages ss to ask *yes/no* questions and *Wh*-questions to guess its meaning. Assemble ss in pairs and distribute poster paper and markers. Ask ss to create their own hazard signs that aren't real. Encourage them to be creative. Afterwards, hang up signs with tape and have class feedback with questions for the creators who would give clues to what the sign means by providing example sentences with modals. | S → S |
| 0.55 | Closing | To summarize | T elicits example sentences using the target modals of everyday hazards | |

Lesson Evaluation:

-there was no time to do the closing
-although ss had fun, not enough time was spent on the uncontrolled practice
-ss had some difficulty differentiating the scale of obligation: "have to",
 "must", "ought to"

Format 4: Individual Tutoring

Topic:	Date:
Aids:	
Warm-Up	
Review	

Language Learning Stage 1

Break

Language Learning Stage 2

Closing

Lesson Evaluation

Sample Format 4: Individual Tutoring

<u>Topic:</u> Asking for things in shops and prepositions of place　　<u>Date:</u> June 21
<u>Aids:</u> picture cards, shopping lists, sample dialogue, blank paper
<u>Warm-Up:</u>
elicit simple *yes/no* questions and *Wh*-questions.
<u>Review</u>
review vocabulary of common grocery items and areas of a store (eg. aisle, cashier, etc.)
review question on how to ask for the price of an item
ask personal questions surrounding shopping and shopping habits

<u>Language Learning Stage 1</u>
set-up a situation where T wants to make a cake. Elicit what ingredients does the T need to make a cake. T writes down the list of elicited ingredients. T needs to go to the store. The store is very big and the T needs to ask a worker in the store for these items. What does the T say to the worker?
target language is elicited or orally presented. Focus on pronunciation and substitute target sentence (Have you got any _____?) with different grocery items.
have student practice making the target sentence with the list of cake ingredients
practice example responses from the clerk, including vocabulary for directions
distribute sample shopping lists. Have student request items on the list that match the picture cards. Student should cross off all items "purchased" from the T (to prepare for the next activity).

<u>Break</u>—Present some brochures advertising a community festival and offer to take the student.

<u>Language Learning Stage 2</u>
ask concept questions about the items that weren't crossed off the shopping lists.
set up a situation where the T really needs these "missing" items so the T goes to another store to buy them. The T asks a store clerk who directs where these items can be found by saying sentences with prepositions of place. Introduce example sentences of prepositions of place and ask concept questions to verify meaning of the prepositions
Elicit the previous target sentence with the "missing" items to the T to model an example response "Yes, the flour is in aisle 4 next to the sugar". Repeat with another item and another response, "Yes, the honey is between the bakery and the frozen food section".
Model an example drawing of a store using the T's responses.
Give student a blank piece of paper to draw responses from questions using the target sentence, "Have you got _____?"
As responses are made, T should keep a note of the prepositions used to check the student's drawing afterwards.

Closing: Summarize and elicit sentences from the student with non-food items around the house, objects outside, and places in the world.

Lesson Evaluation

Student enjoyed the shopping exercise and was enthusiastic with learning prepositions.
Next week, introduce returning items in a store, and prepositions of time.

COURSE SYLLABUS

Course Title:	Listening & Speaking (Intermediate Level)
Duration:	8 weeks—3 hours per class biweekly (48 hours)
Proposed Time:	Monday and Wednesday, 6:30–9:30 p.m. (Negotiable)
Remuneration:	Negotiable
Instructor:	Ms. Ima Teacher, B.A., TESOL
	8740 No. 3 Road
	Richmond, BC
	V7N 2Y3 CANADA
	Phone: (604) 555-1234
	Fax: (604) 555-5678
	E-mail: hireme@immediate.com
Availability:	Immediately
Text:	Jones, Leo and Kimbrough, Victoria. Great Ideas. Cambridge University Press: 1997. ISBN 0-521-31242-6
	Handouts.

Course Description:

The purpose of this course is to help intermediate E.S.L. students improve their listening and speaking skills. Students will be engaged in a variety of activities designed to help students feel comfortable in communicating with others. Students will learn new vocabulary, useful expressions, and participate in role-plays and thought provoking discussions designed to stimulate expressions of ideas.

Course Highlights (Textbook Based):

Week 1—The present/speaking and social interaction
Week 2—The past
Week 3—The future
Week 4—The shopping experience/going out/staying home
Week 5—The workplace
Week 6—Vacation
Week 7—Current events
Week 8—The world around us

Bi-weekly schedule:

Theme	Week 1	Time	Topics
The Present/Social Interaction	Monday	6:30–7:00	Getting acquainted
		7:00–8:00	Cross-cultural awareness
		8:00–8:15	Break
		8:15–9:30	Social interaction skills
	Wednesday	6:30–7:30	Telephone skills
		7:30–8:00	Information seeking
		8:00–8:15	Break
		8:15–9:30	Information seeking
Theme	**Week 2**	**Time**	**Topics**
The Past	Monday	6:30–8:00	Canadian history
		8:00–8:15	Break
		8:15–9:30	Family history
	Wednesday	6:30–8:00	Antiquities
		8:00–8:15	Break
		8:15–9:30	Treasured memories
Theme	**Week 3**	**Time**	**Topics**
The Future	Monday	6:30–8:00	Predicting the future
		8:00–8:15	Break
		8:15–9:30	Hope for the future
	Wednesday	6:30–8:00	A Vision of the future
		8:00–8:15	Break
		8:15–9:30	Solving future problems
Theme	**Week 4**	**Time**	**Topics**
Shopping/Going Out/Staying Home	Monday	6:30–8:00	The shopping experience
		8:00–8:15	Break
		8:15–9:30	Consumer interaction
	Wednesday	6:30–8:00	Going out
		8:00–8:15	Break
		8:15–9:30	Staying home
Theme	**Week 5**	**Time**	**Topics**
The Workplace	Monday	6:30–8:00	The work world
		8:00–8:15	Break
		8:15–9:30	What is my job?
	Wednesday	6:30–8:00	A typical day at work

		8:00–8:15	Break
		8:15–9:30	A job interview
<u>Theme</u>	<u>Week 6</u>	<u>Time</u>	<u>Topics</u>
Vacation	Monday	6:30–8:00	Vacation memories
		8:00–8:15	Break
		8:15–9:30	Travel information
	Wednesday	6:30–8:00	Giving and receiving directions
		8:00–8:15	Break
		8:15–9:30	Practice giving and receiving directions
<u>Theme</u>	<u>Week 7</u>	<u>Time</u>	<u>Topics</u>
Current Events	Monday	6:30–8:00	What is in the news
		8:00–8:15	Break
		8:15–9:30	Finding news information
	Wednesday	6:30–8:00	The news report
		8:00–8:15	Break
		8:15–9:30	Reporting the news
<u>Theme</u>	<u>Week 8</u>	<u>Time</u>	<u>Topics</u>
Capital Punishment	Monday	6:30–8:00	Exchanging opinions
		8:00–8:15	Break
		8:15–9:30	Capital punishment
	Wednesday	6:30–8:00	Crime
		8:00–8:15	Break
		8:15–9:30	Taxes

Sample Lesson Plan: Week 8 (Monday)

<u>Time</u>	<u>Topic</u>	<u>Procedure</u>	<u>Expenditure</u>
6:30–8:00	Exchanging Opinions	-Survey students for their opinions on public protests	5 minutes
		-Introduce newspaper article on a protest and assemble students in pairs for discussion and responses	20 minutes
		-Introduce listening activity with audio cassette. Students will listen and record the opinions of 3 voices on the tape and decide who had the most convincing argument	15 minutes
		-Introduce useful debating expressions/rules Assemble students in pairs for a disagreement	50 minutes

		role play activity. They will disagree over loud noise in an apartment building. Class review.	
8:00–8:15		BREAK	
8:15–9:30	Capital Punishment	-Introduce listening activity with audio cassette. Students will listen and record the opinions of 2 friends on capital punishment	15 minutes
		-Class discussion on the pros and cons of punishment and the cultural views on capital punishment.	15 minutes
		-review debating expressions/rules	10 minutes
		-In pairs, have students engage in a debate using the learned debating expressions to present the pro and con sides of capital punishment. Observe responses. Class review of debate afterwards	35 minutes

<u>Target Market:</u>
Intermediate E.S.L. students—academic, immigrants, business people, professionals

<u>Pre-requisites:</u>
Students must have intermediate level written and oral skills.

<u>Materials for Student Purchase:</u> students are to purchase: <u>Great Ideas</u>. Leo Jones and Victoria Kimbrough. Cambridge University Press:1987. ISBN 0-521-31242-6.

<u>Materials Supplied by Instructor:</u> Handouts

<u>Aids Required:</u> Audio cassette player (to be supplied by the employer)

<u>Evaluation:</u>   Quizzes and assignments 15%
                    Group presentation 20%
                    Mid-term oral 25%
                    Final oral presentation 30%
                    Attendance/participation 10%

Short quizzes will be based on homework. Weekly assignments are based on textbook themes. Group presentation will be an oral presentation conducted in groups of 4. The mid-term oral will be 15 minutes in length. The final oral presentation will be 25 minutes in length.

References

Jones, Leo and Kimbrough, Victoria. (1997). *Great Ideas*. Cambridge University Press.

Weekly Teaching Record

Teacher: Term:
Course:
Text books:
Supplemental books:

Date	Daily Teaching Activities
Monday	
Tuesday	
Wednesday	
Thursday	
Friday	

Monthly Timetable

for the month of _____

	Monday	Tuesday	Wednesday	Thursday	Friday
Week 1					
Week 2					
Week 3					
Week 4					

EXAMPLE GRAMMAR LESSON

Topic: *To Be* in the simple past   Time: 1 hour
Level: Low Beginner

Aims: To introduce *To Be* in the simple past and to practice its use.
Assumed Knowledge: Ss are familiar with *To Be* in the simple present
Anticipated Problems: Ss may have had previous knowledge of do/does which
may influence on their formation of negative statements and questions.
Solutions: Put heavy emphasis on how To Be is special and not like other
verbs, thus requires special structural rules. Ask concept questions to check
for understanding.
Aids: blown-up balloon, picture of a girl, transparency of a model dialogue,
overhead projector, picture of a favorite celebrity

Warm-Up/Review   Time: 15 minutes
Aims: To practice sentence structures using *To Be* in the simple present
Focus: T → S
Aids: a blown-up balloon
Procedure:

1) Orally drill from the class an example affirmative and negative sentences,
    yes/no questions, and Wh-questions using the To Be verb in the simple
    present. Verbally tell the ss that the class will be divided in the middle so
    there will be 2 teams
2) Introduce a balloon, volley it in the air so it would randomly go to a stu-
    dent. Ask the "chosen" student to make either: (a) an affirmative sen-
    tence with *am/is/are* (b) a negative sentence with *am/is/are* (c) a yes/no
    question with *am/is/are* or (d) a Wh-question with *am/is/are*. The student
    only has ten seconds to reply or the balloon is volleyed to the other side
    of the class for an opposing member to answer and take away the turn.
3) if the student answers correctly, he scores a point for his side (mark
    points on the board). If the students doesn't answer correctly, no point is
    given and the other side of the class gets a chance to answer and "steal"
    the other team's turn.
4) A member on the other team gets a turn when the balloon is volleyed to
    their side.
5) The more times a team "steals" the other team's turn and answers their
    questions, the more chances they'll win.

Language Acquisition/Learning Stage   Time: 10 minutes
Aims: To introduce the *To Be* verb in the simple past
Focus: T → S
Aids: picture of a girl
Procedure:

1) Present a picture of a girl. Elicit the name and details with To Be in the simple present. Write down student responses on the board
2) Draw a timeline on the board with a series of different years

| | | | | | | |
| 1980 | 1985 | 1990 | 1995 | 2000 | NOW | FUTURE |

Verbally deliver sentences with To Be in the past for each of those years. (ex. In 1980, Julie was a high school student in Mexico; in 1985 Julie was in university; in 1990 Julie was married; in 1995 Julie and Tom [husband] were in Canada; in 2000 Julie and Tom were on vacation). Repeat example questions 3 times. Ask concept questions to check for understanding (Was Julie single in 1990?, Was Julie in school in 2000?....)

3) Ask random ss to repeat the example sentences for each of the years and write their responses on the board. Elicit the negative form. Elicit the yes/no question and Wh-question forms.
4) Go over pronunciation and stress. Ask ss random yes/no questions and Wh-questions with *To Be* in the simple past.
5) Ask ss to ask other ss yes/no or Wh-questions with *To Be* in the simple past.

Controlled Practice Stage   Time: 15 minutes
Aims: To provide guided practice with *To Be* in the simple past
Focus: T → S
Aids: textbook exercise, listening exercise tape, listening worksheet
Procedure:

1) Have ss listen a conversation between 2 friends who haven't seen each other for a long time. Play tape and inform ss not to take any notes the first time because you'll play the tape again. Ss should just listen for the first playing.
2) Ask ss to take down any notes for the second playing. Play tape.

3) Distribute exercise sheets that ask questions on what the 2 friends said. The conversation focuses on *To Be* in the past so the exercise sheets will ask for information based on *To Be* in the past.
4) Go over answers in class after 8 minutes.
5) Have ss turn to the unit on *To Be* in the simple past in their textbooks and begin work on exercises.
6) Go over answers in class afterwards.

Uncontrolled Practice Stage   Time: 15 minutes
Aims: To provide less controlled-practice for *To Be* in the simple past.
Focus: S → S
Aids: transparency of a model dialogue, overhead projector

Procedure:

1) Present a transparency showing a model dialogue on an overhead projector. The dialogue is of 2 friends who haven't seen each other for a long time and they're using *To Be* in the simple past a lot. Arrange 2 students to read the dialogue. Note the yes/no and Wh-questions in the dialogue.
2) Ask 2 other students to repeat the dialogue except change the yes/no and Wh-questions into different ones. Answers may be changed to correspond to the new questions
3) Arrange ss into pairs and have them practice a dialogue similar to the one on the overhead.
4) Class presentations afterwards.

Closing   Time: 5 minutes
Aims: To reinforce the To Be structure in the past tense
Focus: S → S
Aids: picture of a favorite celebrity

Procedure:

1) Elicit the meaning of celebrity. Entice a student to ask me who my favorite celebrity is and why is this person my favorite celebrity. Use *To Be* in the past for my answers. Present picture of your chosen celebrity.
2) Ask a student who their favorite celebrity is and why.
3) In pairs, have ss discuss who their favorite celebrity is and why they chose him/her.

Lesson Evaluation:

-ss enjoyed the balloon activity
-ss had some difficulty with the listening exercise > next time more emphasis
 on fast pronunciation is needed
-good response to practice activities

EXAMPLE READING LESSON: CRIME

Topic: Crime Time: 1.5 hours

Class: Upper Intermediate College Prep Students

These are international students in their early 20s in a class of about 20–25.

Objective: To build practice for students in formulating and expressing their thoughts and opinions on a current social issue (crime), to read for main ideas and supporting details, and to use relevant vocabulary for for social issues.

Assumptions: The students are already familiar with other social issues such as unemployment, housing, and education. They have read newspaper articles concerning the above issues and have analyzed and studied the vocabulary related to them.

Aids: photo of a man being arrested, map of the country, graph of homicide rates, story on youth crime, vocabulary exercise sheet, comprehensive exercise sheet

Pre-Reading (20 minutes)

1) In order to prepare ss for the article, ask: "Has anyone phoned the police before?"

   "When and what was the problem?", "Has anyone seen a crime?", "What number do you call in an emergency?". As ss share their experiences to the class, contribute my own experience.

2) Pre-teach some vocabulary that will be read in the passage. Assemble ss in pairs to discuss the following questions and encourage them to use the new vocabulary:

   Do you think crime is increasing in ____(your city)____?
   If yes, what kinds of crime and why?
   Do you feel safe where you are living now?

Reading (35 minutes)

SURVEY

1) Hold up a photo of a man being arrested. Ask ss to describe it and how they feel when they look at it. Ask ss to skim the accompanying story for any unfamiliar vocabulary and go over it. Ask ss to predict what the story is about and how it relates to society today.

QUESTION

2) Ask ss to change the title of the passage and its headings into questions. Ask ss to brainstorm questions that the story may have answers to.

READ

3) Ask ss to read aloud short segments of the passage. After each segment, ask comprehensive questions to test understanding. After certain points, ask ss to flip over the passage so they can't look at it. Ask ss to make predictions of what would happen next. Prediction discussions can be made in pairs or small groups.

RESPOND

4) In small groups, have ss take turns recalling the main points in each passage by having a group leader provide clues from each passage. Teacher may have to demonstrate this exercise first before commencing. Next, hang up a map of the country and an accompanying graph showing homicide rates region-by-region (the same graph is in the passage). Ask literal questions based on the graph.

REVIEW

5) In small groups, have ss take notes of the main points in each paragraph by paraphrasing them. Go over the paraphrases with the class to check for accuracy.

Post-Reading (35 minutes)

1) Distribute vocabulary exercise sheet containing sentences with blanks. Ss are to fill in the blanks with the new vocabulary they've just learned.

2) Homework: Have ss complete a comprehensive exercise sheet on the passage.

3) Assemble ss in groups of four to play the role of city council. They would work on solutions to reduce crime in the city. What policies would they implement, what would be the costs to the budget, what programs or rehabilitation ideas would they have, etc. Each group would be given a large sheet of paper and a "secretary" would write down their ideas. They must also discuss and write down why they chose their ideas by using the new vocabulary they've learned. Later each group will hang up their work on the board and the class would examine each other's work.

EXAMPLE PROCESS WRITING UNIT: POVERTY AMONG STREET KIDS

Topic: Poverty Among Street Kids

Level: Upper Intermediate writing class of college prep students who are in their early 20s at a public college.

Time: 2 hours daily/5 times per week

Objective: To give ss practice in formulating and expressing their thoughts on a variety of current social issues. The ss may understand and evaluate other people's opinions through a writing assignment and by the integration of all 4 language skills. This lesson will allow ss to feel comfortable giving a written or oral presentation and gain an understanding of Canadian social values while improving their language skills.

Assumptions: ss are already familiar with previously taught social problems like housing, crime, education, and so forth and they are familiar with the associated vocabulary (standard of living, politics, unemployment, inflation, etc.); ss are also familiar with doing webbing activities, writing different kinds of sentence structures, paraphrasing, and peer revisioning.

Aids: video clip on Vancouver street kids, *Life is a Struggle* and *By the Numbers* articles and pictures from Christine Hoppenrath and Wendy Royal's <u>The World Around Us</u> (1997, Harcourt Brace), exercise sheet on video, exercise sheet on article, handout on discussion topics, poster paper, markers

Context for Writing

Listening

Day 1

- survey ss on their background knowledge on youth poverty
- introduce new vocabulary that would be useful in discussions
- introduce vocabulary from the upcoming video clip for discussions
- introduce common idioms, phrases and other street language expressions that kids would use

Speaking

- following the short video clip, assemble ss in pairs to discuss focus questions on the video

- introduce new vocabulary and expressions from the upcoming reading passage (ex. *cycle of poverty, dead-end jobs, runaways, exploit, etc.*)
- distribute handout on discussion topics and encourage ss to use the new vocabulary
- from the discussion topics, ss are to discuss with their partners the differences between the lives of Canadian street kids and the street kids from their native countries and the long-term results if this problem continues

Reading

- distribute article, *Life is a Struggle* from the textbook: The World Around Us by Christine Hoppenrath and Wendy Royal (1997, Harcourt Brace)
- ask ss to survey the article for unfamiliar vocabulary, graphics, and identify the main players in the story.
- have ss turn the heading into a question; then brainstorm other possible questions that the article may have answers to.
- have ss read aloud the article a few lines at a time and ask concept questions following each paragraph to reinforce understanding
- in small groups, have ss answer comprehensive questions on the reading without looking back at it
- correct the previous exercise with the class and have ss review the reading by discussing the main points and paraphrasing the main ideas on paper with a partner.
- assemble ss in new groups of 4; each group represents city officials who are given "$100,000" to spend in helping street kids; the whole amount does not necessarily have to be used.
- on a large sheet of paper each group is to write down how they would allocate the money on programs in helping street kids
- afterwards each groups' budget will be put on the board to be reviewed by the whole class
- this activity further integrates the speaking component of this unit

Writing Assignment

Pre-Writing

Day 2

- present a picture from <u>The World Around Us</u> by Christine Hoppenrath and Wendy Royal (1997, Harcourt Brace) of a street kid sleeping in a stairwell
- pose the questions: Who is this person? What is he doing? How old is he? Why is he in the basement? Do you think he has a home?
- inform class that the person is a runaway and ask class the question: Have you ever seen poor kids in Canada? If so, where and what were they doing? How did it make you feel?
- have ss do a webbing activity on poverty among street kids
- next, experiment with another pre-writing activity → on blackboard, write:

Problem: Poverty Among Street Kids

Causes————————————————————————————-Effects

- assemble ss in pairs to discuss the causes and effects of poverty among street kids

Planning

- inform ss they are going to write an essay (3–4 pages) on the causes and effects of youth poverty and how they may alleviate the problem.
- ask ss to look at the two pre-writing exercises they did (the webbing and the cause and effect listings), categorize the main points and discard the irrelevant ones
- have ss make an essay outline using their points to form a thesis statement
- outlines will be assigned for homework

First Draft

Day 3

- with the class, review the parameters of sentence structure and how to paraphrase
- ask ss to begin writing an essay (3–4 pages) on the causes and effects of youth poverty and how they may alleviate the problem

- ask ss to use the cause and effect list and the webbing exercise to assist them with organizing ideas.
- remind ss to keep all of their work in a portfolio, which includes invention strategies and all drafts
- uncompleted first drafts will be assigned for homework

Peer Editing for Coherence and Unity

Day 4

- assemble ss into peer revision groups
- ask ss to read their classmates' essays primarily for content and organization and ignore errors in grammar and mechanics
- while ss are editing, have them go over a checklist of items on what to look for in this stage of the editing process
- remind ss to check if there is a clear theme in the introduction, supportive paragraph bodies and a logical progression to the conclusion
- assign the second draft for homework
- distribute a schedule for the next day's teacher-student conferencing

Conferencing Day

Day 5

- for each essay, verify the understanding of each essay's content and organization
- if a trend of certain errors are found, provide clues to the student to identify the common problems being made
- work with the student to correct for vocabulary usage, sentence structure and grammar but don't correct the entire essay
- make sample corrections for the student and encourage the student to watch for particular repeated errors in the rest of the paper
- list the types of errors that are being made the most and at the same time give some positive feedback
- during conferencing, the other ss will conduct a reading exercise on the article *By the Numbers* in <u>The World Around Us</u> by Christine Hoppenrath and Wendy Royal (1997, Harcourt Brace)
- on the board, write the headings: **Your Culture   Canadian Culture**

- for each of the 12 lists of facts in the article, ss are to compare the articles' statistics with possible generalized statistics from their own cultures.
- in groups of 3, ss are to compare their findings
- go over *By the Numbers* exercise with class
- third drafts are assigned for homework

Peer Editing for Grammar and Mechanics

Day 6

- assemble ss in groups of three to begin peer proofreading stage.
- ss would edit for vocabulary usage, sentence structure, grammar, and mechanics
- while ss are editing, have them go over a checklist of items on what to look for in this stage of the editing process
- upon completion, ss will write the final drafts of their essays (Draft # 4) to be handed in on the first day of next week

Evaluation

- essays will be marked out of 30 points
- a maximum of 8 points for organization and unity, 7 points for grammar and mechanics, and 15 points for logical progression and content.

EXAMPLE PRONUNCIATION LESSON: SEGMENTAL

Level: Mid Intermediate
Time: 1.5 hours
Aim: To help my Polish students to say /|θ/ instead of /t/
   To help my Polish students say *thank you* instead of *tank you*.
Assumed Knowledge: They know the parts of the tongue and oral cavity from seeing cross-sectioned diagrams from before. They know what air flow, puff of air, minimal pairs, voiced and voiceless mean.
Anticipated Problems: listening perception of the error and target sound
Possible Solution: extend perception practice; make audio recordings of student feedback to help them distinguish the sound difference
Aids: drawing of oral cavity showing the target and error sounds, lip drawings, audio recording of minimal sentences, minimal pair answer exercise with answer sheets, vocabulary bingo cards, bingo prize, tongue twister and cued dialogues, mutual dictation exercise

A. PLANNING STAGE

Target Sound /θ/

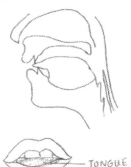

Voiceless
Interdental
Fricative

Error Sound /t/

Voiceless
Alveolar
Stop

Error of place & manner

Non-technical description of the target sound:
The tip of your tongue is between your teeth. There is a little air flow, but it isn't stopped. The air comes out through the tip of your tongue and the edge of the front teeth. It is a voiceless sound.

Non-technical description of the error sound:
The tip of the tongue touches the tooth ridge. There is a puff of air that is stopped when the tongue moves down and away from the tooth ridge.

Common spelling patterns: **th**
Uncommon spelling patterns: non-applicable

B. PERCEPTION STAGE (30 minutes)

1. Tell ss to listen to these minimal pairs said aloud.

/θ/	/t/
than	tan
three	tree
there	tear
with	wit
weather	wetter
thank	tank
thought	taught
wrath	rat
math	mat
bathe	bait

Present illustrated drawings of both sounds. Introduce which one is the target sound.
Present non-technical description of target sound and write in point form on board.
Present non-technical description of error sound and write in point form on board.
Elicit articulation difference from students.

2. Perform minimal pairs drilling with the class using the above list.

3. Repeat above but repeat one of the words twice and ask ss to circle which one sounds different on a worksheet:

1.	a	b	c
2.	a	b	c
3.	a	b	c
4.	a	b	c
↓			
10.	a	b	c

4. Present any applicable common and uncommon spelling patterns associated with the target sound.

5. Play pre-recorded audio tape on minimal sentences. Ask ss to circle the letter of the sentence that they hear.

eg.   1 a) I suffered because of the wrath.
      b)   I suffered because of the rat.

      2 a) I saw the three over there.
      b)   I saw the tree over there.

      3 a) Did you see how big the bath was?
      b)   Did you see how big the bat was?
      ↓
      10.

6.   Distribute answer sheets for minimal pair answer exercise. Call out questions and have ss circle the correct answer to the questions.

eg.   1.   (read: Where is the author?)
      (a)   In Victoria.
      (b)   In the water.

      2   (read: Do you always tell people about the baseball myth?)
      (a)   Yes, I love stories.
      (b)   Yes, I've worn it for 20 years.
      ↓
      10.

C. CONTROLLED PRACTICE (30 minutes)

7)   Distribute vocabulary bingo cards with containing the target and error sounds. Call out random words and have ss check for them on their cards. Distribute bingo prize to a winner.

8)   Assemble ss in groups of 3–4. Have each group brainstorm vocabulary with the targeted sounds under certain categories. (Eg. Group 1 will list personal names with the targeted sound, Group 2 will list food items with the error sound, Group 3 will list nouns and adjectives with the target sound, etc.)

9)   Distribute tongue twister dialogues for pairs practice.

10) Distribute mutual dictations to pairs. Each dictation will have the same story but with missing information. Student A will have missing information that Student B will have and vice versa. The missing information will have words with /t/ and /θ/ that act as minimal pairs. Students will practice dictating to each other with the correct pronunciation.

11) Distribute cued dialogue exercise for ss to improvise a role play and integrate targeted vocabulary.

D. LESS CONTROLLED PRACTICE (30 minutes)

12) Display a model poem that uses words with the target sound in a rhyme. Go over the rhyming pattern with ss. Assign ss in pairs to write a rhyming poem under certain themes (love, money, friendship, school, etc.)

LESSON EVALUATION

There wasn't enough time to complete all the activities. The less controlled practice had to be carried over to the next day.

SAMPLE SUPRASEGMENTAL ACTIVITY

Intonation for Tag Questions

Speaking Activity: Intonation Board Game
Aim: To provide students with speaking and listening practice in using the appropriate intonation pattern for contexts of certainty and uncertainty.
Type of Exercise: Less controlled practice
Class Level: Low-upper intermediate
Approx. Time: 45 minutes
Aids: Game boards, 1 die for each board, bingo chips, box of baked treats (grand prize and participation prizes), tag question cards
Pre-Lesson Prep: Prepare game board and tag question cards, prizes (edible treats) for added motivation (!)
Classroom Set-Up: Students should be in groups of 3 and assembled around each of their game boards. There should be room between each of the groups for the teacher to monitor.

Procedure

- ss are assembled in groups of 3–4
- T gives each group a game board, bingo chips, 1 die, and a pile of tag question cards (to be laid out in the middle of the board) and player pegs
- object of the game is to go around the board as many times as possible collecting as many bingo chips as he can. The one collecting the most bingo chips wins. Bingo chips are collected when tag questions are answered correctly and whenever a player passes the "Start" square.

- to begin, each player puts their names in the boxes with a small "x" on the game board. All names should have an equal distribution around the game board

- each player can roll a die to determine the order of play. The highest roll goes 1st.

- player A begins the game by rolling the die and moving his peg to the corresponding square

- when player A lands on a square with a player's name (other than his own), he picks up a tag question card. He reads the tag question card according to the context indicated on the card (the context is not to be revealed by player A in the reading). The player's name in the square must correctly indicate if the tag question expressed certainty or uncertainty. If the answer is correct, then player A gets the right to stay in that square and collects a bingo chip; the player who answered also collects a bingo chip. If the answer is incorrect, no chips are given out and player A cannot stay in the square and must return to his originating square.

- if player A lands on a square with his name in it, he must roll the die again until he is able to land on a square not containing his name.

- in addition, each time a player goes around the board and passes the start square, he collects a chip.

- at the end of the game, the player with the most bingo chips wins teachers may provide special edible treats as prizes for added incentive to winners and participants

Sample Tag Question Cards

The basketball team played well, didn't they? Context: Uncertainty	It's nice outside, isn't it? Context: Certainty
The door is open, isn't it? Context: Certainty	The window is open, isn't it? Context: Uncertainty
She left the house, didn't she? Context: Certainty	He bought the car, didn't he? Context: Certainty
You paid him, didn't you? Context: Uncertainty	You like country music, don't you? Context: Uncertainty
John and Bill left, didn't they? Context: Uncertainty	The dog is sick, isn't it? Context: Certainty
Her daughter likes chocolate, doesn't she? Context: Certainty	My son is home now, isn't he? Context: Uncertainty
Your dress is blue, isn't it? Context: Uncertainty	We're going to be late, aren't we? Context: Certainty
The test is tomorrow, isn't it? Context: Uncertainty	I got an "A", didn't I? Context: Certainty
Sally called you last night, didn't she? Context: Certainty	You went out with Bill, didn't you? Context: Uncertainty
The train leaves at midnight, doesn't it? Context: Uncertainty	Their flight is late, isn't it? Context: Certainty
They broke up last Saturday, didn't they? Context: Certainty	Her dog is big, isn't it? Context: Uncertainty

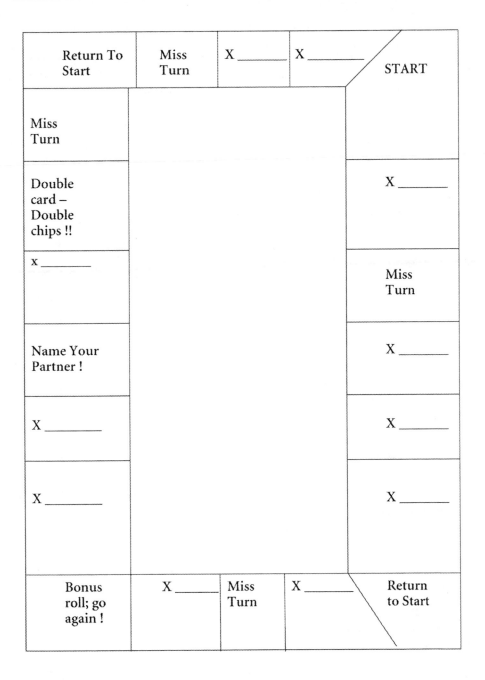

EXAMPLE LISTENING LESSON: FASHION

<u>Topic</u>: To introduce clothing trends with a listening exercise   <u>Time</u>: 1 hour
<u>Level</u>: Low intermediate academic students
<u>Aim</u>: To introduce new vocabulary and associated expressions with fashion
<u>Assumed Knowledge</u>: Ss are familiar with some basic clothing vocabulary (shirt, pants, sweater, dress, etc.) and fabric patterns (plaid, polka dot, etc.)
<u>Anticipated Problems</u>: Adjective word order describing the clothes
<u>Solutions</u>: Review adjective work order prior to presenting the lead-in stage.
<u>Aids</u>: audio recording of two people talking about the latest fashions, pictures of models in designer clothing, pictures of latest fashion trends, sample fabric patterns (polka dot, plaid, stripes, etc.), unusual clothing

<u>Warm-Up/Review</u>   <u>Time</u>: 20 minutes
<u>Aim</u>:   To review adjective word order and to survey student tastes in fashion in order to pique interest.
<u>Focus</u>: T → S
<u>Aids</u>: pictures of models in designer clothes, pictures of latest fashion trends, fabric sample of common swatch patterns, unusual clothing
<u>Procedure</u>:

1. Walk into class wearing some unusual clothing. Note student response to you. Ask for student opinion on your choice of clothing. Ask ss why they have their opinions and inquire into what they prefer to wear (for daily routine, sporting events, special occasions, weddings, etc.)

2. Distribute pictures of models in designer clothes to individual students. Ask ss to show them to the class one-by-one and elicit a description of the clothing with sentences using 3 consecutive adjectives from other students. Repeat by having ss include fabric pattern into their descriptions. Student response will test for their knowledge of adjective word order.

3. If ss have trouble with adjective word order, quickly review the order on the board.

4. Repeat step # 2 by distributing pictures of latest fashion trends to other students.

5. Introduce new vocabulary for any clothing in the pictures that ss may not know (toque, mini dress, suspenders, long johns, etc.). In pairs, have ss tell each other in detail what they are wearing today.

6. Introduce vocabulary from the upcoming audio recording: scarf, mittens, ear muffs

Listening Task   **Time**: 25 minutes
Aim: To have ss identify a description of the new clothing vocabulary
Focus: S → T
Aids: audio recording, comprehension worksheet on recording
Procedure:

1. Tell ss they are going to listen to two boys talking about what their mothers bought them for the winter. The two boys are 10 years old and are talking at school. Remind ss which new vocabulary is in the recording.

2. Write an easy focus question for the first listening stage: When did Tommy's mother buy his new clothes?

3. Play the tape for the 1st time.

4. Elicit the answer to the focus question from the class and write responses on the white board. (Aim: to give students confidence in completing tasks related to the recording)

5. Hand out further comprehension questions on a worksheet. Give learners time to read them. (Aim: to guide learners to a deeper understanding of the recording)

6. Play tape for the 2nd time.

7. Assemble students in pairs (pair stronger ones with the weaker ones) to discuss their answers. (Aim: to promote communication between students; to give the teacher an opportunity to check for the task's level of difficulty).

8. If necessary, play the tape for the 3rd time. Play strategic spots in the recording if necessary.

9. Whole class check. Nominate individual students when eliciting answers and check for agreement from 1 or 2 other students. For trickier questions, ask a student to justify his answer. Write all answers up on the white board. (Aim: to ensure comprehension of text).

Closing   **Time**: 15 minutes
Aim: To reinforce the new clothing vocabulary learned today
Focus: S → S
Aids: drawing paper
Procedure:

1. Distribute drawing paper to students and have them discreetly draw a picture of a person wearing clothing from the new vocabulary learned today. Tell ss the person should have at least six different pieces of clothing from

the new vocabulary. Encourage them to put patterns on the clothing. Give them 5 minutes.

2. Assemble ss in pairs and have them sit back to back. Distribute a new pieces of drawing paper to one partner.

3. For 5 minutes, one partner describes his/her drawing of the person and the clothes he/she is wearing while the other partner who can't see the drawing has to listen and try to duplicate that drawing on the new blank drawing paper that's been given.

4. Switch partners for the last 5 minutes and repeat Step # 3. Distribute more drawing paper.

Lesson Evaluation

Students enjoyed the closing. If there is more time left in the class, colored crayons could be distributed to make the closing activity even more challenging.

Appendix

Reports, Observations, Assessment Forms

Appendix

Student Progress Report

Student: _____

Teacher: _____

Class: _____ Term and Date : _____

Mid-term Mark: _____

Report Categories	Comments
Attendance Student attends class at least 90% of the time. Student arrives on time for class.	
Participation Student participates fully in class discussions and activities.	
Study Habits Student respects the classroom rules and the learning environment of other students.	
Homework Student regularly does his/her assigned homework.	

Assignments and Projects Student completes all assignments and projects in the course.	
Tests Student writes all tests and quizzes given in class.	

Other Comments:

_____

_____

_____

_____

Teacher Observation

Teacher: _____

Class: _____

Term and Date: _____

Observed By: _____

Externals	Comments
Teacher is enthusiastic, professional and friendly in the classroom.	
Students provide feedback and respond positively to teacher's elicitation.	
Teacher is punctual, organized, and delivers the lesson with good efficiency of time.	
Lesson Content	
Teacher introduces interesting and useful material in a lesson with a clear objective.	
Teacher's lesson satisfies the objectives of the course curriculum (ex. reading, writing, grammar building, idioms, etc.)	
Teacher utilizes a variety of materials and activities that enhance student-centered learning.	
The activities are relevant to the lesson's focus.	
Teacher is knowledgeable with the target language	
Delivery	
Teacher delivers the lesson in a clear and logical manner which provides direction for the students.	
Teacher is animated in the lesson's delivery.	

Teacher guided activities are proceeded by student-centered activities.	
The duration of activities is appropriate to the lesson progression.	
Teacher circulates around the class to monitor students.	
The class is managed effectively.	
Teacher is able to effectively answer questions from the students and deal with any problems or concerns.	
Teacher asks various students questions to check for acquisition of target language	

Other Comments:

_____
_____
_____
_____

EXAMPLE INTERVIEW QUESTIONS FOR ENGLISH PLACEMENT TESTING

<u>Closed-Ended Low Level Questions</u>

What is your name?
How do you spell it?
Where do you live?
How long have you been in _____?
Do you have a job?
Have you studied English before?

<u>Open-Ended Intermediate Level Questions</u>

Tell me about your country.
Tell me about your city.
Tell me about your education.
Tell me about your experience with learning English.
What do you do for fun?
Tell me about your family.

<u>Open-Ended Advanced Level Questions</u>

What do you want to do in the future? Why?
What are the main cultural differences between _____ and
                                                    (country of origin)
_____?
           (host country)
What are the main differences between educational system in
_____ and in _____?
  (country of origin)   (host country)

❖ Ask the student about his knowledge and opinion on a current event or issue.

E.S.L. Learning Center
Interview Form

Date:_____

Name (Surname, Given Names): _____

Gender M/F: _____   Date and Place of Birth: _____

Student Registration No.: _____ Interviewer: _____

Status: ABC Citizen _____

     Landed Immigrant _____   Length of time in the country: _____
     International Student _____   Estimated Date of Arrival: _____

First Language: _____

Correspondence Address:

_____

_____

_____

Residential Address (if different):

_____

_____

_____

E-mail: _____ Phone Number: _____

Fax Number: _____

Education Experience (place, time, courses, and personal comments)

In country A:

_____

_____

_____

Elsewhere:

_____

_____

_____

Language Needs (What do you wish to learn?):

_____

_____

_____

Future Goals (In 5 years):

_____

_____

_____

Speaking Evaluation

1-poor   2-needs improvement   3-satisfactory   4-good   5-excellent

	1	2	3	4	5
1. Can engage in a conversation at a regular pace.					
2. Can understand the interviewer without inquiry.					
3. Can communicate his/her meaning with few errors.					
4. Makes appropriate responses to questions.					
5. Makes appropriate responses to common idioms.					
6. Makes appropriate responses to commonly used vocabulary.					
7. Can express opinions on familiar topics.					

8. Makes an effort in discussions of unfamiliar topics.

9. Makes appropriate responses about the past.

10. Makes appropriate responses about the present.

11. Makes appropriate responses about the future.

12. Can converse with other teachers/students.

Additional Comments (vocabulary usage, complexity of sentences, phrasal verbs, etc.)

_____

_____

_____

<u>Conversational English Level:</u>

Beginner: _____

High Beginner: _____

Intermediate: _____

High Intermediate: _____

Advanced: _____

High Advance: _____

E.S.L. Learning Center
Reading Assessment Form

Date: _____

Name (Surname, Given Names): _____

Gender M/F: _____

Student Registration No.: _____

Reading Level: _____

Problem Words:

_____

_____

_____

Reading Errors:

Hesitation: _____
Stress Problems: _____
Intonation Problems: _____
Miscellaneous Pronunciation Problems: _____
Word Linking Problems: _____
Omits letters, words, lines: _____
Repeats portions of the text: _____
Changes vocabulary: _____
Changes work order: _____
Other: _____

Other comments:

_____

_____

_____

_____

Comprehensive Question Results:

_____

_____

_____

_____

Final Instructional Reading Level: _____

Beginner Writing Evaluation Grid
for a Dictated List Task

Note: There is no writing task for students at the low-beginner reading level.

Place a check √ according to the strength of the writing skill	Needs Improvement	Satisfactory	Strong
1. Student can follow instructions.			
2. Student is able to write his name.			
3. Student can write numbers.			
4. Student can write legibly.			
5. Student can transcribe initial position consonants and consonant clusters.			
6. Student can transcribe final consonants.			
7. Student can transcribe irregular phonetic words.			
8. Student can transcribe digraphs.			
9. Student can.........			

Comments:

Intermediate Writing Evaluation Grid
for a Short Response Task

Place a check √ according to the strength of the writing skill	Needs Improvement	Satisfactory	Strong
Coherence and Unity			
1. Unity: The student talks about the main topic only			
2. Coherence: Sentences have logical connections with the topic and logically presented with transition signals.			
3. Sentences express the student's ideas, although there may be frequent errors in fragments and run-on sentences.			
4. Student provides sufficient support for his controlling idea without irrelevant details.			
Vocabulary			
1. Correct word form is used: gerunds, infinitives, etc			
2. Adjectives, adverbs, clauses and phrases are correctly used.			
3. Non-standard English expressions and idioms are correctly used.			
4. Spelling is correct.			
Grammar & Mechanics			
1. Verb tenses are correctly used.			
2. Sentences are structurally correct.			

Place a check √ according to the strength of the writing skill	Needs Improvement	Satisfactory	Strong
3. Punctuation is correct.			
4. Student's handwriting is legible.			
Comments can be made on the reverse side of this sheet.			

Advanced Writing Evaluation Grid
for a Letter Writing Task

Place a check √ according to the strength of the writing skill.	Needs Improvement	Satisfactory	Strong
Coherence and Unity			
1. Unity: The student talks about the main topic only.			
2. Coherence: Sentences have logical connections with the topic and are logically presented with transition signals.			
3. Ideas are clear.			
4. Ideas are strongly supported with relevant details.			
5. Letter follows the appropriate structural format.			
Vocabulary Fluency			
1. Simple, compound, complex, and compound-complex sentences are used for variety.			
2. Student uses appropriate descriptive and complex words.			
3. Ideas are connected with transition signals.			
4. Spelling is correct.			
5. Non-standard English expressions and idioms are correctly used.			
6. Correct word form is used: gerunds, infinitives, etc			

Place a check √ according to the strength of the writing skill.	Needs Improvement	Satisfactory	Strong
Grammar & Mechanics			
1. Verb tenses are correctly used.			
2. Sentences are structurally correct.			
3. Punctuation is correct.			
4. Student's handwriting is legible			
5. Other…….			

Comments:

Diagnostic Pronunciation Profile
E.S.L. Center
123 Fifth Avenue
City, Region, COUNTRY

PERSONAL PROFILE

Date: _____ Evaluator: _____

Student: _____ Student No. _____
E.S.L. Assessment Level: _____ Age: _____
Length of residence in host country _____
First language: _____ Other languages spoken: _____
Highest level of education: _____
Standard Test Score(s): _____
Occupation: _____
English use in the workplace: □ none   □ a little   □ some   □ a lot
English use in other environments: □ none   □ a little   □ some   □ a lot

GENERAL COMMUNICATION
1 = poor   2 = needs improvement   3 = satisfactory   4 = good   5 = excellent

	1	2	3	4	5
1. Intelligibility					
2. Speed					
3. Volume					
4. Appropriate pauses					
5. Appropriate facial expressions					
6. Eye contact					
7. Appropriate body language					

8. Other: _____

CONSONANTS
Prepare a list of words that encompass all 24 consonant sounds and some clusters. Make a note beside each word on any sound substitutions, deletions, aspiration difficulties, cluster problems, and general articulation problems.

Example:

Consonant	Model Word	Model Cluster
/d/	Dog	Drank [dr—initial cluster]
/t/	Tail	Talent [nt—final cluster]
/b/	Beef	Blank [bl—initial cluster]

VOWELS

Prepare a list of words that encompass all 20 vowel sounds. Make a note beside each word on any general articulation problems, inappropriate lip shaping, sound substitutions, incorrect vowel length, reductions, etc.

Example:

Vowel	Model Word
/uw/	Glue
/ey/	Play
/æ/	Bank

WORD AND SENTENCE STRESS

Ask student to read example sentences to test for performance in word and sentence stress.

1 = poor   2 = needs improvement   3 = satisfactory   4 = good   5 = excellent

	1	2	3	4	5
1					
2					
3					
4					
5					

1. Word stress

2. Content words expressed in a sentence:
    Larry and Bill are going to the mall to meet her.

3. Focus stress: new information
    I bought a new car.

4. Focus stress: contrast emphasis
   I bought a blue car, not a red one.

5. Focus stress: special emphasis
   I bought my first car today.

INTONATION

Ask student to read example sentences to test for performance in intonation.

1 = poor   2 = needs improvement   3 = satisfactory   4 = good   5 = excellent

	1	2	3	4	5
1					
2					
3					
4					
5					
6					
7					

1. Rising-falling
   What are you going to do today?

2. Rising
   Do you live in Richmond?

3. "Or" Question
   Do you have a pen or pencil?
   Do you want to go in the afternoon or the evening?

4. Tag Question
   It's a beautiful day, isn't it?

5. Listing
   I have to buy a sweater, a pair of pants, a shirt, some shoes, some socks, and a hat.

6. Social address
   Hi John, how are you?

7. Conditionals
   If you follow me, I'll show you the way.

LINKING, REDUCTION, SOUND TRANSFORMATION

Prepare a list of sentences that test for linking between word borders, contractions, vowel reduction, consonant deletions, and sound transformations.

Example: $C_1 + C_1$: *I see a big girl.*
$C + C$: *He was in Norway.*
Final consonant cluster + C: *I read my first book*

978-0-595-34221-1
0-595-34221-3

Printed in the United States
58953LVS00003B/115